Hegel and His Critics

SUNY Series in Hegelian Studies
William Desmond, Editor

Hegel and His Critics

Philosophy in the Aftermath of Hegel

Edited by
William Desmond

State University of New York Press

Hegel and his critics

Published by
State University of New York Press, Albany

©1989 State University of New York

For information, address State University of New York
Press, State University Plaza, Albany, N.Y., 12246

Library of Congress Cataloging-in-Publication Data

Hegel and his critics.

Includes index.
1. Hegel, George Wilhelm Friedrich, 1770-1831—
Influence. 2. Philosophy, Modern—19th century.
3. Philosophy, Modern—20th century. 1. Desmond,
William, 1951-
B2948.H3175 1988   193   87-16185
ISBN 0-88706-667-4
ISBN 0-88706-668-2 (pbk.)

10 9 8 7 6 5 4 3 2 1

Contents

INTRODUCTION

William Desmond

In recent centuries perhaps no philosopher has been rejected as often as Hegel. A roll call of his critics would include many of the major philosophers who have succeeded him. Yet an equally impressive list could be drawn up of thinkers who in different ways have been dependent on him. Some of his critics have even fed on the *disjecta membra* of his system, developing one of its strands in an effort to dismember the system's fuller claims. Post-Hegelians philosophers have repeatedly tried to determine, in Croce's now hackneyed words, what is living and what is dead in Hegel. One critic declares dead what another detects as still vibrant with life, and vice versa. Such contrary evaluations might imply that there is something inherently ambiguous in the Hegelian enterprise. Many commentators have admitted as much. But even this is barely a beginning in coming to terms with Hegel. If ambiguity hovers over Hegel, this evokes many responses, two of the chief being the following.

First we have the response that Hegelianism is humbug. This is a variation of Schopenhauer's denunciation of the "charlatanry" of Hegel and other self-proclaimed heirs of Kant. Schopenhauer thought Hegelianism was humbug partly because he had his own rival metaphysical wares to peddle and was envious of Hegel's success. But the majority of those subscribing to this view take their sights from more empiricist, analytically oriented philosophizing. On this view, Hegelianism undergoes repeated resurrection only because human credulity is perennial and lets itself be repeatedly taken in by pseudo-science. To the analytical philosopher Hegel presents a double scandal, of course. The analytical philosopher prides himself on fidelity to logic's precisions. Hegel's double affront is to claim to effect a revolution in philosophical logic. He carries the insult into their Holy of Holies.

A second response is less dismissive. The fact that Hegel *needs* to be *repeatedly* "refuted" makes one suspect that he is not being "refuted" at all. Here the critics find themselves with growing respect for the thinker they are intent on "refuting." Something about the complexity, indeed greatness of Hegel's thought resists reduction to more manipulable, univocal concepts. It is not so easy to put Hegel in his place. Instead of being a straw man to be knocked down, Hegel may become a living voice in the conversation of post-Hegelian thought. This has happened in the best of Continental thought, even when Hegel is explicitly seen as an antagonist to be strongly opposed. Hegel's ambiguity is doubled here, in that Hegel, the antagonist of post-Hegelian thought, proves to be absolutely necessary to the life of that opposing thought. Kierkegaard and Marx, critics of Hegel from significantly different perspectives, already knew this, perhaps more deeply than later critics.

The different chapters in this book will look at most of Hegel's major critics and the basic issues that are at stake. Most of the contributors attempt to speak for Hegel in response to his critics. But this does not mean that Hegel escapes criticism. Prescinding from individual critics, many of the major criticisms cluster around a set of striking oppositions that the reader may find helpful to keep in mind. I will single out four such oppositions for brief mention.

The first opposition deals with the criticism that Hegel was a "panlogist," *and* also helped precipitate "irrationalism" in subsequent thought. Panlogism is the view that Hegel's system is entirely a logical system, that the genuinely real is the fully rational. Hence Hegel the panlogist is absolutely insistent that being conform to the requirements of logical thought. This Hegel is unremittingly hostile to the "irrational." Yet opposite to this is the Hegel of many analytical philosophers, the Hegel who helped unhinge the flood gates of the "irrational." The logic of this Hegel is merely an apotheosis of the illogical. It is significant that Hegel's apotheosis of reason historically coincides with the onset of "irrationalist" philosophies of existence. But to castigate Hegel for this is another thing. Yet in the eyes of these critics, Hegel becomes the ancestor of all the metaphysical absurdity and "woolly nonsense" that Continental thought has supposedly spawned ever since. Hegel seems to have two faces: panlogist and harbinger of logic's humiliation. Perhaps this reflects his thought as both faithful to the requirements of philosophical reason, and yet facing towards what normally resists reason, struggling with this to make philosophy itself more concrete and comprehensive.

A second striking opposition relates to religion. On the one hand, Hegel has been denounced as being an insidious "atheist." Reasons for this include Hegel's view that the philosophical concept is more ultimate than religious representation. To the religious critic this is a sign of Hegel's will to pluck the heart of mystery out of religion, to reduce its sacred enigmas to abstract, poverty-stricken concepts. This is part of the Kierkegaardian criticism. But the opposite criticism has been levelled, namely that he was too timid to follow the path of his thought all the way to atheism and instead "mystified" the rational kernel of his philosophy with religious obscurantism. This is part of the Marxist and generally the Left-Hegelian view. This Hegel took religion too seriously; and though he claims to transcend religion philosophically, Hegel ends up reinstating religious "mystification" once more in the end. Is this doubleness just philosophical duplicity? Or does it testify to a commitment that philosophy must be double, that is dialectical, in being at once both respectful and critical of what is other? His critics sometimes split this doubleness into two starkly opposed polarities, each of which inevitably is found wanting for exactly opposite reasons.

A third important opposition might be expressed as the contrast between foundationalists and deconstructionists. Some critics of Hegel, call them the deconstructionists, see his doctrine of the absolute as one of the most extreme versions of foundationalism. In current debates foundationalism is itself a very ambiguous conception. (Hegel is not a foundationalist, if we simply think of the ultimate grounds as immediately given; against the Schellingian contact with the absolute as like "shot from a pistol," for Hegel the ultimate grounds must be mediated.) But Hegel's absolute, in one interpretation, does provide an ultimate ground or foundation for the intelligibility of being and the rationality of the categories we require to make being intelligible. The deconstructionist is an anti-Hegelian in claiming to expose the illegitimacy of any appeal, immediate or mediated, to such ultimate grounds. But once again Hegel has been seen as the exact opposite of a foundationalist, in this sense. This Hegel is seen as a radical historicist, where this means that there are no transtemporal grounds of intelligibility or meaning. All truth is historically mediated; reason itself is an historical product; there is no leap outside history to an eternal standpoint that would comprehend time within itself. It is interesting that the deconstructionists themselves exploit this historicist side in their own crusade against foundationalism. In Anglo-American analysis, Rorty has intoned the name of Hegel with the same intent of radical historicism.

A more abstract way of putting this opposition of foundationalism and deconstruction would be to point out that Hegel has been repeatedly criticized as a philosopher of identity in supposedly reducing all multiplicity to a conceptually totalitarian monism. And yet, at the same time, Hegel is sometimes seen as a philosopher of *difference*.

Indeed Derrida, who excoriates all philosophies of identity, speaks of Hegel as the first philosopher of difference. Hegel strangely is both a Hegelian and a post-Hegelian philosopher. Perhaps also Hegel wished neither an historicist excess of temporality without grounding rational intelligibility, nor an ahistorical absence of temporality, in which eternity has nothing intelligible to do with the productions of time. If Hegel were placed dialectically between these extremes, the two opposed interpretations would appear to be abstractions from Hegel's fuller vision. The more complex intentions of Hegel's dialectic are certainly evident in his trenchant repudiation of any "either/or" between identity and difference.

A fourth important opposition is between what I will call the scientistic and aestheticist criticisms. The former sees Hegel as an enemy of science, where this means the empirical and mathematical sciences of recent centuries. Did he not support Goethe's theory of color against Newton's? Does he not resort to a priori reasoning with respect to nature, as opposed to the humility of patient observation? The picture unrolls of a somewhat strange, antiscientific rationalist, whose reason is only disguised metaphoric imagination. This picture is unfair to Hegel who, though he did not invest finite science with the same ultimacy as art, religion and philosophy (absolute spirit), does seem to have been abreast of the scientific developments of his day. It is hardly scientific to accuse him of lack of clairvoyance with respect to science's future findings. By contrast, the aestheticist criticism sees Hegel as too enamored of science and even as hostile to art. Did he not say that philosophy must take the shape of science and system, and imply that art was something past for modern rational self-consciousness? Apart from the involved theme of the "death" of art, this contrast between scientism and aestheticism has been a continuing problem in Hegel's wake. Hegel is criticized from both sides which are not so opposed in Hegel himself. The scientistic critic does not situate Hegel's defense of science's rationality within a more embracing concept of philosophical reason. The aestheticist critic, perhaps because of a similar neglect of this notion of reason, fails to notice that Hegel, after all, does put art in the same community of absolute spirit, along with religion and philosophy. Hegel raises more possibilities for thought in excess of this opposition of scientism and aestheticism.

These four oppositions testify, I believe, to the power of Hegel's thought to provoke thought and not just to evoke criticism. As I already said, most of the major post-Hegelian philosophers take some stance with respect to Hegel, revealing something about their own philosophical concerns as well as Hegel's challenge. The list is by no means exhausted by the different critics treated in this volume.

Whatever else one might say, Hegel emerges as a living thinker at the end of the twentieth century. Hegel emerges as our contemporary. Indeed I suspect he emerges as our contemporary in a way helpfully *beyond* the split of Continental and analytical thought, a split which some have recently sought to surpass. He is beyond because he is before the split, and the split is partly conditioned by the different responses of Anglo-American and Continental thought to his legacy. He is beyond the split, first because of his commitment to philosophical reason, something the analytical philosopher ought to ponder. This commitment rescues him from simply celebrating the inarticulate, something that analytical philosophy suspects of his Continental successors. Nevertheless, he commits philosophical reason to the articulation of issues of fundamental importance, issues that may resist being thought of in standard, traditional logical terms; thus he is clear of the suspicion that Continental thought sometimes thrusts at analysis, namely, that its logical virtuosity dissipates itself on the inconsequential. Analysis, as technique for its own sake, risks the loss of philosophical depth; Continental thought dives for the depths but sometimes does not resurface with the rational thought. Hegel tries to think beyond those extremes and so in his distinctive way fulfill Kant's *desideratum:* intuitions without concepts are blind, concepts without intuitions are empty.

The different chapters and commentaries of this volume were first delivered at the Ninth Biennial Meeting of the Hegel Society of America, which was held at Emory University, 9–11 October 1986. For very generous assistance in the preparation of this volume, I would like to thank Loyola College in Maryland, and especially Frank Cunningham, Assistant to the Provost.

Chapter One

Presidential Address
THE USE AND ABUSE OF HEGEL BY
NIETZSCHE AND MARX

George L. Kline

As a preliminary to consideration of the "use" and "abuse" of Hegel by Nietzsche and Marx, I wish to challenge three common but erroneous characterizations of these two seminal thinkers. The first applies to both Marx and Nietzsche, the second to Nietzsche only, the third to Marx only.

(1) I deny what is widely but uncritically assumed, namely, that both Nietzsche and Marx are *existentialists*, or at least proto-existentialists (in the case of Marx this claim is usually limited to the early writings). As existential or proto-existential thinkers, both of them allegedly "revolted" against Hegel's "impersonal" speculative system. This I deny: neither Nietzsche nor the youngest possible Marx was an existential thinker in any meaningful sense. If we—quite properly—take Kierkegaard as exemplary of "existential philosophy," it is evident that both Nietzsche and Marx are much closer to Hegel than they are to the anti-Hegelian Kierkegaard. Neither of them valued subjectivity, existential decision, inwardness, passion, or spiritual suffering as such. Rather, they assigned them a certain instrumental value insofar, and only insofar, as they issue in cultural products (Nietzsche) or in socio-economic products (Marx). In Kierkegaard's quarrel with Hegel, both of them sided squarely with Hegel, lusting mightily after what Kierkegaard scornfully dismissed as the "banquet-table of the world-historical."[1]

(2) I also deny the related claim that Nietzsche was an *individualist*, in revolt (like Kierkegaard) against Hegel's anti-individualistic system. On my reading, Nietzsche valued human individuals only, or at least primarily, as creators of cultural values, not as persons having intrinsic value. Nietzsche's stress on the individual character of cultural creativity resulted in part from his quite understandable

1

skepticism about the creative prowess of crowds or collectivities of any kind. Of course, in any comparison of strong and creative individuals with the "herd" (*die Herde*), Nietzsche's clear preference was on the side of the individuals.[2]

(3) I deny that Marx, even the oldest possible Marx, was a philosophical *materialist*, i.e., a theorist who developed, or at least defended, a materialist ontology, in clear opposition to Hegel's idealist ontology. Such a claim is canonical with both followers and critics of Marx, but is nonetheless groundless. It is to Marx's philosophical credit that he did not share the naive commitment to an uncritical and simplistic materialist ontology that one finds in Engels, Plekhanov, Lenin, et al. I have made this case in detail elsewhere[3] and must for present purposes regard it as established, noting only that the denial that Marx was a philosophical materialist does not entail the assertion that he was a philosophical *idealist*. His philosophical position would be more accurately, if somewhat inelegantly, characterized as a "dialectico-historical, socio-economic objectivism." Such a position is measurably closer to Hegel's position than to any sort of materialist ontology.

I

When I speak of the use of Hegel by Nietzsche and Marx, I refer to their positive or non-abusive appropriation of certain general and specific aspects of the Hegelian philosophy of history and culture. Both of them, in this appropriation, reveal themselves as decisively post-Hegelian thinkers.

(1) The general aspect is Hegel's central stress on historical development and on *objektiver Geist*—the articulated network of dialectically interrelated social, economic, cultural, and political institutions and practices. Both thinkers were aware, at least dimly, of their debt to Hegel in this regard, but neither of them was conspicuously generous in acknowledging that debt.

(2) Two specific aspects of Hegel's thought which Nietzsche appropriated were:

(a) The Hegelian emphasis on *Werden*, becoming, development. Nietzsche singled this out, along with Schopenhauer's stress on the value-character of existence, as a powerful and original (and German!) contribution to philosophical thought (WM § 1058). However, in this posthumously published text Nietzsche did not mention either Hegel or Schopenhauer by name.

(b) Hegel's doctrine of the few decisive world-historical individuals (*welthistorische Individuen*) is, I would suggest, echoed in Nietzsche's doctrine of the few decisive *Übermenschen*, imagined as possessing unprecedented energy of will and cultural creativity. Hegel's favored world-historical individuals include Alexander the Great, Julius Caesar, and Napoleon. The last named was the object of Nietzsche's particular admiration; for Nietzsche Napoleon was not just a military and political genius who had brought about the unification of Europe when that large and difficult task was on the world-historical agenda (Hegel's view), but also, and especially, a kind of *uomo universale*, an "artistic" genius who imposed form upon the world of culture as well as that of politics and strategy.[4]

Even if I am right about the (partially) Hegelian genealogy of Nietzsche's *Übermenschen*, a crucial difference needs to be emphasized: Hegel's world-historical individuals have already lived and acted, they belong to the world-historical *past*. In sharpest contrast, none of Nietzsche's *Übermenschen* has yet lived or acted, all of them are anticipated or projected to appear in the remote world-historical *future*.

One would hardly expect Nietzsche to give Hegel any credit for the doctrine of the *Übermensch*; in fact, it is likely that if this suggestion had been presented to Nietzsche he would have roundly rejected it.

(3) The two specific aspects of Hegel's thought which Marx appropriated were:

(a) The doctrine of the "cunning of reason [in history]"—*die List der Vernunft* [*in der Geschichte*]— was reformulated in Marx's claim that the bourgeoisie, in its quest to maximize surplus-value and profit, unknowingly, and of course quite contrary to its own interests, brings about the historically rational and necessary emergence of its own "gravediggers (*Totengräber*),"[5] namely, those united class-conscious industrial workers whose historical mission is to put an end to the class rule of the bourgeoisie and, eventually, the rule of *every* socio-economic class.

(b) The second specific aspect of Hegel's thought which Marx appropriated also involves both historical projection and evaluative idealization. I would suggest, as an interpretive hypothesis, that Marx's free, unalienated, just, and harmonious communist society may be seen as a projection into the remote world-historical future of the *Sittlichkeit* or *sittliches Leben* which Hegel admired in the ancient Greek *polis*—a solidary, free, unalienated, harmonious community, whose members were at home (*bei sich*) with one another and at home in the cosmos.

The common philosophical debt which Nietzsche and Marx owe to Hegel and the largely parallel way in which they reacted to key elements of his speculative system do not, of course, imply any general community of doctrine. It is evident that they differ sharply on a central issue of socio-economic, political, and cultural policy and program, which could be encapsulated in the formula that Nietzsche's position is "elitist" and "radically aristocratic,"[6] whereas Marx's is "egalitarian" and "radically democratic." For Nietzsche, after all, the egalitarian ideal was no more than a secularization of the despised Judeo-Christian "slave morality."

Marx hated the dominant socio-economic, cultural, and political institutions and practices of his historical present because they were not egalitarian or democratic enough, because they were marked by pervasive exploitation. Nietzsche, who reached intellectual maturity a generation later, hated the socio-economic, cultural, and political institutions and practices (e.g., public welfare, "mass culture," extension of the suffrage) of *his* historical present because they were far too egalitarian, democratic, and unexploitative—in a sense to be elucidated below—and because they pointed toward an even more egalitarian, democratic, and unexploitative future. In this he agreed with Kierkegaard, equally (with him) scorning the "newspaper readers and balloting idlers"[7] of his time.

Marx envisaged an eventual "levelling up"—economic, social, cultural, and political. In contrast, Nietzsche insisted that all levelling is a "levelling down," and he bitterly opposed it. On Marx's view, all human beings will eventually be economically productive, independent, and nonconformist, whereas on Nietzsche's view only a tiny elite group of human beings will ever be culturally creative, independent, and nonconformist, the vast majority remaining, as they have always been, timidly conformist, dependent, and uncreative.

II

What I am calling the "abuse" of Hegel by Nietzsche and Marx might be described as "negative" or "abusive" appropriation of key elements of Hegel's system. It is a threefold process, involving (a) critique, (b) reduction, and (c) reversal. Although the first of these negative appropriations is probably the most familiar, it is the third— less noticed—of them which, in my judgment, is the most important and has the most fateful consequences. In this abusive appropriation both Nietzsche and Marx reveal themselves as profoundly anti-Hegelian thinkers.

There is ample evidence that Marx had closely and critically studied a number of Hegel's major works, including the *Phenomenology of Spirit*, the *Science of Logic*, and the *Philosophy of Right*. In contrast, Nietzsche—as a judicious commentator has recently noted—"did not study Hegel's texts in any depth and relied mainly on secondary sources [Schopenhauer, Jacob Burckhardt, and perhaps F.A. Lange's

Geschichte des Materialismus (1866)] for his interpretation and. . . evaluation of Hegel's thought."[8]

The philosophical atmosphere at the University of Leipzig when Nietzsche was reaching intellectual maturity (1865–1867) was pro-Schopenhauerian and anti-Hegelian. And Wagner, whom he met in 1868, "would have reinforced Nietzsche's early Schopenhauerian prejudice against Hegel."[9] It was not until the early 1880s, when he was becoming increasingly critical of both Schopenhauer and Wagner, that Nietzsche began to express more positive evaluations of Hegel.

(a) Nietzsche, no less than Marx, despite his less intimate knowledge of Hegel's works, unerringly identified their common philosophical enemy, namely, the ontological and axiological priority which Hegel placed on the world-historical *present* and on the past which has led, by a rational dialectical process, to that present. In the words of Nazi commentator Alfred Baeumler, Nietzsche immediately sensed an adversary in Hegel's philosophy of history.[10] Baeumler's clear implication is that Nietzsche, like the Nazis later, was entirely justified in this reaction. The doctrinal reversal of Hegel's position, carried out independently by the two thinkers (to be discussed in a moment) involved a decisive displacement of that priority to the world-historical *future*.

Thus, applying his celebrated "hermeneutics of suspicion," Nietzsche, as early as 1873, heaped scorn on the "Hegelian worship of the real (*das Wirkliche*) as the rational," which he further castigated as a "deification of success" (DS § 7, 1: 169). He accused Hegel of offering an "apotheosis of the commonplace [or 'everyday'] (*Vergötterung der Alltäglichkeit*)" in order to ingratiate himself with the "cultural philistine, who . . . conceives himself alone to be *real* (*wirklich*) and treats his reality (*Wirklichkeit*) as the standard of *reason* in the world" (DS § 2, 1: 146, italics added). According to Nietzsche, David Strauss is being a faithful Hegelian when he "*grovels* before the realities [or 'conditions'] (*Zuständen*) of *present-day Germany*" (DS § 6, 1: 165; italics added). In the following year Nietzsche went on to accuse Hegel of "a naked admiration for success" and an "idolatry of the factual (*Götzendienst des Tatsächlichen*)" (HL § 8, 1: 263).

Marx's more theoretical, less abusive attack—in the *Holy Family* (1845)—makes a closely related critical point.

> The philosopher is only the organ whereby the creator of history, the Absolute Spirit, *retrospectively* (*nachträglich*) becomes conscious *after* the movement of history has ended. The philosopher's participation in history is reduced to this retrospective consciousness. . . . Thus the philosopher appears [only] *post festum*. . . . Since the Absolute Spirit becomes conscious as the creative World Spirit in the

philosopher and only *post festum*, its making (*Fabrikation*) of history
exists only in consciousness, in the opinion (*Meinung*) and conception (*Vorstellung*) of the philosopher, only in speculative imagination
(*Einbildung*).[11]

Nietzsche, no less clearly than Marx, had grasped the point of the
famous "Owl of Minerva" passage in the Preface to Hegel's *Philosophy of Right*, namely, that the task of the speculative philosopher of
history is to exhibit the rational and dialectically "necessary" pattern
of *past* historical development that has led to the world-historical
present. But, emphatically, it is not such a philosopher's task to predict, or to urge, how the world-historical *future* will, or should,
develop.

Nietzsche even formulated his polemical point in a pair of scathing, not to say hooting, couplets in which he contrasted his own
favorite *future*-oriented eagle to Hegel's *past*-oriented ("backward-
gazing") owl:

> Schwermütig scheu, solong du *rückwärts* schaust,
> Der *Zukunft* trauend, wo du selbst dir traust:
> O Vogel, rechn ich dich den *Adlern* zu?
> Bist du *Minervas* Liebling *U-hu-hu*?
>
> (FW, "Vorspiel in deutschen Reimen," # 53, 2: 29; italics added)
>
> (Shy, gloomy, when your looks are *backward* thrust,
> Trusting the *future* where yourself you trust,
> Are you an *eagle*, mid the nobler fowl,
> Or are you like *Minerva's* darling *owl*?)
>
> (Trans. by Paul V. Cohn and Maude D. Petrie; another transla-
> tion, by Walter Kaufmann, is included in his edition of *The Gay
> Science* [New York: Vintage, 1974], p. 63.)

Both Nietzsche and Marx scorn the *post festum* ("after-the-party-
is-over") character of Hegel's philosophy of world history, urging
instead that the world-historical *future* be treated, in the present, as
having both ontological and axiological priority, that future historical
developments should not only be anticipated but also, in a sense,
described and interpreted *before* they occur.

On two less central points Nietzsche and Marx raise rather different objections to the Hegelian position. Nietzsche, echoing Schopenhauer, complains loudly about Hegel's philosophical style, speaks of
sinking "into the Hegelian mud (*in den Hegelschen Schlamm*)," and
accuses the "Hegelians and their deformed offspring" of being the
"most infamous of all corrupters of German" (DS § 12; 1: 197, 196).
And in a jibe which was probably directed at Schelling as well as at
Hegel, he applauded those anti-Hegelians—presumably, in the first

instance, Schopenhauer—who had repudiated "with a shrug of the shoulders the brew of fantastic and language-twisting philosophies and tendentious historiographies (*schwärmerisch-zweckbewusster Geschichtsbetrachtung*)" which was current in Germany in the early nineteenth century (DS § 2, 1: 145).

Marx's criticism of a key point of Hegel's philosophical doctrine strikes me as no less unfair than Nietzsche's criticism of Hegel's philosophical style. I refer to Marx's claim that, for Hegel,

> [o]bjectivity (*Gegenständlichkeit*) as such is regarded as an *alienated* human relationship which does not correspond to the *essence of man*. . . . *Reappropriation of the objective essence of man, developed as something alien, . . . means not only the overcoming (aufzuheben) of alienation but also of objectivity*—that is, man is regarded [by Hegel] as a *non-objective, spiritual* being (ein *nicht-gegenständliches, spiritualistisches* Wesen).[12]

Marx is wrong, and wrong-headed, to assume that for Hegel human existence is something purely "spiritual" (even "spiritualistic") and as such non-objective. More generally, Marx is wrong to treat the Hegelian *Geist* and *Idee* as a kind of disembodied spirit-subject standing over against the social and historical world. Hegel, after all, was the philosopher who breakfasted on brass tacks.[13] As a recent commentator has put it: "The pith and marrow of [Hegel's] whole philosophy is that it is embodied in and articulates the self-changing [social] world in its historical development."[14] In a word, Hegel is no less committed to socio-historical *objectivism* than is Marx himself.

(b) The specializing or particularizing *reductions* which Nietzsche and Marx carried out on the rich and complex content of Hegel's *objektiver Geist* are contrasting and, in a sense, complementary. *Objektiver Geist* is a comprehensive and inclusive totality. Nietzsche focuses upon *one* of its aspects, namely, high culture; Marx focuses upon *another* aspect, namely, socio-economic institutions and practices. Nietzsche tends to treat the aspect upon which Marx focuses in a reductionist way—as no more than one of the (minor) conditions for the development of high culture. Marx, in turn, tends to treat the aspect of *objektiver Geist* upon which Nietzsche focuses in a comparably reductionist way—as no more than one of the (minor) conditions for the development of economic production and human self-realization.

(c) Nietzsche and Marx come together in the reversal, or inversion, which they carry out on Hegel's speculative philosophy of history.[15] Both of them repudiate the Hegelian prudence and wisdom of the "owl of Minerva" and the "affirmation of the actual (*Bejahung des Wirklichen*),"[16] placing a decisive, even obsessive, emphasis upon the world-historical *future*. The emotional and evaluative counterpart of the "will to the future *(Wille zur Zukunft)*"[17] which characterized both Nietzsche and Marx was their shared hatred and contempt for the world-historical *past* and, especially, *present*, which both of them saw as radically defective—as obstacles to be overcome, reduced to *means* in the service of the future as *end*.

In the words of a recent commentator, "both [Nietzsche and Marx] understand man's life activity as a creative [future-oriented] process which requires constant striving to destroy what has gone before."[18] Another commentator adds that for Nietzsche present mankind is "defective or contemptible, able to justify itself only in the achievement of something higher than itself." Zarathustra's "appeals to live and die for a future a long way off present themselves as a pure love of . . . mankind in the form of the superman, aided by contempt for the present. . . ."[19]

Nietzsche praises the wise man's "icy rejection of the present *(Kälte gegen das Gegenwärtige)*."[20] His Zarathustra declares passionately:

> I walk among [present] human beings *(Menschen)* as among the fragments . . . of human beings! . . . The present *(das Jetzt)* and the past *(das Ehemals)* upon the earth . . . is my most intolerable burden *(mein Unerträglichstes)*; . . . I should not know how to live, if I were not also a seer of that which must come [in the future]. . . . I walk among human beings as among fragments of the future: of the future which I scan *(schaue)*. (Z II, 2: 393, 394.)

In a word, what is more basic than Nietzsche's noisily proclaimed *amor fati* is what I would call his *amor temporis futuri* and its corollary, an embittered *odium temporis praesenti*.

For Marx, of course, what has mutilated and dehumanized the world-historical present is the capitalist system of production and exchange. As Tabora has recently put it, "The future in Marx's thought . . . impels [i.e., motivates and activates] the criticism and overthrow of the . . . dehumanized present. . . . The future is humanity raised *(emporgehoben)* from the human ruins [of the present] through the necessitated insurrection *[Empörung]* of the proletariat. . . ."[21]

Marx himself, in *The Class Struggles in France* (1850), expressed the point in a way even closer to Nietzsche's formulation:

> The revolution is . . . no short-lived revolution. The *present* generation is like the Jews whom Moses led through the wilderness. It not only has a new world to conquer *(erobern)*, it *must* [also] *go under* [or *'perish'*] *(untergehen)* to make room for [future] human beings who are [i.e., will be] able to cope with a new world *(einer neuen Welt gewachsen sind)*. (T 592; MEW 7: 79.)

For both Nietzsche and Marx the Hegelian focus (both ontological and axiological) on the world-historical present involves an unacceptable neglect and denial of the rights of the world-historical future. Both of them strongly urge a reversal of the abnormal situation in which—as Nietzsche put it—"the present [is] living *at the expense of the future* (die Gegenwart *auf Kosten der Zukunft* lebt)" (GM Pref. § 6, 2: 768). For the future to live at the expense of the present—as both, in different ways, would have it—involves a harsh negation and *Entwertung* of the world-historical present for the sake of a decisive affirmation and *Verwertung* of the world-historical future.

This shared future orientation—despite the contrasting ends-in-view of the two thinkers, which might be concisely formulated as the creation of an unprecedentedly high culture, on the one hand, and the construction of a classless society, on the other—represents the core of Nietzsche's and Marx's ultimate repudiation and reversal of Hegel's orientation toward the world-historical past and, especially, the world-historical present.

III

But, it may be objected, is there not an orientation toward the world-historical future in Hegel's own thought? Consider: (a) his assertion that "ours is a time of birth and transition (*Zeit der Geburt und des Übergangs*) to a new era" and his reference, in this connection, to "heralds of approaching change (*Vorboten, dass etwas anderes im Anzuge ist*)" (PhG, Pref., § 11); (b) Hegel's characterization of America as the "country of the future" whose "world-historical importance is yet to be revealed in the ages which lie ahead";[22] and (c) the influential commentaries of Alexandre Kojève and Albert Camus, which find just such a future orientation in Hegel himself.

I shall try to respond to each of these points in turn.

(a) This relatively early (1807) statement has no counterpart in Hegel's later writings, where—especially in the *Philosophy of Right* (1821)—he scrupulously avoids such rhetoric. Moreover, even in the *Phenomenology*, Hegel has in mind a relatively brief transition period, one measured in years or at most in decades (*Jahrzehnte*). This is a crucial difference from the transition periods typically envisaged by Marx, which are measured in centuries (*Jahrhunderte*), or those envisaged by Nietzsche, which are measured in millennia (*Jahrtausende*). (See Sections V and VI below). In other words, even this early statement, which is *not* typical of the mature Hegel, expresses a modestly *short*-term future orientation in contrast to the immodestly *long*-term future orientations of both Nietzsche and Marx.

(b) No comment about America (or any other country) being the "country of the future" appears in any work which Hegel himself prepared for publication. And this comment is vague, offering no estimate of *when* America will come into its own. In terms of Hegel's speculative philosophy of history it is incautious and unfortunate, not because it names a specific country, but because it refers to *any* country (or institution, culture, or practice) as belonging to the world-historical future. Hegel himself admits as much when, in the same passage, he adds the pregnant remark: "[A]s a country of the future, [America] is of no interest to us here, for prophecy (*das Prophezeien*) is not the business of the philosopher."[23]

(c) The relevant claims of both Kojève and Camus strike me as seriously misleading. I refer to Kojève's assertion that for Hegel "historical time is characterized by the primacy [or 'priority'] of the future," and that "only the Present . . . determined by the Future and the Past is a human or historical Present."[24] In an even more surprising formulation, Kojève asserts that in historical time "the *Future* that *determines* the *Present* by way of the Past takes *priority* [or 'primacy']."[25] But surely none of this applies to the Hegel of the *Philosophy of Right* or the *Lectures on the Philosophy of World History*. Rather, this is a thoroughly "Heideggerianized" Hegel (though Kojève makes no explicit reference to Heidegger in this context), and thus a radically distorted Hegel. My guess is that Kojève is thinking of such dark but characteristic passages as that in *Being and Time* in which Heidegger insists that pastness or "having-been-ness" (*Gewesenheit*) springs from the future, that the future—"*die gewesend-gegenwärtigende Zukunft*"—produces the present by somehow "rendering itself past."[26] This clearly implies that the future performs an action or completes a process in the course of which, by being "past"ed, or "past"ing itself, it generates the present.

According to Heidegger's etymological gloss, the word *Zukunft* means "that which *comes toward us*" (Die Zukunft ist das, was *zu uns kommt*). But surely this is a mistake; the *Zukunft*, rather, is that which is yet "to come" (*zu kommen*). Kojève appears to accept, and to apply to Hegel, three highly dubious Heideggerian assumptions: (i) that the future enjoys both ontological and phenomenological priority over the present and past; (ii) that the temporal relation between future and present (and past) is strictly analogous to a spatial relation; (iii) that the future is, or contains, an agent or agents. All three assumptions, I would insist, are both false and utterly foreign to Hegel's position on these questions.

Camus's remark that for Hegel "values are . . . only to be found at the end of history,"[27] though seriously misleading as applied to Hegel, is revealing as applied to both Nietzsche and Marx (see Section VI below). The notion of an "end of history" is a difficult and controversial one, although certain Hegelian texts appear to support it. But one thing is reasonably clear: if, for Hegel, there is an end—in the sense of both *telos* and termination—of world history, that end is not to be reached, as in Nietzsche and Marx, in the remote world-historical *future*, but rather in the world-historical *present*, that twilight present in which the Owl of Minerva takes its flight.

Franz Grégoire makes the sensible comment that for Hegel history has substantially "come to an end" or "has no future" only in the sense that there will not be radical future changes in presently established political and socio-economic institutions and practices.[28] In the Owl of Minerva passage, according to Grégoire, Hegel is simply saying,

> in reaction against those people who are dissatisfied on principle and against the builders of utopias, that the philosopher's task is to disclose the rational character of present reality, and not to determine [or 'define'] (*déterminer*) the future, since "in any case" (*ohnehin*), i.e., supposing that the future should happen to bring us something new, the philosopher would be able to concern himself with it only after the fact. . . .[29]

There *is* a sense—not, I think, the one intended by Camus—in which values may be said to be found "only [or, at least, preeminently] at the end of history." If, as just suggested, we place that end not in the remote world-historical future but in the world-historical present, then such values as the freedom and dignity of human persons would, on Hegel's account, be more adequately realized in that present than in any previous stage of world history. That this is *not* what Camus meant is clear from his further claim, in the same passage, that, according to Hegel, "[o]ne must act and live in terms of the future."[30] Like Camus's claim about values, this strikes me as grotesquely inappropriate as applied to Hegel's position, but strikingly appropriate as applied to the positions of both Nietzsche and Marx.

IV

This is not the place even to sketch my own ontology of time—a task which I have begun in another place.[31] However, since I shall be charging both Nietzsche and Marx with committing the (ontological) "fallacy of the actual future" and the related (axiological) "fallacy of deferred value," I need to say a word about the ontological status of present, past, and future as I understand that status. (The order of these terms is the order of the ontological priority which I would assign them. In this I am, I think, agreeing with Hegel.)

The future is marked by pure possibility; it is empty of what is *actual* in either of the two senses of that term which I have distinguished in another context: it is neither actual$_1$, i.e., *active*, as the present is, nor actual$_2$, i.e., *efficacious*, as the past is.[32] Only present existents are agents: past existents, as efficacious, provide real potentialities for actualization in the present. To put the point in Hegelian terms (although this is not precisely Hegel's doctrine): the present is characterized by *Wirklichkeit* in the active or "process" sense of *ein Verwirklichen*. The past is characterized by *Wirklichkeit* in the passive or "product" sense of *das Verwirklichte*. The future, of course, is not characterized by *Wirklichkeit* in *either* of these senses, but only by timeless possibilities.

To commit the "fallacy of the actual future" is thus to treat what is merely possible as though it were actual (either actual$_1$ or actual$_2$), to treat the future as though it were either the present or the past. To commit the "fallacy of deferred [or 'historically postponed'] value" is to treat abstract value-ideals as though they were concrete achievings of value or determinate value-achievements. This again is to treat the future as though it were either the present or the past.

Nietzsche and Marx uncritically shared a baseless assumption—one nearly as widespread in our day as it was in theirs—namely, that historical improvements can be appropriately expressed in terms of forward or upward movement along a linear spatial series. They were equally uncritical in assuming that what makes certain individuals or classes more "progressive" or "avant-garde" than others is either their more advanced position on, or their more rapid motion along, such a spatial series. This model or metaphor involves an unacceptable spatialization of the temporal order and other incoherences which I have discussed in another place.[33] My conclusion, in brief, is that locomotion—from whatever starting point, in whatever direction, and at whatever rate—provides a grossly inappropriate model or metaphor for both historical improvements and historical worsenings (the latter, of course, being standardly expressed as backward or downward movements).

Historical change generally is much more adequately expressed by Hegel's (temporal) model or metaphor of organic growth from bud to blossom to fruit.[34] Like the models of spatial motion, it emphasizes that historical development is a process; but unlike them it also suggests that this process is temporal, cumulative, irreversible, and categoreally distinct from locomotion.[35] Hegel's model definitely does not suggest, as the spatializing models do, that when the (present) bud opens, the (future) fruit is in some queer sense "already there." On Hegel's account, (past) bud and (past) blossom are indeed *aufgehoben*—negated, preserved, and raised to a higher dialectical level—in the (present) fruit. But it would make no sense to reverse the process, to say that the fruit was *aufgehoben* in the bud or blossom. *Aufhebung* is an asymmetrical relation: if *a* is *aufgehoben* in *b*, then *b* cannot be *aufgehoben* in *a*.

Spatial models of historical change, according to which movement from past to present is strictly analogous to movement from present to future (since both are simply forms of locomotion), strongly and misleadingly suggest that there is an ontological and axiological symmetry of past and present, present and future, and even past and future. "Future existents" are said to have the same kind of being, and the same or higher value, compared to present or past existents.

In thinkers like Nietzsche and Marx such assumptions entail a further, and unacceptable, devaluing and instrumentalizing of present and past existents, a denial of their intrinsic value. Each such existent—each community, culture, practice, or person—is held to have only instrumental value—positive instrumental value if it facilitates, negative instrumental value if it obstructs—the establishment, in the remote world-historical future of existents—communities, cultures, practices, and persons—which eventually will, or at least may, have non-instrumental, intrinsic value. (This is truer of Marx's position than of Nietzsche's. For Nietzsche, even the ultimate *Übermenschen* will be valued not for what they *are* but for what they *contribute* to the creation of the unimaginably high culture of the most remote world-historical future.)

As great instrumentalizers, both Nietzsche and Marx were faithful philosophical sons of the French Enlightenment; Hegel, in contrast, was the first and most penetrating of the critics of that Enlightenment's instrumentalizing tendencies (cf. PhG, §§ 562, 580, 582).

Both Nietzsche and Marx assume that, since the present socioeconomic, cultural, and political order is marked by negative values, disvalues, present existents may legitimately be restricted, repressed, or eliminated in order to facilitate the emergence of "future existents" that will be marked exclusively by positive values. For Nietzsche the chief negative values may be summarized as humility, pity, the quest for security, and equality; their chief positive counterparts are pride, pitiless creativity, risk-taking, and hierarchy. For Marx the chief negative values are alienation, exploitation, injustice, and unfreedom; their chief positive counterparts are disalienation, harmonious cooperation, justice, and freedom.

For both thinkers the world-historical present (and, indirectly, the world-historical past) is reduced to a locus of *means* and the world-historical future exalted to a locus of *ends*. On their shared spatial model of historical development, the past is analogized to a large but finite space, the present to an extremely small space, and the future to a huge and infinitely expanding space. Thus for Nietzsche the (indefinitely expansible) sum of future cultural values will enormously exceed the (non-expansible) sum of present cultural values as well as the (non-expansible) sum of the cultural values accumulated throughout past history. For Marx the (indefinitely expansible) sum of future goods produced by free, unexploited producers will enormously exceed the (non-expansible) sum of goods produced in the present and the past. There is also a "qualitative" difference: the future goods will not be *commodities*, destined for the market, but *products*, destined for human use; in the present and the (post-feudal) past the goods have all been commodities, destined for the market.

On this model, it makes perfect sense for both Nietzsche and Marx, to urge, and work for, the sacrifice of the trifling and non-expansible sum of past and present cultural values and socio-economic goods for the sake of the huge and indefinitely expansible sum of future values and goods.

V

Nietzsche and Marx borrowed one of the concepts which Hegel had made philosophically current and central to his own philosophy, that of transition (*Übergang*) and of "transitional periods" or "times of transition" (*Übergangs-Perioden, Übergangszeiten*). However, as with Hegel's philosophy of history generally, they carried out a drastic reversal of its use. Hegel was always scrupulously careful to locate such transitions in the historical *past*.[36] For example, the early eighteenth century was a transitional period (*Übergangs-Periode*) in the history of Western philosophy—between the mid-seventeenth century and the mid-eighteenth century, roughly, between Descartes and Kant. The philosophers active during this transitional period included Berkeley, Hume, and certain Scottish and French philosophers.[37]

In sharpest contrast, Nietzsche and Marx typically place the historical transitions with which they are concerned in the "space" between present and *future*, less frequently between past and future. As we have seen, on the spatial model of historical change, which both Nietzsche and Marx accept, there is a strong symmetry of present-to-past or past-to-present relations and present-to-future relations. This entails the false and dangerous claim that there is no significant ontological or socio-political difference between transitions in those cases where the *terminus a quo* and *terminus ad quem* are both past or where the former is past and the latter present, on the one hand ("Hegelian" transitions), and transitions in those cases where the *terminus a quo* is either past or—more typically—present and the *terminus ad quem* is future ("Nietzschean" and "Marxian" transitions), on the other.

Marx tends to use the term *Übergang* without metaphorical embellishment. Thus, to take a relatively early and a relatively late example, he writes in 1852 that

> the [present] class struggle necessarily leads to the [short-term future] dictatorship of the proletariat [and] that this dictatorship itself only constitutes the transition (*Übergang*) to the [long-term future] abolition (*Aufhebung*) of all classes and to a classless society.[38]

In 1875, in the "Critique of the Gotha Program," Marx added:

> Between [present] capitalist and [future] communist society lies the period of the revolutionary transformation of the one into the other. There corresponds to this also a political transition period (*Übergangsperiode*) in which the state can be nothing but the revolutionary dictatorship of the proletariat (T 538; MEW 19: 28).

I shall come back in Section VII below to the question of the dictatorship of the proletariat. For the moment, the point to note is that the "transition period"—like the future itself—is indefinitely expansible, of indeterminate duration.

Nietzsche repeatedly refers to his own time as a "time of transition" (*Übergangszeit*) (e.g., FW 356, 2: 223) and, with striking alliteration, as *zerbrechliche, zerbrochene Übergangszeit* ("fragile, broken time of transition") (FW § 377, 2: 251). Presumably, although the transition itself is fragile and broken, the future to which it will lead will be firm and unshakable. Nietzsche's images of present-day mankind as a transition to the future *Übermensch* are embellished with a series of powerful—though uniformly spatializing—metaphors.

> Man is a rope, fastened between animal and Superman (*Übermensch*)—a rope over an abyss.
> A dangerous going-across (*Hinüber*), . . .
> What is great in man is that he is a bridge and not a goal; what can be loved in man is that he is a transition (*Übergang*) and a perishing (*Untergang*) (Z Pref. § 4, 2: 281).

Nietzsche italicizes the words *Übergang* and *Untergang*, to bring out his punning but deadly serious point that the "going over" of mankind to the *Übermensch* is at the same time a "going under" or perishing of present-day mankind. The image of this transition in terms of a rope, or a bridge, stretched between past and future across the abyss or wasteland of the present appears in several key passages of *Thus Spoke Zarathustra* (cf. Z I, 2: 301; Z II, 2: 393; Z IV, 2: 519). See also GM II § 16, 2: 826.

VI

I have now laid out my principal theoretical and interpretive claims concerning the use and abuse of Hegel by Nietzsche and Marx. The aim of this and the following Section is to provide a certain amount of doctrinal detail and textual support for my claims concerning the will to the world-historical future and the instrumentalizing of the present for the sake of that future as these are exhibited in Nietzsche (this Section) and in Marx (Section VII). I shall also indicate briefly the kind of philosophical defense that Hegel provides against these dangerous positions.

Although Nietzsche made no effort to develop an ontology of time, he did refer, shockingly, to "*time* as a property of *space* (*Zeit* als Eigenschaft des *Raumes*)" (WM § 862, italics added). This philosophical prejudice, combined with a rhetorical predilection for spatial imagery to express temporal relations (in which he was not, of course, alone), has, I suspect, been one of the reasons why Nietzsche's powerful future orientation has been so little noticed by commentators.

Thus, the noun *Ferne* ("distance") and the adjective *fern* ("distant"), as well as the adjective *lang* ("long") standardly refer to remoteness in the world-historical past and especially the world-historical future. Nietzsche's phrase "Alle *lange* Dinge sind schwer zu sehen" (GM I § 8, 2: 780) is typical in two respects: (1) it expresses a temporal duration with a spatial term, and (2) it offers a clue to this usage by including the temporal expression *zwei Jahrtausende* ("two millennia") in the same passage. Kaufmann's rendering—"All *protracted* things are hard to see"—although acceptable as a translation, is misleading as an interpretation. What Nietzsche means is that those processes or developments which began a long time ago are hard to discern now. In the given case it is hard to grasp that the origin of present-day Christian *agapē* and good Samaritanism lies in the Jewish resentment and hatred of two thousand years ago.

Nietzsche's celebrated coinage *Fernsten-Liebe* ("love of the most distant") (Z I, 2: 324–25) refers not to what is spatially most remote— not the Chinese the Australians, or the Martians (if such there be)— nor even to what is temporally most remote in human history—not the ancient Egyptians or Assyrians—but to what is temporally most remote in the world-historical *future*. (I shall have something to say below about the punning, but wholly serious, opposition of Nietzschean *Fernsten-Liebe* to Christian *Nächstenliebe*.) Clues as to the temporal meaning of this spatial term are provided by such expressions as "of the most distant and of the future (*zum Fernsten und Künftigen*)" (2: 324)[39] and the even more explicit phrase "the future and the most distant (*Die Zukunft und das Fernste*)" (2: 325).

Nietzsche uses such spatial terms as *hinter sich* ("behind one") to mean "in the past" (FW 337, 2: 198) and *rückwarts* ("backwards") to mean "toward the past": (FW "Vorspiel" # 53, 2: 29). *Vor sich* ("in front of one") means "in the future" (FW § 337, 2: 198). "Toward the future" is expressed by several different terms, including *vorwärts* ("forward") (HL § 8, 1: 259: MA I § 292, 1: 623), *weiter* ("further" (FW § 20, 1: 51), and *hinweg* ("away," "hence") (GB Pref., 2: 565; EH Pref. § 4, 2: 1067).

Participles and gerunds formed from certain verbs of locomotion are also used to mean "future" or "the future." *Das Vertrauen auf das Kommende* means "confidence in the future" (HL § 1, 1: 214), and *eine kommende Zeit* means "a future time" (HL Pref., 1: 210). *Diese kommenden Philosophen* are identified a few lines further on with philosophers of the future (*Zukunft*) (GB § 43, 2: 605).

Nietzsche uses the substantives formed from the adverbs *morgen* ("tomorrow") and *Übermorgen* ("the day after tomorrow") to express the shorter and longer-term future, respectively, as in the phrase *ein . . . Mensch des Morgen und Übermorgen* ("a man of tomorrow and the day after tomorrow") (GB § 212, 2: 677). Note that the *Über-* in *Übermorgen* echoes and reinforces the use of the same prefix in such key terms as *Übermensch* and *Übergang*.

In an important fragment from the *Nachlass*, omitted by the editors of *The Will to Power*, Nietzsche declared:

> In order to be able to create [we need] liberation from morality and relief (*Erleichterung*) by means of festivals. Anticipations of the future! to celebrate the *future* not the past! To compose [or "write the poem of" (*dichten*)] the *myth of the future!*[40]

The "myth of the future"—set out most lyrically in *Zarathustra* (Part I of which was written in the same year as this fragment)—is of decisive rhetorical significance for Nietzsche. He develops this myth by using a cluster of images and metaphors, mostly borrowed from the Romantics, who used them to symbolize the lofty and sublime, namely, images for the "higher man," the "higher race," and especially, the "higher culture" of the future. These include stars (which in Nietzsche stand for cultural values or ideals), mountain peaks, cliffs, treetops, and the birds, particularly eagles, which wing toward them and nest in them. The word *Stern* ("star") has the further lyrical advantage that in the plural or dative singular (*Sterne*) it rhymes handily with Nietzsche's favorite term for the remote world-historical future: *ferne/Ferne*. And, as Goethe had made clear in one of his most familiar and moving short lyrics, *Gipfel* ("mountain peak") rhymes nicely with *Wipfel* ("treetop"). Rhyme is a device used by serious poets for bringing together, and holding in tension, images and concepts which would not otherwise be related. Nietzsche uses both internal rhymes and end-rhymes on *fern/Stern* to associate the future with cultural ideals or values (*Sterne*), as in the early phrase *die fernen*

Sternbilder zukünftiger Kulturen ("distant stellar images of future cultures") (MA I § 292, 1: 624). Compare his overly Romantic evocation of *purpurglühenden Sternbildern und ganzen Milchstrassen des Schönen* ("purple-glowing stellar images and whole Milky Ways of the beautiful"), which ends with the apostrophe: *Wo seid ihr, ihr Astronomen des Ideals?* ("Where are you, you astronomers of ideals?") (M § 552, 1: 1271). If stars symbolize cultural values or ideals, then Zarathustra's admonition to "give birth to a dancing star" (Z I, 2: 284) means to "create a vibrant cultural value or ideal."

Nietzsche's end-rhymes are most effective in such lines as these:

Er hat des Adlers Auge für die *Ferne*,
Er sieht euch nicht!—er sieht nur *Sterne, Sterne*!

(He has the eagle's eye for what is *far*,
He does not see you, he sees only *stars*.)

(FW, Vorspiel # 40, 2: 26, italics added)

Nah hab den Nächsten ich nicht gerne:
Fort mit ihm in die Höh und *Ferne*!
Wie würd er sonst zu meinem *Sterne*?

(I do not love my neighbor near,
But wish he were high up and *far*
How else could he become my *star*?)

(FW, Vorspiel # 30, 2: 23, italics added: both translations by Walter Kaufmann)

Nietzsche's myth of the future not only includes such lyrical but overspatialized imagery; it also assumes that the future is a *place*—distant and difficult to reach, but perfectly actual. The future is a mountain, a tree,[41] a nest; there are "realms of the future (*Reiche der Zukunft*)" around which the "will to power . . . flies and flutters covetously" (GB § 227, 2: 691). Zarathustra declares: "I flew too far into the future. . . . Then I flew back . . . and so I came to you, you men of the present (*ihr Gegenwärtigen*)" (Z II, 2: 375). Thus the future is a place to which one can travel and from which one can return into the present! The spatialization of temporal relations could hardly be carried further than this.

When Nietzsche writes, "We children of the future . . . much prefer to live on mountains, apart, 'untimely', in past or future (*kommenden*) centuries . . ." (FW § 377, 2: 252, 253), he is suggesting something that in other places—particularly his letters—he makes explicit, namely, that there is a *personal* future orientation which runs parallel to his *philosophical* future orientation. He appears to be almost pathologically sensitive to his fateful place among the centuries and millennia, and obsessed with the expectation that his work, now neglected on almost all hands, will come to be appreciated a century, or several centuries, after his death, and that it will then exercise a decisive influence, shaping that more distant future for thousands of years.

During his last lucid months Nietzsche wrote, with evident annoyance, to his sister:

> You haven't the remotest conception of the fact that you are closely related to a man and a fate in whom and in which the question of the millennia (die Frage von Jahrtausenden) has been decided. I hold the future of humanity, quite literally [!], in my hands. (Draft of a letter to Elizabeth Förster-Nietzsche, mid-November 1888.)

A year earlier he had declared that people would come to realize what he had been saying "some hundred years from now (etwa heute über hundert Jahre)" (letter to Franz Overbeck, November 12, 1887). He sent a long-time correspondent a copy of Beyond Good and Evil but advised her against reading it, saying that people would not find it readable until the year 2,000 (letter to Malwida von Meysenbug, September 24, 1886).

During the final days before his collapse Nietzsche reported excitedly that among his (very few) readers was August Strindberg, a man of genius, who considered him the "deepest spirit [or 'mind'] of all the millennia (den tiefsten Geist aller Jahrtausende) (letter to Meta von Salis, December 29, 1888). Nietzsche boasted that Zarathustra was "a book that will sound through [future] millennia" (EH Pref. § 4, 2: 1067).[42] He appears to be assuming that his work will have the sort of lasting impact that the works of Homer and Heraclitus have had—"voices" that have resounded over the course of more than two thousand years into our present.

Heidegger, in a parallel way, declared in his 1937 Nietzsche Seminar that his own confrontation with Nietzsche and with Western philosophy as a whole was "a matter for this century and for the century to come (eine Sache dieses und des kommenden Jahrhunderts)."[43] He added, grandiloquently, that if we fail to grasp Nietzsche's central doctrines in their relation to Western metaphysics (of which they are the culmination), "we will comprehend nothing of the twentieth century and of the centuries to come (den künftigen Jahrhunderten)."[44]

The term "life" which appears in the title of one of Nietzsche's important early works—Vom Nutzen und Nachteil der Historie für das Leben—has been much misunderstood. (I shall return to the term Historie in a moment.) Das Leben is often taken to mean either individual life or biological life in general. A few scattered texts can be read in a way that supports such interpretations. But Nietzsche's central intention is clear enough. Das Leben, or das Lebendige ("what is living") means "the life of culture" or "cultural vitality." Nietzsche says that *das Lebendige* can be either "a man, a people, or a *culture* (ein Mensch oder ein Volk oder eine *Kultur*)"; he refers to the "plastic power" and the "health" (or sickness) of "a man, a people, or a *culture*" (HL § 1, 1: 213, 219, italics added). He asserts that "an excess (*Übermass*) of history (*Historie*, i.e., "historical consciousness," "our interpretation and assessment, in the present, of what has happened in the past" [which Nietzsche distinguishes as *Geschichte*]) is harmful to what is alive (*dem Lebendigen*)" (HL § 2, 1: 219). In other words, a sense of the past which is too heavy and pervasive is an obstacle to future-oriented cultural creativity in the present.

Heidegger rightly notes that for Nietzsche " 'Life' is neither 'biologically' nor 'practically' intended; it is meant 'metaphysically'," and that it does not mean merely "human life," adding that the essence of "creative life" as "will to power" is not Darwinian self-preservation but "self-transcending enhancement" (*Steigerung über sich hinaus*)."[45] But Heidegger's positive characterization of how Nietzsche uses *das Leben*, namely, as "the term for what is (*jegliches Seiende*) and for beings as a whole (*das Seiende im Ganzen*)"[46] unduly "ontologizes" and thus distorts Nietzsche's position. Houlgate is closer to the truth, characterizing life (for Nietzsche) as "a creative artistic reality" marked by "dynamic aesthetic creativity."[47]

Nietzsche provides abundant clues to his rather special use of the term "life." Thus he closely associates and appears to identify the ideal of the "highest degree of powerfulness of the spirit [i.e., culture] (*der höchsten Mächtigkeit des Geistes*)" with that of the "most overabundant life (*des überreichsten Lebens*)" (WM § 14). In using *Geist* to mean "culture" rather than, or in addition to, "spirit," Nietzsche is following Hegel. Thus he often uses *der deutsche Geist* as a synonym for *die deutsche Kultur* (cf. DS § 1, 1: 137). And the prima facie puzzling, even paradoxical, characterization of *Geist* as the "life that itself strikes [or 'cuts' (*schneidet*)] into life" (Z II, 2: 361) means quite straight-forwardly that the life of culture, or cultural vitality, uses and exploits individual or biological life for its own purposes.

Examples of the achieved high culture—which is a "unity of artistic style in all the expressions of the life of a people (*Lebensäusserungen eines Volkes*)" (DS § 1, 1: 140)[48]—of the historical *past* are ancient Greece and Renaissance Italy, the former being pre-Christian, the latter (on Nietzsche's somewhat idiosyncratic reading) anti-Christian.

But the life of culture in which Nietzsche is most passionately interested is *future*-oriented. As he put it, "the main concept of [cultural] life (*der Hauptbegriff des Lebens*)" is "the concept 'future' (*der Begriff 'Zukunft'*)" (letter to Georg Brandes, May 23, 1888). It is in the remote world-historical future that higher and ever higher cultures will be created. Understood in this way, another recent commentator's claim that "Life [i.e., the life of culture] in all its moments [i.e., aspects or components] is affirmed [by Nietzsche] as an end in itself"[49] is both to the point and illuminating.

I sometimes wish that Nietzsche had seen fit to apply his "hermeneutics of suspicion" to that feature of the German language which makes it possible for the words *Jahrtausend* and even *Jahrmillion* to flow as trippingly from the future-oriented tongue as their relatively innocuous counterparts *Jahrzehnt* ("decade") and *Jahrhundert* ("century"). Although the term *Jahrtausend* occurs in Hegel, it is invariably used with respect to the historical past, never with respect to the historical future. For example, Hegel speaks of the history of philosophy as "the work of [past] millennia ([*die*] *Arbeit von Jahrtausenden*)," i.e., from the pre-Socratics to his own time (Enz. § 13). He refers to events that happened in and around Babylon "several thousand years ago (*seit mehreren tausend Jahren*)."[50] Even the less grandiose term *Jahrhundert* is used by Hegel exclusively with respect to the past, e.g., when he speaks of the "philosophical spirits [or 'minds'] of all the [past] centuries (*die philosophischen Geister aller Jahrhunderte*),"[51] or notes that the opposition between faith and reason has been a concern "for centuries" (*das Interesse von Jahrhunderten beschäftigt ist*).[52]

There is nothing in Hegel—or for that matter in the future-oriented Marx—to compare with the rhetorical extravagance of Nietzsche's claim that "in the long run (*auf die Dauer*)" in the present context means "a hundred thousand years [in the future] (*auf hunderttausend Jahre hin*)" (FW § 133, 2: 131). Earlier Nietzsche had written that the human race is a "tough and persistent thing and will not permit its progress (*seine Schritte*)—forwards [i.e., toward the future] or backwards [i.e., toward the past] to be viewed in terms of [mere] millennia (*Jahrtausende*) or indeed even in terms of hundreds of thousands of years (*Hunderttausenden von Jahren*)" (HL § 8, 1: 259). Perhaps, in speaking of hundreds of millennia of future history, Nietzsche was following Fichte's extravagant example. Referring to the future time when mutual respect and benevolence will prevail in human affairs, Fichte exclaimed "and even if it takes millions or trillions[53] of years—what is time!—surely a time will come when. . . ."[54]

It is difficult to take such rhetorical excesses seriously. One is at a loss to conceive of a historical situation which will occur millions or trillions—or even, with Nietzsche, hundred of thousands—of years in the future. Possibly Fichte intended this rhetorical flourish as a stratagem for deflecting suspicions in official circles that he in fact favored an early or immediate "revolution" in social relations. It may be that Nietzsche's remarks about *Hunderttausenden von Jahren* in the future are equally unserious. It is true that, in contrast to Fichte, Nietzsche spoke of millions or trillions of years in the future only in connection with the cosmic time of the eternal recurrence, not in connection with human history.[55] But I would insist that his characteristic, and repeated, references to *Jahrtausende* in the world-historical future are both serious and sinister—the latter for reasons suggested in Section IV above, and to be spelled out more fully below.

Typically, Nietzsche's claims about the world-historical future are limited to two or three thousand years, presumably because—given his spatial model of historical change and his controversial assumption of past-future symmetry—he sees the future as mirroring the past history of Europe, back to the Greeks and the Egyptians. Thus he celebrates the "bliss" of the creative few, speaking to them directly, "to press your hand upon [future] millennia (*Jahrtausende*) as upon wax" and "to write upon the will of [future] millennia (*Jahrtausende*) as upon metal [or 'bronze' (*Erz*)]" (Z III, 2: 460).

In a similar image Nietzsche writes of "men of the future," i.e., those with a powerful orientation toward the world-historical future, who "in the present" forcefully set the "will of [future] millennia (*Jahrtausende*) upon *new* tracks" (GB § 203, 2: 661). And, deploring the contemporary absence of a long-term future orientation, he asks rhetorically, "who would still dare to undertake [cultural] projects (*Werke*) that would require [future] millennia (*Jahrtausende*) for their completion?" (FW § 356, 2: 225).[56]

When Zarathustra speaks of "our great, far-off [future] empire of man (*Menschen-Reich*), the thousand-year empire of Zarathustra (*das Zarathustra-Reich von tausend Jahren*)" (Z IV, 2: 480), he is playing on the two senses of "millennium": (1) a perfected realm, purged of present flaws, and (2) a realm that will endure for a very long time in human history. This thousand-year realm or empire may also be a mirror image, projected into the world-historical future, of the thousand-year past history of the Holy Roman Empire (*das Heilige Römische Reich*), which lasted from ca. 800 until 1806. The *Zarathustra-Reich* is of course envisaged as something wholly secular, un-Roman, and anti-Christian.

More fundamentally, it seems to me, the *Zarathustra-Reich* is a radically secularized version of the Biblical doctrine that "[they] shall reign [with Christ] a thousand years (*basileusousin [meta tou Christou] chilia etē*)" (Rev. 20.4, 6).[57] Chiliasm is the belief that Christ will return to earth, displace its evil rulers and reign over the good and faithful in peace and harmony for "a thousand years," after which the world will end with the Last Judgment. Nietzsche's version—which might be called "cultural chiliasm" (as Marx's less explicit version might be called "socio-economic chiliasm"—see Section VII below)—omits the

Last Judgment, but insists on the dominance of the creative few, who in a thousand, or several thousand years, will have displaced the uncreative many, ushering in the unprecedentedly high culture of the "Nietzschean millennium."

Such claims are not harmlessly grandiose. They are sinister because, as already suggested, they involve an instrumentalizing of the present, in particular of existing individuals, a rejection of pity, and more generally of decency, and a preaching of what I have called "instrumental cruelty,"[58] cruelty with a purpose, directed at the timid, weak, and uncreative.

Such cruelty is not sadism, not cruelty for its own sake. Nietzsche directs scathing remarks at those who "enjoy" the spectacle of a bullfight—or a crucifixion (Z II, 2: 464). The instrumental cruelty that he advocates is ruthlessness toward the weak and conformist masses; its purpose is to economize and thus maximize the limited energies of the creative few. Nietzsche repudiates the morality of pity and *Nächstenliebe* in both its religious (Christian, Buddhist, "Schopenhauerian"[59]) and secular manifestations (egalitarianism, democracy, socialism, the "welfare state"). A key passage—already referred to in terms of its strong future orientation, is that entitled *Von der Nächstenliebe* ("On Love of One's Neighbor"), in which Nietzsche punningly, but with deadly seriousness, urges the displacement of *Nächstenliebe* by *Fernsten-Liebe*: "Do I exhort you to love of your neighbor? I exhort you rather to flight from your neighbor and to love of the most distant. Higher than love of one's neighbor stands love of the most distant and of the future; higher still than love of man I account love of causes (*Sachen*) and of phantoms (*Gespenster*)" (Z I, 2: 324, 325). Nietzsche's placing of *Sachen* and *Gespenster* above human beings is deliberate; in Stirner's anarchist and nominalist view—with which Nietzsche was familiar—all the components of what Hegel called *objektiver Geist* are scornfully repudiated as *Gespenster*. And this definitely includes high culture. Thus Nietzsche is calling not for the love of future generations as such, or even future individuals (*Übermenschen*) but rather for the love of the cause or enterprise (*Sache*) of building a future high culture (a Stirnerian *Gespenst*).

The summons to *Nächsten-Flucht* ("flight from one's neighbor") is incomplete and misleading as it stands. Nietzsche also intends a summons to acts of cruelty directed at the weak and faltering: "O my brothers, am I then cruel? But I say: That which is falling should also be pushed [down] (*was fällt, das soll man auch noch stossen!*)! Everything of today—it is falling, it is decaying . . . but I—want (*ich will*) to push it [down] too! . . . And him you do not teach to fly [creatively toward the future], teach—to fall faster!" (Z III, 2: 455).

Earlier he had spoken explicitly of *Nächsten-Hass* ("hatred of one's neighbor") (M § 63, 1: 1053).

In the previously quoted complaint that the present lives at the expense of the future, Nietzsche made clear that it was the morality of pity, functioning as a poison and narcotic, that brought about this abnormal situation (GM Pref. § 6, 2: 768).

In this light two of Nietzsche's prima facie paradoxical claims make good Nietzschean sense. (1) The "entire history of higher culture" is a *Vergeistigung* of cruelty (GM II § 6, 2: 807). Here *Vergeistigung* means not "spiritualization" (as Kaufmann has it), but—taking *Geist* in the sense of "culture"—rather "culturization," i.e., the placing of cruelty in the service of the building of high culture. This is precisely Nietzsche's claim for his favored instrumental cruelty. The claim is both historical and descriptive, on the one hand, and projective and programmatic, on the other. Nietzsche maintains that slavery and instrumental cruelty toward the conformist and uncreative masses have *always* been conditions for the creation of high culture, and that this relationship should and, if he has anything to say about it, *will* continue into the remotest world-historical future.

Scornfully rejecting the socialist claim that exploitation will be eliminated in the future, Nietzsche asserted bluntly that life (*das Lebendige*) itself is "essentially . . . injury (*Verletzung*), . . . suppression (*Unterdrückung*) . . . and . . . at its mildest, exploitation (*Ausbeutung*) . . ." (GB § 259, II, 729). Of course, here as elsewhere, Nietzsche means by *das Lebendige* not only, or primarily, individual or biological life, but the life of culture, cultural vitality.

(2) "The weak and the [creative] failures should perish: [this is] the first principle of our love of man (*Menschenliebe*). And one should help them do so" (AC § 2, 2: 1166). The paradox disappears when we realize that Nietzsche's *Menschenliebe* is not a *Nächstenliebe* but a *Fernstenliebe* and that the latter is not a love of (future) persons but a love of what they will create, the *Gespenst* of an unimaginably high culture.

Devotion to the building of high culture and concern for one's suffering neighbor are, for Nietzsche, incompatible. He is entirely serious when he complains bitterly at the fading of the future-oriented fundamental faith (*Grundglaube*) that "a [present] human being has value and meaning only insofar as he is *a stone in a great* [cultural] *edifice* (der Mensch nur insofern Wert hat, Sinn hat, als er *ein Stein in einem grossen Baue* ist) . . ." (FW § 356, 2: 225; Nietzsche's emphasis). The instrumentalizing of living human beings for the sake of the high culture of the remote world-historical future could hardly be more clearly formulated.

VII

Although Marx's orientation toward the world-historical future is less extravagantly expressed than Nietzsche's, with fewer poetic images, it also functions as a "conceptual mythology" or—in Marx's own language—an "ideology," i.e., a false or distorted consciousness of its object.

For example, Marx's doctrine of *Verelendung*, the increasing impoverishment of the proletariat (stubbornly maintained in the face of, and with deliberate suppression of, the growing counterevidence), his doctrine of "beneficent catastrophe" ("the worse it is now, the better it will be in the future"), and his doctrines of class struggle and the revolutionary "dictatorship of the proletariat" are broadly parallel to Nietzsche's doctrine of instrumental cruelty. In the words of a perceptive critic of the 1930s both thinkers were seeking

> a substitute for God in the form of the Kingdom of Heaven on Earth. [Both Nietzsche and Marx] treated the human being of today as a [mere] means to [the attaining of] the human being of tomorrow (*Mittel des Menschen von morgen*). Only the human being of the future, who is to be created by violence (*Gewalt*), justifies the contingent, unintended (*unbeabsichtigten*) human being who has gone before [in the present and the past]. . . . In both [thinkers] human beings lose their . . . intrinsic value (*Eigenwert*). . . . The doctrine of the *Übermensch* aims at an earthly God, [Marx's] socialism [aims at] a Kingdom of Heaven on earth. Both [doctrines] are pseudo-religions, opposed to Christianity, which betray the idea of love to the idea of violence. . . . Nietzsche and Marx are alike in preparing the way intellectually and culturally for [20th-century] dictatorship and the destruction of moral freedom.[60]

Like Nietzsche, Marx urges a "progressive" move into the future, beyond (bourgeois-Christian) "good and evil." An early commentator noted that Marx and the Marxists viewed "stateless communism" (and the classless society) as a "perfected condition, i.e., as a millennium or empire of a thousand years (*tausendjähriges Reich*)."[61]

Camus, who noted that both Nietzsche and Marx treated the historical future as a substitute for God and transcendence of any kind, added: "[T]here remains of Marx's prophecy [of a just classless society] only the passionate annunciation of an event that will take place in the very far future." When it fails to arrive, Marxists will say that the "delays are simply longer than was imagined and . . . one day, far away in the future, the end will justify all."[62]

The proletariat—the class "which holds the future in its hands" (T 481; MEW 4: 471)—will, in Marx's words, "have to pass through *long* struggles, through a *whole series* (*eine ganze Reihe*) of historical processes" (T 635; MEW 17: 343, italics added) before reaching the future.

A recent commentator adds that Marx's account of an "absolute . . . future-in-the-making . . . entails . . . a necessary ideologization [in Marx's sense, see above] of the future."[63]

Much of all this is summed up in Marx's use—in several key passages, dating from 1850 to 1875—of the expression "revolutionary dictatorship of the proletariat."[64] To be sure, Marx knew both the Latin language and Roman history; he appears to have used the German word *Diktatur* in roughly the sense of the Latin *dictatura*, namely, to designate the absolute and unlimited but temporary power delegated to a ruler or group of rulers to meet a specific emergency—military, economic, or social. However, the "dictatorship" of the bourgeoisie, which Marx describes in considerable detail in several works, will have lasted some three hundred years by the time the proletarian revolution puts an end to it for good. Marx offers no timetable for the disappearance of the dictatorship of the proletariat, and there is no good reason to suppose that it will be of significantly shorter duration—indeed it might be of much longer duration—than the dictatorship of the bourgeoisie. This doctrine, as presented by Marx, throws open the doctrinal door to "transitional totalitarianism" and "temporary terror," where what is held to be both transitional and temporary may in fact be of unlimited duration.

As one commentator has noted, in Marxist-Leninist practice the transitional condition or state has become an end in itself. And the end-in-view which it was supposed to lead to and bring about has been indefinitely postponed.[65]

The distinguished theologian Karl Rahner has put the point succinctly:

> Christianity, through its hope for an absolute [i.e., trans-historical] future, protects man from the temptation to strive so violently for a this-worldly (*innerweltliche*) future that every [present] generation is brutally sacrificed for the sake of the next [i.e., future] generation, and so on, and thus the future becomes a Moloch at whose altar real human beings are slaughtered for the sake of human beings who are never actual [but] always absent or not-yet there (*nie wirklichen, immer ausständigen*).[66]

Whether one puts the point in such theological language, or in the language of ethical humanism, there is nothing in Marx's own position to preclude the situations here described, situations all too familiar from the history of Stalinism in the Soviet Union. As I have argued in detail elsewhere, Marx accepts a future-oriented "humanism of ideals" but rejects any present-oriented "humanism of principles" with its defense of the rights and the dignity of living individuals.[67] And a humanism of ideals is fully compatible with the instrumentalizing of the present, and indeed with transitional totalitarianism, in which the humanist ideal is—in conformity with what I have called the "fallacy of deferred value"—repeatedly and endlessly postponed to the yet more remote world-historical future.

Tobora has put the point in forceful, if less than lucid, language. For Marx present individuals, as "degraded, enslaved, . . . and despicable beings," function as "fit [i.e., appropriate] means [for] the humanization of all men in the future," but in the meantime "alienative situations in the present" may be indefinitely extended in the name of the future end-in-view. The remoteness of the envisaged future, together with the "loftiness" (i.e., vagueness, unreality?) of the communist ideal, invites the "fanaticism" of inhuman practices in the present.[68]

VIII

The obsessive orientation toward the world-historical future on the part of both Marx and Nietzsche is the obverse of their intense hatred of and contempt for the historical present, in which—unlike Hegel—they are constitutionally unable to feel "at home" (bei sich). They are prepared to unmask and "deconstruct" what Hegel has to say about the "life and freedom of the present (Lebendigkeit und Freiheit der Gegenwart)."[69] But as a perceptive commentator, a non-Marxist Russian writing in Moscow in 1921, expressed it, Hegel emphasizes the rationality which is "realizing itself in history, in every historical moment, in every 'present', thus acknowledging historical existence and the historical process at every moment as a self-contained existence [i.e., as having intrinsic value], not predestined to serve as a step or a means in some Providential plan or in the program . . . of progress [as defined by some future-oriented theorist or activist]."[70]

The point has been vividly expressed by Dwight Macdonald, who wrote in 1946 that

> Marxists . . . habitually regard the Present as merely the mean entrance-hall to the spacious palace of the Future. For the entrance-hall seems to stretch out interminably; it may or may not lead to a palace; meanwhile it is all the palace we have and we must live in it. . . . [W]e shall live in it better and even find the way to the palace (if there is a palace), if we try living in the present instead of in the Future.[71]

Camus made a parallel point when he declared that "[r]eal generosity toward the future lies in giving all to the present."[72]

It is in their instrumentalizing and devaluing (*Entwertung*) of the present—of present communities, cultures, practices, and, especially, persons—that Nietzsche and Marx most unambiguously exhibit the abusive reversal and inversion of Hegel's doctrine which both of them have undertaken.

NOTES

1. Sören Kierkegaard, *Concluding Unscientific Postscript* [1846], trans. David F. Swenson and Walter Lowrie (Princeton University Press, 1941), p. 128.

2. Friedrich Nietzsche, *The Will to Power*, trans. Walter Kaufmann and R. J. Hollingdale (New York: Random House, 1967), § 766. Hereafter references to Nietzsche's works will be given by means of sigla in the text. The sigla, and corresponding works, in chronological order are as follows: "DS" (*David Strauss, der Bekenner und der Schriftsteller/David Strauss, the Confessor and the Writer*); "HL" (*Vom Nutzen und Nachteil der Historie für das Leben/On the Uses and Disadvantages of History for Life*); "MA" (*Menschliches, Allzumenschliches/ Human, All-Too-Human*; followed by "I" and "II" for vols. 1 and 2, respectively); "M" (*Die Morgenröte/ The Dawn*); "FW" (*Die fröhliche Wissenschaft/The Gay Science*); "Z" (*Also sprach Zarathustra/Thus Spoke Zarathustra*; followed by "I," etc. for Part 1, etc.); "GB" (*Jenseits von Gut und Böse/Beyond Good and Evil*); "GM" (*Zur Genealogie der Moral/ On the Genealogy of Morals*); "GD" (*Die Götzen-Dämmerung/The Twilight of the Idols*); "EH" (*Ecce Homo*); "AC" (*Der Antichrist/The Antichrist*). Volume, part, and section numbers will be given (where appropriate), followed by volume and page numbers in Karl Schlechta's edition, *Werke in drei Bänden* (Munich: Hanser, 1960). "2: 345" will mean "vol. 2, p. 345." I have quoted and sometimes revised the translations by Walter Kaufmann (of FW, GB, GM, and EH), by R. J. Hollingdale (of DS, HL, and Z), and—as indicated above—by Kaufmann and Hollingdale (of WM). Nietzsche's letters are cited by addressee and date. The fullest collection of letters to and from Nietzsche (in sixteen volumes) is to be found in the *Kritische Gesamtausgabe*, ed. Giorgio Colli and Mazzino Montinari (Berlin: de Gruyter, 1975–1984), but many of the most important of Nietzsche's own letters are included in Schlechta, 3: 927–1352. All translations from Nietzsche's letters are my own. Schlechta's arrangement of the *Nachlass* of the 1880s (3: 415–925) is less convenient than that of other German editions, to which the section numbers of the Kaufmann-Hollingdale translation correspond. The index volume of Schlechta contains a double concordance for cross-reference between his arrangement and the standard one (4: 485–514). A few texts from the *Nachlass* not included in WM are cited (with footnote references) from earlier and more complete editions of Nietzsche's *Werke*.

3. See my essay, "The Myth of Marx's Materialism" in *Philosophical Sovietology: The Pursuit of a Science*, ed. Helmut Dahm, Thomas J. Blakeley, and George L. Kline (Dordrecht and Boston: Reidel, 1988), pp. 158–203.

4. Nietzsche's characterization of Napoleon as a "synthesis of the *inhuman* and *superhuman* (*Unmensch* und *Übermensch*)" (GM I § 16, 2: 797) is well known. Less well known are three specific claims that Nietzsche makes

about Napoleon. The first two are close to Hegel's points; the third is distinctively "Nietzschean."

(a) Napoleon's life exhibited a "miracle of meaning (*Wunder von Sinn*)"; he was "a *force majeure* of genius and will . . ., strong enough to create a unity out of Europe, a political and *economic* unity for the sake of a world government (*Erdregierung*)" (EH, 2: 1148; cf. also Nietzsche's letter to Franz Overbeck, Oct. 18, 1888). As a result Europeans owe to Napoleon "almost all of the higher hopes of this century" (WM § 27).

(b) Napoleon is included, with Julius Caesar and Alexander the Great, among the great men of history—precisely Hegel's list (WM § 751). In one place Nietzsche adds Mohammed to these three (M § 549, 1: 1269). On a list of great men who behaved "immorally" Alexander the Great is omitted and Frederick the Great is added—along with Homer, Aristophanes, Leonardo da Vinci, and Goethe (WM § 380; in the Kaufmann-Hollingdale translation both Napoleon and Frederick the Great are erroneously omitted from this list).

(c) Napoleon is an *ens realissimum* [!] (GD § 49, 2: 1025), who, with Julius Caesar, belongs among the "highest human beings" and represents the "future of the highest human beings" (WM §§ 544, 975). Napoleon is grouped with poets, novelists, composers, and philosophers—in one list with Stendhal, Goethe, Heine, Beethoven, Wagner, and Schopenhauer (GB § 256, 2: 724), in another with Dante and Michelangelo (WM § 1018). In the latter passage Nietzsche quotes with approval a journal article in which Hippolyte Taine spoke of Napoleon as the "posthumous brother of Dante and Michelangelo," a man who is "*leur égal: son génie a la même taille et la même structure*" as theirs.

5. Marx and Engels, *Manifesto of the Communist Party* in *The Marx-Engels Reader*, ed. Robert C. Tucker, 2nd ed. (New York: Norton, 1978), p. 483; German text in *Marx-Engels-Werke* ([East] Berlin: Dietz, 1969), 4: 474. Hereafter such references will be given in the text in the form "(T 487; MEW 4: 474)." References to works not included in the *Marx-Engels Reader* will be given separately in footnotes. Hegel's discussion of the "cunning of reason" is in the *Lectures on the Philosophy of World History: Introduction*, trans. H. B. Nisbet (Cambridge University Press, 1975), p. 89; German text in *Sämtliche Werke*, ed. Hermann Glockner (Stuttgart: Frommann, 1928), 11: 63.

6. Nietzsche was delighted with Georg Brandes' characterization of the Nietzschean position as an "aristocratic radicalism," declaring, "That is . . . the cleverest expression that I have read about myself up to now (*Das ist . . . das gescheuteste* [i.e., *gescheiteste*] *Wort, das ich bisher über mich gelesen habe*") (letter to G. Brandes, Dec. 2, 1887).

7. *Concluding Unscientific Postscript*, p. 135. Nietzsche's agreement with Kierkegaard on this specific point does not, of course, make him an "existentialist."

8. Stephen Houlgate, *Hegel, Nietzsche and the Criticism of Metaphysics* (Cambridge University Press, 1986), pp. 24, 27. Heidegger's claim—that Nietzsche's hectic decade (1879–1888) of work on his magnum opus "did not grant him the time to linger in the vast halls [or 'edifices' (*Bauten*)] of

Hegel's and Schelling's works"—strikes me as misguided. If Nietzsche had had more leisure, it is highly *unlikely* that he would have used it for a close study of either Hegel or Schelling. (See Martin Heidegger, *Nietzsche* [Pfullingen: Neske, 1961], 1: 75–76; English version in *Nietzsche by Martin Heidegger*, trans. David F. Krell [San Francisco: Harper & Row, 1984], 1: 63.)

9. Houlgate, *Hegel, Nietzsche and the Criticism of Metaphysics*, pp. 229–230n.23.

10. Alfred Baeumler, "Nietzsche" [1930] in *Studien zur deutschen Geistesgeschichte* [1937], 3rd edition (Berlin: Junker & Dünnhaupt, 1943), p. 252.

11. *Writings of the Young Marx on Philosophy and Society*, ed. and trans. Loyd D. Easton and Kurt H. Guddat (New York: Doubleday, 1967), p. 383; MEW 2: 90, italics modified.

12. "Economic and Philosophic Manuscripts" (1844) in *Writings of the Young Marx*, p. 322; MEW Ergänzungsband 1: 575.

13. John Herman Randall, Jr., *The Career of Philosophy*, Vol. 2: *From the German Enlightenment to the Age of Darwin* (New York: Columbia University Press, 1965), p. 277.

14. Richard Kilminster, *Praxis and Method: A Sociological Dialogue with Lukács, Gramsci and the Early Frankfurt School* (London: Routledge & Kegan Paul, 1979), p. 57.

15. There is no evidence that Nietzsche was aware of Marx's critique of Hegel on this point. That critique is mainly contained in the "Economic and Philosophic Manuscripts," which were not published until long after Nietzsche's death.

16. Fritz Gerlich, *Der Kommunismus als Lehre vom Tausendjährigen Reiche* (Munich: Bruckmann, 1920), p. 206.

17. Although Nietzsche did not use the expression *Wille zur Zukunft* in any of his published writings, this key expression occurs in a fragmentary text from the period 1882–1885: "Jedesmal die Mitte, wenn der *Wille zur Zukunft* entsteht: *das grösste Ereignis steht bevor!*" (*Nietzsches Werke* [Leipzig: Naumann, 1904], 14: 263). It seems clear that this passage should have been included in the collection of fragmentary texts and drafts published (in 1901, 3rd enlarged edition, 1906) as *The Will to Power* (*Der Wille zur Macht*)—which in fact might well have been given the more informative title *The Will to Power as Will to the Future* (*Der Wille zur Macht als Wille zur Zukunft*)—and was omitted only because the original editors, prominently including Nietzsche's sister, Elizabeth Förster-Nietzsche, failed to recognize its theoretical importance. Cf. Karl Löwith's suggestive remark about the impact of Wagner's *Zukunftsmusik* upon "Nietzsches zeitlichen *Willen zur Zukunft*" (*Von Hegel zu Nietzsche: Der revolutionäre Bruch im Denken des 19. Jahrhunderts* [1941], [4th ed., Stuttgart: Kohlhammer, 1958], p. 192, italics added). Nietzsche had used the related expression *Wollust des Zukünftigen* ("voluptuous delight in the future") (Z III, 2: 467), and the editors of *The Will to Power* had included the parallel expression *Lust am . . . Zukünftigen* ("joy in . . . the future") (WM § 417). Earlier, Nietzsche had spoken of learning "to desire the future more vehemently (*die Zukunft heftiger begehren*)" (HL § 1, 1: 217).

18. Nancy S. Love, *Marx, Nietzsche, and Modernity* (New York: Columbia University Press, 1986), p. 52.

19. Laurence Lampert, *Nietzsche's Teaching: An Interpretation of* Thus Spoke Zarathustra (New Haven and London: Yale University Press, 1986), pp. 19, 79.

20. *Nachlass* (1884) in *Nietzsches Werke* (Leipzig: Naumann, 1903), 13: 37.

21. Joel Tabora, S.J., *The Future in the Writings of Karl Marx* (Frankfurt, Bern, New York: Peter Lang, 1983), pp. 353, 354-55.

22. *Lectures on the Philosophy of World History*, p. 170; *Sämtliche Werke*, 11: 129. Hegel makes a parallel remark about "epic poems that would perhaps appear in the future (*Epopoeen . . . die vielleicht in Zukunft sein werden*)," suggesting that they would express the "victory of a future living American rationality (*den Sieg dereinstiger amerikanischer lebendiger Vernünftigkeit*)" over endlessly repeated but limited depictions of particular European events (*Vorlesungen über die Aesthetik* in *Sämtliche Werke*, 14: 355).

23. *Lectures on the Philosophy of World History*, p. 171.

24. Alexandre Kojève, *Introduction to the Reading of Hegel*, ed. Allan Bloom, trans. J. H. Nichols, Jr. (New York: Basic Books, 1969), pp. 134, 136.

25. Ibid., p. 140, italics added. The French original of this phrase reads: "le Temps où *prime l'Avenir* qui *détermine* le *Présent*, en passant par le *Passé*" (*Introduction à la lecture de Hegel* [Paris: Gallimard, 1947], p. 372, italics added).

26. The key passage reads as follows: "*Die Gewesenheit entspringt der Zukunft, so zwar, dass die gewesene (besser gewesende [!]) Zukunft die Gegenwart aus sich entlässt*" (*Sein und Zeit* [1927] [Tübingen: Niemeyer, 1960], § 65, p. 326, italics added).

27. Albert Camus, *The Rebel* [1951], trans. Anthony Bower (New York: Vintage, 1956), p. 142.

28. Franz Grégoire, *Études Hégéliennes: Les Points capitaux du système* (Louvain: Publications Universitaires; Paris: Éditions Béatrice-Nauwelaerts, 1958), pp. 121n.1, 209, 264, 316.

29. *Ibid.*, pp. 354-55.

30. Camus, *The Rebel*, p. 142.

31. See my essay, " 'Present', 'Past', and 'Future' as Categoreal Terms, and the 'Fallacy of the Actual Future'," *Review of Metaphysics*, Vol. 40 (1986-1987), esp. pp. 219-220, 223-25, 229-230.

32. See my essay, "Form, Concrescence, and Concretum" in *Explorations in Whitehead's Philosophy*, ed. Lewis S. Ford and George L. Kline (New York: Fordham University Press, 1983), esp. pp. 104-107.

33. " 'Present', 'Past', and 'Future' . . .," pp. 226-27.

34. Cf. PhG, Pref. §2. Hegel applies the metaphor of bud-blossom-fruit explicitly to the history of philosophical doctrines, but I consider it generalizable to world history, at any stage of which—as one might put it—some buds are opening into full blossom while others have been nipped by the frost: some fruits are ripening while others are rotting. Such a metaphor is measurably superior to the spatial models or metaphors according to which historical improvements or positive developments are expressed as forward or upward movements and historical worsenings or negative developments as backward or downward movements.

35. Although Hegel did not accept the spatial model of historical change, he did frequently use the term 'progress' (*Fortschritt* or *Fortschreiten*) to characterize historical improvements or positive developments. A key formulation in the *Lectures on the Philosophy of World History* is "World history is the *progress* (*Fortschritt*) of the consciousness of freedom" (*Philosophy of World History*, trans. Nisbet, p. 54, italics added). Equally suggestive of locomotion, and hence equally misleading, are the terms "decline" (*Untergang*) and "fall" (*Verfall*) (ibid., p. 199; *Sämtliche Werke*, 11: 153). But Hegel also used two non-spatializing terms, terms appropriate to the bud-blossom-fruit metaphor of historical change: "becoming" (*Werden*) as in "religion's process of becoming (*das Werden der Religion*)" (PhG § 680) and "development" (*Entwicklung*) as in another key formulation from the *Vorlesungen über die Philosophie der Geschichte*, "world history is nothing but the development of the concept of freedom (*die Weltgeschichte ist nichts als die Entwicklung des Begriffs der Freiheit*)" (*Sämtliche Werke*, 11: 568).

36. One partial and relatively early exception was noted in Section III above. But there the future orientation, as we saw, was modestly short-term.

37. *Vorlesungen über die Geschichte der Philosophie*. vol. 3, ch. 2, in *Sämtliche Werke*, 19: 485–87. In the *Vorlesungen über die Philosophie der Geschichte* a typical *Übergang* is that between the Oriental World (China, India, Persia, etc.) and the world of ancient Greece (*Sämtliche Werke*, 11: 292).

38. Letter to Joseph Weydemeyer, March 5, 1852, in T 220; MEW 28: 508, italics removed.

39. Hollingdale, whose translation of *Zarathustra* is generally accurate and readable, quite unjustifiably renders "die Liebe zum *Fernsten* und *Künftigen*" as "love of the most distant *man* and of the *man* of the future" (*Nietzsche: Thus Spoke Zarathustra* [Harmondsworth: Penguin Books, 1969], p. 87, italics added). I prefer Kaufmann's straightforward rendering: "love of the farthest and the future" (Walter Kaufmann, *The Portable Nietzsche* [New York: Viking, 1954], p. 173).

40. *Werke: Kritische Gesamtausgabe*, ed. Giorgio Colli and Mazzino Montinari (Berlin: de Gruyter, 1977), Abt. 7, Bd. 1, p. 638.

41. Even before he had come to characterize the future as a "tree" (*Auf dem Baume Zukunft bauen wir unser Nest*: "We build our nest in the tree Future"— Z II, 2: 356, repeated in EH, 2: 1081), Nietzsche had spoken of the "uprooting of a vigorous [i.e., culturally powerful] future (*Entwurzelung einer lebenskräftigen Zukunft*)" (HL § 4, 1: 231; cf. § 7, 1: 252).

42. Walter Kaufmann, whose Nietzsche translations are generally accurate, unaccountably renders "mit einer Stimme *über Jahrtausende* hinweg" as "with a voice bridging *centuries*," thus reducing Nietzsche's grandiose "thousands" to mere "hundreds" (*Nietzsche: On the Genealogy of Morals and Ecce Homo* [New York: Random House, 1967], p. 219, italics added).

43. Heidegger, *Nietzsche*, 1: 340; *Nietzsche by Martin Heidegger*, 2: 83.

44. Heidegger, *Nietzsche*, 1: 26; *Nietzsche by Martin Heidegger*, 1: 17.

45. Heidegger, *Nietzsche*, 1: 253, 186, 406, 488; *Nietzsche by Martin Heidegger*, 1: 219, 159; 2: 144; 3: 15.

46. Heidegger, *Nietzsche*, 1: 488; *Nietzsche by Martin Heidegger*, 3: 15. Without going into the details of Heidegger interpretation, one should note that for him *das Seiende/die Seienden* is something quite different from *das Sein*, the latter being "ontological," the former merely "ontic." Thus it is confusing when in one place Heidegger characterizes "life" for Nietzsche as *das Sein* conceived as *Werden* (*Nietzsche*, 1: 253; *Nietzsche by Martin Heidegger*, 1: 219).

47. Houlgate, *Hegel, Nietzsche and the Criticism of Metaphysics*, pp. 188, 85.

48. Hollingdale inexplicably omits the word *künstlerisch* ("artistic") in translating this passage (*Nietzsche: Untimely Meditations* [Cambridge University Press, 1983], p. 5). However, he restores the missing adjective in the later passage in which Nietzsche repeats this formulation (HL § 4, 1: 23), ibid., p. 79.

49. *Love, Marx, Nietzsche, and Modernity*, p. 193.

50. *Vorlesungen über die Philosophie der Geschichte* in *Sämtliche Werke*, 11: 241.

51. *Enzyklopädie der philosophischen Wissenschaften im Grundrisse*, ed. F. Nicolin and O. Pöggeler (Hamburg: Meiner, 1969), Pref. to 1st ed., p. 22.

52. Hegel's Preface to Hermann Hinrichs, *Die Religion in inneren Verhältnisse zur Wissenschaft* (Heidelberg: Karl Groos, 1822, rpt. 1970), p. i.

53. Fichte's term is *Billionen*, i.e., "million-millions," which in American usage is "trillions" rather than "billions."

54. J. G. Fichte, *Vorlesungen über die Bestimmung des Gelehrten* [1811] (East Berlin: Aufbau, 1956), p. 58.

55. In discussing the doctrine of eternal recurrence, Nietzsche says in the *Nachlass* that between successive "recurrences" of the same (*des Gleichen*) there will be only the briefest moment, "even if living creatures measure [that interval] in terms of trillions of years (*Jahrbillionen*)." (cf. *Nietzsches Werke* [Leipzig: Naumann, 1904], 12: 66. This is one of a number of passages which make it clear that the doctrine of eternal recurrence is a *cosmic* and not a historical doctrine.

56. Other uses of *Jahrtausende* to refer to the world-historical future may be found at FW § 337, 2: 198 and § 380, 2: 255. The cognate term *jahrtausendelang* occurs at FW § 108, 2: 115. Of course, like Hegel, Nietzsche also uses *Jahrtausende* to refer to past stretches of history; but in certain of these cases he places himself imaginatively at the given point in past time and thus treats the elapsed millennia as though they referred to the future, i.e., the future as viewed from that past. An example is his remark that "[t]he dogmatist' philosophy was . . . only a promise across millennia [i.e., from ancient times to the present]" (GB Pref., 2: 565). For similar usages, see GB § 195, 2: 653; GD § 35, 2: 1010; AC §§ 58, 59, 2: 1229, 1230; WM § 1043.

57. In Luther's translation this reads "sie werden . . . mit [Christo] regieren tausend Jahre." Nietzsche uses this as a subtext for a late, sarcastic remark: "Das 'Reich Gottes' . . . kommt *nicht* in 'tausend Jahren' " (AC § 34, 2: 1197; italics added).

58. See my Foreword to *Nietzsche in Russia*, ed. Bernice G. Rosenthal (Princeton University Press, 1986), p. xiii.

59. Schopenhauer referred to *Nächstenliebe* and *Mitleid* ("pity" or "compassion") as the "most necessary of things" (*das Nötigste*) (*Parerga und Paralipomena* in *Werke* [Wiesbaden: Brockhaus, 1966], 6: 323).

60. Walter Schubart, *Europa und die Seele des Ostens* [1938] (Lucerne: Vita Nova, 1947), p. 196. This intriguing book has been freely translated by Amethé von Zeppelin as *Russia and Western Man* (New York: Ungar, 1950), in which edition the passage quoted is on p. 184.

61. Gerlich, *Der Kommunismus als Lehre vom Tausendjährigen Reiche*, p. 160.

62. *The Rebel*, pp. 226, 222. The expression "one day, far away in the future" is a very free rendering of Camus's phrase *un jour encore invisible* (cf. *L'Homme révolté* [Paris: Gallimard, 1951], p. 275).

63. Tabora, *The Future in the Writings of Karl Marx*, p. 320; cf. also p. 371.

64. The works in question are *The Class Struggles in France* (1850), the letter to Joseph Weydemeyer quoted above (1852), and the *Critique of the Gotha Program* (1875). The expression "dictatorship of the proletariat" occurs twice in the first and last of these texts and once in the second of them. Cf. T 220, 538, 590, 592–593.

65. Heinz-Dietrich Wendland, "Christliche und kommunistische Hoffnung," *Marxismus-studien*, Vol. 1 (1954), 225.

66. Karl Rahner, "Marxistische Utopie und christliche Zukunft des Menschen" in *Schriften zur Theologie* (Einsiedeln: Benziger, 1965), Vol. 6 ("Neuere Schriften"), p. 84.

67. See my essay, "Was Marx an Ethical Humanist?" *Studies in Soviet Thought*, Vol. 9 (1969), 91–103.

68. Tabora, *The Future in the Writings of Karl Marx*, pp. 371, 363, 374.

69. *Lectures on the Philosophy of World History*, p. 21; *Sämtliche Werke*, 11: 31.

70. Gustav G. Shpet, *Filosofskoe mirovozzrenie Gertsena* (Herzen's Philosophical World View) (St. Petersburg: Kolos, 1921), p. 48.

71. Dwight Macdonald, "The Root is Man," *Politics*, vol. 3 (1946), 98; quoted in Steven Lukes, *Marxism and Morality* (Oxford University Press, 1985), pp. 139, 145.

72. Camus, *The Rebel*, p. 304.

Chapter Two

HEGEL AND THE PROBLEM OF DIFFERENCE

Carl G. Vaught

In the hands of his most persistent critics, philosophy in the aftermath of Hegel has focused upon three pervasive themes: first the problem of existence and individuality,[1] then the problem of theory and practice,[2] and finally the problem of identity and difference.[3] From a systematic point of view, this final problem is the most important, for it epitomizes the fact that Hegel's critics have always attempted to stand outside his comprehensive philosophical system. The philosophies of existence, individuality, praxis, and difference which have been Hegel's most visible philosophical legacy are rooted in the primacy of difference and in the conviction that philosophy after Hegel is possible only if the omnivorousness of his system can be transcended from an external point of view.

Despite the force of these familiar responses to Hegel, there are two obvious difficulties with any external attack upon the Hegelian enterprise. First, Hegel makes the phenomenon of negation the central element of his system so that any attempt to stand outside it becomes an indirect way of being imprisoned within it. As he expresses the point in both the *Phenomenology* and the *Logic*, the kind of negation, opposition, and difference that appears to be external to the system is included in it as the moving principle that allows his thought to become a living unity.[4] The critic who adopts an external point of view in relation to Hegel is therefore placed from the outset at the center of his dynamically developing philosophical system. In the second place, Hegel claims that even if non-dialectical difference were possible, it would be absolutely unintelligible. He demands repeatedly that we say what we mean, but if we intend to speak on behalf of radical externality, we are unable to do so without embracing the universality that is one of the marks of the dynamic logos

under external attack.[5] Hegel insists that difference is always dialectical and that by itself, bare difference is just as unintelligible as
simple identity.[6]

In order to avoid these difficulties, my own criticism of Hegel will
be internal and will examine the problem of difference as a way of
exploding his dialectical project from within. I will also focus my
attention primarily on the *Phenomenology*, for it is the most perspic-
uous place to exhibit the presence of non-dialectical difference in
Hegel's thought. The first example of the kind of difference I have in
mind is to be found in sense-certainty, where Hegel begins with
what is given, moves to the attempt to articulate it in terms of an
abstract universal, and then suggests that the truth of sense-certainty
is the process in which the particular articulated in this way both
vanishes and is preserved as a constituent element of a concrete
plurality. In describing the temporal dimension of experience, Hegel
first suggests that it is present *now*, and that we might attempt to
capture its conceptual content by claiming that the "now" is night.
But if we make this abstract claim, it is negated by the temporal
process as it moves from night to day, and the process itself becomes
the "now" as a concrete universal that is neither day nor night but
both together. The "now" preserves itself by negating abstract universality and its self-identity is constituted by the fact that it remains
utterly unaffected by its own negativity. Thus, the momentary "now"
with which we begin, and the abstract "now" with which we might
attempt to bring time to a standstill, finally become the "now" as a
self-identical process generated by its own self-negation.[7]

An even more forceful formulation of this point is to be found in
Hegel's brief characterization of the act of pointing to the temporal
aspect of experience. In this formulation he says:

> (1) I point out the "Now," and it is asserted to be the truth. I point it
> out, however, as something that *has been*, or as something that has
> been superseded; I set aside the first truth. (2) I now assert as the
> second truth that it *has been*, that it is superseded. (3) But what has
> been, *is not*; I set aside the second truth, its *having been*, its superses-
> sion, and thereby negate the negation of the "Now" and thus return
> to the first assertion, that the "*Now*" is. The "Now," and pointing
> out the "Now," are thus so constituted that neither the one nor the
> other is something immediate and simple, but a movement which
> contains various moments.[8]

The movement in question is temporality understood as the Absolute
Process, and the moments to which Hegel refers are a unified plurality of "nows," bound together by negating the negation of abstract
universality.

In his phenomenological description of sense-certainty, Hegel provides us with a profound account of the dialectical structure of time, where in Kantian terms we find a dynamic reconstruction of the synopsis of sense and of the temporal dimension of sensible intuition. His characterization of the "now" is an attempt to articulate the nature of this synopsis, and his explication of the act of pointing is a dialectical reformulation of the nature of pure intuition.[9] However, in this same section Hegel implies that space is equally dynamic and dialectical, and it is here that he begins to ignore a non-dialectical dimension of difference we must not overlook. Hegel claims that having referred to a particular spatial region, we find that *when we turn around*, it has been replaced by another. As a result he says that the truth of space is universal, not simply because a description of a particular spatial region must be universal, but because space remains constant when a particular "here" vanishes as it is replaced by another.[10] Yet Hegel fails to notice that this transition is mediated by my own act of turning around and that this act is clearly non-dialectical. The sequence of statements that results when I attempt to articulate the determinate content of particular spatial regions as I turn from place to place can be understood dialectically. But this is due to the fact that they form a temporal series and does not imply that space is inherently dialectical. In fact, space must be presupposed as the non-dialectical context in which I turn around before these statements can be formulated, and from a transcendental point of view, it becomes the non-dialectical dimension of sensibility and pure intuition.

The difference between space and time as forms of intuition is that space is non-dialectical while time is not. The temporal dimension of the phenomenological process unfolds of itself, and as Hegel reminds us, the philosopher can simply observe this self-developing process without any outside interference.[11] However, the spatial dimension of the process does not take care of itself in the same way, for it unfolds dialectically only after the subject makes a non-dialectical transition. And it does so even then only when this same subject formulates a sequence of utterances that can be taken up into a dialectical context. The most important conclusion to be drawn from this fact is that when the spatial and temporal dimensions of experience are taken together, the spatial element must not be sublated, since it is the non-dialectical presupposition that makes a series of "spatial" utterances possible. To move from one "here" to another is structurally quite different from moving from one temporal moment to another in terms of a determinate negation. This structural difference should be acknowledged by admitting that there is a radical externality about the relation between one "here" and another that is not to be captured in dialectical terms. Difference is not always reducible to negation and space is constituted by a non-dialectical dimension of difference that is not reducible to the negative moment of a temporal process.

This non-dialectical element is also reflected in Hegel's account of the role of the subject of consciousness in sense-certainty, though he refuses to acknowledge its presence in this admittedly more complex dialectical context. The transition to the subject first occurs in order to allow us to remain in contact with the particularity of the object with which we began. The transmutation of the "now" and the "here" into universals can be prevented only if *I* hold them fast and because *I* see and hear that "now" is day rather than night and that "here" is a tree rather than a house. But as Hegel reminds us, another "I" can make a different assertion, and when it does, the dialectical development we have traced already re-emerges. One bare assertion cancels out the other, and all that survives is the "I" understood as a universal that is mediated by any particular claim.[12] In Kantian terms, this "I" is to be understood as the transcendental ego, transmuted into a dynamic center of activity, just as sensibility and pure intuition have been transformed dialectically in the earlier account.

In developing his account from an exclusively dialectical perspective, Hegel has overlooked once more the non-dialectical element at the heart of his position. He fails to acknowledge the fact that when a *different* "I" makes a different assertion than the first, there are two senses of difference involved, the first of which is the non-dialectical ground of the second. The two "I's" do not differ from one another in the same way that the contents of their utterances do, for both may speak independently, even though what they say may be subjected to subsequent dialectical transformations. Indeed, this independence is necessary if there is to be another "I" who makes a different utterance which may then take its place within a larger dialectical context. The transcendental ego thus proves to have two sides which parallel the earlier contrast between the two forms of pure intuition, one of which is dialectical, while the other is the non-dialectical ground of ordinary discourse.

It remains to be seen whether we can state philosophically what we mean to do in drawing this distinction, for unless this can be done, non-dialectical difference can at best be pointed out rather than articulated. It would then remain wordless; articulation would once again prove to be exclusively dialectical; and the *empirical* differences between the "now" and the "here" and between two distinct centers of consciousness would have no *philosophical* significance. It is therefore of the utmost importance that a mode of discourse be developed that will enable us to articulate both the spatial and the temporal aspects of experience and both the dialectical and the non-dialectical dimensions of the experiencing subject.

Perhaps we can take our clue from Hegel's own procedure in this respect. In discussing the contrast between saying and meaning, Hegel confronts the problem of framing an adequate philosophical language by introducing an ambiguous sense of universality.[13] He suggests that we can say what we mean straight-forwardly by using abstract universals, and it is articulation of this kind that he some-times seems to demand of the non-philosophical consciousness.[14] By contrast, Hegel acknowledges the fact that the concept of a concrete universal is inherently difficult to articulate and that it is by no means clear that we can say what we mean in this respect without straining language almost to the limit. As he formulates the point himself,

. . . the proposition in the *form of a judgment* is not suited to express speculative truths . . .

[Moreover,] it is the form of simple judgment, when it is used to express speculative results, which is very often responsible for the paradoxical and bizarre light in which much of recent philosophy appears to those who are not familiar with speculative thought.[15]

Hegel responds to this problem by expanding the unit of meaning to include both the product and the process of reflection, generating a mode of discourse that is adequate to express speculative insights. But if he is able to remedy the defects of propositional language by developing a dialectical framework, perhaps we should stretch language a bit further to say what we mean by the concept of non-dialectical difference. In this way, we could satisfy Hegel's demands for articulation at the distinctively philosophical level at least as well as he satisfies them himself.

Before we turn to this problem directly, we can take the next step in framing an intelligible account of difference that is not exclusively dialectical by turning to the perception section of the *Phenomenology* where once more the subject confronts an object that stands in radical contrast with it. Since the object to be encountered is in space and time, and since the synopsis of sense and pure intuition have been articulated dialectically, both the universal and the particular dimensions of the earlier discussion are present in the object at the outset.[16] Indeed, Hegel suggests that if we have understood the dialectical consequences of the examination of sense-certainty, we can stand in between the subject and the object as abstractable aspects of a concrete process in which they both participate, where immediacy and abstract universality interplay with one another as a way of "taking things truly."[17] The ordinary consciousness fails to occupy this standpoint because it always makes the mistake of beginning with the primacy of the object,[18] and I am willing to embrace it only if this middle ground is not understood as a process that overrides the non-dialectical dimension of sensibility, pure intuition, and the transcendental ego. From the philosophical perspective I have been developing, this dimension expresses itself as a non-dialectical difference between the subject and the object, where particularity and abstract universality fall on both sides, and where to stand in between is to occupy the standpoint of dialectical and non-dialectical difference simultaneously.

But what is the fate of non-dialectical difference in Hegel's own discussion of the dialectic of perception? With respect to ordinary consciousness, he argues that it cannot he sustained and that under the pressure of dialectical reflection both the subject and the object of perception prove to be identical in content. More accurately, he claims that the same dialectical transitions occur on both sides of the subject-object distinction, and that as a result, each term is an expression of the self-articulation of the same process. If we begin with the object of perception, it first presents itself as a unity, and the diversity of its properties falls within the subject as the conceptual elements that serve to make it cognitively accessible. But we might also regard the object as a plurality of properties and construe the subject as the seat of unity. In this case, unification is made possible by the transcendental unity of apperception, where the plurality of objective properties is understood as the unified content of synthetic activity.

When these two ways of proceeding are taken together, Hegel claims that the subject and object are identical since both can be understood in terms of unity and diversity. According to the Leibnizian principle, two things that are indiscernible are identical and may therefore be identified with one another.[19] But if this proves to be the case the non-dialectical difference between subject and object is canceled and we are returned to the Absolute Process not simply as a dynamic version of the synopsis of sense or of pure intuition, but also as a dialectical reformulation of the nature of pure synthetic activity. Indeed, non-dialectical difference not only appears to be overcome once again, but the truth of the *Phenomenology* reveals itself as both an experiential and a philosophical version of the development of the Absolute toward its final consummation. Like Cronus who devours his children, the Absolute Process is at work within this context, repeatedly devouring non-dialectical difference so it can finally be at peace with itself as it unfolds its absolute content.

There is one problem that blocks the path of the dialectical development of consciousness at this point, and this problem is to be found in the fact that before he identifies them with one another, Hegel ignores the order in which the dialectical transitions occur in the subject and the object respectively. This order differs in each case non-dialectically, and it is this non-dialectical difference that holds the subject and the object apart for the reflective consciousness. In the dialectic of perception, the object moves from unity to diversity before it collapses into the unity of the Absolute Process,[20] while the subject moves from its original diversity into a unity of properties before it collapses into the unity of this same process.[21] This means that the subject and the object traverse different paths in their dialectical development, one beginning with diversity and moving toward unity, while the other begins with unity and moves toward differentiation. However much these two poles might be identical in conceptual content, they are not identical in *directional orientation*, and it is this vector difference that holds them apart as really distinct elements of the perceptual process.

At one point, Hegel himself seems to acknowledge this crucial distinction, for having argued that the act of perceiving and the object of perception are the same he says:

> In essence the object is the same as the movement: the movement is the unfolding and differentiation of the two moments, and the object is the apprehended togetherness of the moments.[22]

Hegel introduces the concept of essence to designate the dialectical development of the subject and the object respectively, and since a developmental dimension is present in each case, he quite naturally assumes that the two poles of the subject-object relation are the same. However, he also seems to suggest that the analytic moment of unfolding and differentiation is to be distinguished from the synthetic moment of apprehended togetherness with respect to directional orientation. But if this is so, and unless it can be shown that vector directionality has nothing to do with the essence of a thing, Hegel will never be able to demonstrate that the subject and the object dissolve into one another in the process of cognition. In fact, just the opposite is the case, since the vector difference displayed by the development of the subject and the object hold them apart in a mirror-image relation that can never be canceled by dialectical considerations alone. In characterizing the essence of both subject and object it is not sufficient to introduce a developmental dimension which will then allow the terms that display it to be identified with one another. Since the subject and the object move in different directions, this non-dialectical fact must be acknowledged explicitly, and when it is, the essence of the perceptual consciousness reveals itself as a non-dialectical separation between two terms that develop in different directions.

The analytic development of the object from unity to diversity and the synthetic development of the subject from diversity to unity are similarities that bind the knower and the known together, but they are also differences that allow these terms to remain separate as really distinct elements in the unfolding process of cognition. This moment of separation can be described most adequately as a representational relation between subject and object in which the intelligibility of the act of representing is grounded by the analogies that preserve both the differences and the identities of its terms. Formulated in somewhat different terms, analogy is the ontological foundation for the intelligibility of non-dialectical difference, and it finally makes it possible for us to say what we mean by this central element of our earlier discussion.

There is a dialectical dimension present in perception, and it is revealed in the fact that both the subject and the object undergo transitions involving identity, difference, and unity. However, these two dialectical poles are held apart by a non-dialectical difference of directionality and this difference can be made mediated only by an imagistic relation of irreducible similarity. As Hegel suggests, this mediation can be articulated by claiming that the subject and the object are the same, but the sameness in question is not to be understood in dialectical terms alone. Instead, a judgment of analogy must be formulated that preserves both the identity and the difference of its terms non-dialectically. To say that the subject and the object are the same does not simply mean that these two poles of consciousness develop dialectically, requiring us to expand the propositional unit of meaning to include both structural and developmental elements. Rather, their sameness presupposes this dialectical dimension and can be expressed in a judgment that asserts that the object develops dialectically from unity to diversity, while the dialectical development of the subject moves from diversity to unity. This judgment of analogy is the foundation for an internal critique of Hegel, and it is the crucial element in preserving the intelligibility of both the dialectical and the non-dialectical dimensions of the experience of consciousness.

It is important to emphasize the fact that both dialectical and non-dialectical elements are present in the subject and the object of consciousness and that non-dialectical intelligibility is not to be confined simply to the representational relation between them. In my earlier discussion of the differences between space and time and between two centers of consciousness, I have suggested that space involves non-dialectical difference while time does not and that a distinction should be drawn between the dialectical difference present in a sequence of utterances and the non-dialectical difference that makes it possible. Since the subject and the object are both in space and time, and since two *different* "I's" can participate in a unified dialectical sequence, we may conclude that both kinds of difference are present in the subject and the object respectively. But what can be said about the intelligibility of non-dialectical difference in these two contexts? In framing his own response to this problem, Hegel attempts to demonstrate that difference of this kind cannot be articulated and that it can be absorbed into the dialectical intelligibility of a larger relational nexus.

As he formulates the problem of difference with respect to two or more objects of consciousness, Hegel claims that the first object can be understood as a One in contrast with a Many. But since this object is what it is only by contrast with others, it is not simply an independent entity, but depends for its integrity upon the relations in which it stands with whatever else there is. These relations thus become essential to the thing, and what began as an independent entity ends as a term in a relational network of other terms that define the being of the thing in question.[23] In this way Hegel attempts to override non-dialectical difference, introducing a set of internal relations to undermine the apparent externality that holds a plurality of objects apart. However, an argument of this kind with respect to either subjects or objects overlooks once more the crucial distinction between conceptual content and vector directionality, mistakenly suggesting that they collapse into one another as terms on the same logical level. A subject or an object is first oriented in space and time and then related to other things, and unless these two moments could be distinguished, there would be no term with respect to which Hegel could generate his own dialectical argument. But if this is so, *order* once more proves to be an essential ingredient in the discussion, not only for establishing the integrity of non-dialectical difference, but also for allowing us to show how difference of this kind can be intelligible.

The importance of the concept of order becomes clear when we notice that if a second term is related to the first, what is *first* for each element is its own vector orientation, and what is *second* is the relational network in which it stands with other things. This means that what is *first* for $term_2$ is *second* for $term_1$, and that what is *first* for $term_1$ is *second* for $term_2$. However much these terms develop dialectically, they also stand in a mirroring relation to one another, and it is the possibility of a cognitive judgment corresponding to this relation that serves to make their non-dialectical difference intelligible. The centrality of a judgment of this kind must therefore be acknowledged, not only with respect to the representational relation between subject and object, but also as it reflects the non-dialectical dimension of the subject and the object of consciousness respectively.

It would be possible to continue these critical reflections at every stage of the phenomenological project, showing how other dialectical transitions are infected by a dimension of difference that is intelligible only in non-dialectical terms. Yet this is unnecessary, for what is at stake is the need for a revised conception of the entire Hegelian enterprise, understood as a dialectical articulation of the Absolute Process. In attempting to move the discussion beyond the level of an empirical protest into a philosophical context, and in attempting to show that both the subject, the object, and their relations can be made intelligible in both dialectical and non-dialectical terms, I have been suggesting that the structure of the Absolute must be reconstrued in terms of a broader conception of philosophical intelligibility. This reconstruction involves the supplementation of the kind of intelligibility appropriate to the concrete universal with the intelligibility made accessible by a non-dialectical concept of analogy. The concrete universal is an appropriate way of articulating the temporal dimension of experience, but we must stretch language even further to do justice to the irreducibility of space and to the truth expressed by the concept of spatial and temporal orientation. I have done this by claiming that an analogical relation can bind together two or more terms that are internally dialectical, where both the orientation and the abstract structure of the process are made intelligible by the mirroring relations in which they stand with other things and by the judgment that relations of this kind obtain.

Just as Hegel extends the traditional concept of the abstract universal to capture the developmental dimension of both substance and subject, I have extended the traditional concept of structural similarity to capture both the structure and the vector directionality that can be mirrored in its ingredient elements. Since this extension is intended to be applicable to the philosophical articulation of experience, it is important to emphasize the fact that it can be applied to the Absolute Process, and not simply to the subject and the object of experience or to the representational relations that bind them together. Sense-certainty and perception are stages in the development of the Absolute within experience, but if an adequate understanding of their "spatial" dimension requires a non-dialectical concept of analogy, this concept must be placed alongside the concrete universal to make the expression of the Absolute intelligible throughout the entire range of human experience. Indeed, the concept of analogy I have introduced is richer than Hegel's concept of dialectical intelligibility, for it includes the dialectical dimension of both the terms and the process that it makes philosophically accessible. This is not to say that this revised conception of analogy is a dialectical sublation of the dialectical process, for it includes this process only in the sense that it allows its structure, its orientation, and its development to be imaged without subordinating the image to the process. As a result, a dimension of radical externality is preserved not only at the level of representation and not simply as an internal constituent of the subject and the object of experience, but also in the kind of judgment that can make the non-dialectical aspect of the Absolute intelligible to the philosophical consciousness.[24]

I do not expect an Hegelian to be persuaded by my argument, not only because it has been formulated so generally, but also because Hegel himself would clearly reject it. At a number of places Hegel says that space is an abstract reflection of the Absolute and that it is merely the skeletal form of time understood as a dynamically developing process.[25] He also claims that directionality has no philosophical significance[26] and that even after it has been perfected by art and religion, the kind of imagistic thinking I have introduced is taken up into the Absolute Process in the transition to Absolute Knowing.[27] Finally, in the *Logic* Hegel describes the Absolute Process in such a way that difference is just as dominant as identity, insisting that the *sameness* of the process is as much the *difference* of identity and difference as it is their identity. In this respect, he is a modern Heraclitean and in a context where he has been freed from the opposition of consciousness, he makes this clear by emphasizing the centrality of the category of becoming for his dialectical enterprise.[28] However, the fact remains that Hegel's system displays a sense of cumulative philosophical progress and that he insists that philosophy is a circle where the beginning and the end of the process are the same.[29] The unrelenting teleological dimension of his thought belies Hegel's claim about the value of vector orientation, for from within the Absolute Process, he is clearly oriented toward the concrete articulation of the Absolute in its richest and most comprehensive form. This comprehensive articulation is the circle of philosophical reflection that Hegel inscribes and it is the completeness with which he does so that forces us to insist on a non-dialectical sense of difference that must be made intelligible in its own terms.

If we are to take seriously Hegel's claim that sameness involves difference in just as primordial a way as identity, it would appear that the sameness of the beginning and the end of the philosophical circle is just as different as it is identical. But this fact serves to rupture the circle, demanding a sense of philosophical articulation that is adequate to the way in which the beginning and the end stand in contrast with one another. The concrete universal is not sufficient in this case, for when it is introduced, the beginning is regarded as an abstract arche that is to be comprehended by dialectical sublation. If the beginning and the end are different in a strong sense, they stand apart in such a way that the kind of imagistic articulation I have introduced becomes appropriate at the most fundamental level. To invert one of Hegel's most suggestive phrases,[30] the beginning and the end of things are God standing over against Himself and over against those who recognize themselves as finite beings, charged with the task of making the Absolute Process philosophically intelligible. My own way of doing this has been to mobilize the concepts of orientation and analogy, where the essence of the Absolute can be articulated by the kind of sameness in which identity and difference are both preserved and held apart by the imagistic thinking. Hegel is correct in claiming that sameness involves the difference of identity and difference just as much as it involves their identity, but an intelligible account of this fact requires the transformation of the Heraclitean flux into analogy as an irreducible ontological nexus.

NOTES

1. The first existential reaction to Hegel was the "positive" philosophy of the late Schelling, and this reaction was developed and accentuated in the writings of Kierkegaard. See F. W. J. Schelling, *Werke*, ed. M. Schroter, (Munich, 1927–28), Vol. I, Part II, pp. 285ff.; Vol. III, p. 46; vol. V, pp. 729–753. See also Sören Kierkegaard, *Concluding Unscientific Postscript*, trans. David F. Swenson and Walter Lowrie (Princeton: Princeton University Press, 1941), pp. 267–282.

2. The attack on Hegel from this perspective began with Marx's early writings. See Karl Marx *The Economic and Philosophic Manuscripts of 1844*, ed. Dirk M. Struik and trans. Martin Milligan (New York: International Publishers, 1964), pp. 170–193. For discussions of some of the same themes by Marx's successors, see Herbert Marcuse, *Reason and Revolution: Hegel and the Rise of Social Theory* (Boston: Beacon Press, 1960) and Jürgen Habermas, *Theory and Practice*, trans. J. Viertel (Boston: Beacon Press, 1973).

3. The most important contemporary representatives of this perspective are Heidegger and Derrida. See Martin Heidegger, *Identity and Difference*, trans. Joan Stambaugh (New York, Evanston, and London: Harper and Row, 1969) and Jacques Derrida, *Margins of Philosophy*, trans. Alan Bass (Chicago: The University of Chicago Press, 1982), pp. 1–27, 69–108.

4. G. W. F. Hegel, *Phenomenology of Spirit*, trans. A. V. Miller (Oxford: Clarendon Press 1977), pp. 48–57 and *Hegel's Science of Logic*. trans. A. V. Miller (New York: Humanities Press, 1969), pp. 112, 118–25, 138–53, 158, 384.

5. Hegel, *Phenomenology of Spirit*, pp. 60, 62, 64, 66.

6. *The Logic of Hegel*, 2nd ed., trans. William Wallace (Oxford: Oxford University Press, 1892), pp. 215–16.

7. Hegel, *Phenomenology of Spirit*, p. 60.

8. *Ibid.*, pp. 63–64.

9. *Ibid.*, p. 63.

10. *Ibid.*, pp. 60–61.

11. *Ibid.*, pp. 53–55.

12. *Ibid.*, pp. 61–62.

13. For the clearest examples of Hegel's failure to distinguish clearly between the abstract and the concrete universal, see *Ibid.*, pp. 60, 61, 66.

14. *Ibid.*, pp. 60, 66.

15. *Hegel's Science of Logic*, pp. 90–91.

16. Hegel, *Phenomenology of Spirit*, pp. 66–67.

17. *Ibid.*

18. *Ibid.*, p. 67.

19. *Ibid.*, pp. 70–74.

20. *Ibid.*, pp. 70–71.

21. *Ibid.*, pp. 71–74.

22. *Ibid.*, p. 67.

23. *Ibid.*, pp. 74–76.

24. I have discussed the concept of analogy and the kind of intelligibility appropriate to it in a variety of contexts. See *The Quest for Wholeness* (Albany, New York: The State University of New York Press, 1982), pp. 178–197; "Categories and the Real Order: Sellars's Interpretation of Aristotle's Metaphysics," *The Monist*, Vol. 66 (1983), 438–449; "The Quest for Wholeness and Its Crucial Metaphor and Analogy: The Place of Places," *Ultimate Reality and Meaning*, Vol. 7 (1984), pp. 157–165; "Metaphor, Analogy, and System: A Reply to Burbidge," *Man and World*, Vol. 18 (1984), pp. 55–63; "Semiotics and the Problem of Analogy: A Critique of Peirce's Theory of Categories," *The Transactions of the Charles S. Peirce Society*, Vol. 22 (1986), pp. 311–326; "Subject, Object and Representation: A Critique of Hegel's Dialectic of Perception," *International Philosophical Quarterly*, Vol. 26 (1986), pp. 117–129; "Metaphor, Analogy, and the Nature of Truth," in *New Essays in Metaphysics*, ed. Robert C. Neville (Albany, New York: The State University of New York Press, 1986), pp. 217–236; and "Participation and Imitation in Plato's Metaphysics," in *Contemporary Essays on Greek Ideas: The Kilgore Festschrift* (Waco, Texas: Baylor University Press 1987), pp. 17–31. I would also like to express my indebtedness to the writings of two of my friends and former students, each of whom has attempted to move beyond dialectical intelligibility in his own way. See William Desmond, *Desire, Dialectic, and Otherness: An Essay on Origins* (New Haven: Yale University Press, 1987), and Brian John Martine, *Individuals and Individuality*, (Albany, New York: The State University of New York Press, 1984).

25. For example, see Hegel, *Phenomenology of Spirit*, pp. 26–27 and *Hegel's Philosophy of Nature*, trans. A. V. Miller (Oxford: Clarendon Press, 1970), pp. 28–30.

26. *Hegel's Science of Logic*, pp. 105–06, 117, 147–48.

27. *Hegel's Philosophy of Mind*, trans. William Wallace (Oxford: Clarendon Press, 1892), p. 302.

28. *Hegel's Science of Logic*, pp. 82–100.

29. *Hegel's Philosophy of Nature*, p. 2.

30. Hegel, *Phenomenology of Spirit*, p. 409.

Commentary on Carl Vaught's "Hegel and the Problem of
Difference"

Ardis B. Collins

Professor Vaught's paper challenges Hegelian philosophy on an
issue that Hegel himself takes to be crucial. In the Preface to the
Phenomenology, Hegel represents the truth not only as the whole, but
also as absolute difference. "Spirit gains its truth," he says, "by
finding itself in absolute dismemberment."[1] If, therefore, the quest
for truth is the quest for wholeness, it is also the quest for difference;
and both wholeness and difference depend on the power of the
negative which separates and unifies absolutely. But Vaught claims
that some differences are independent and unconnected; they cannot
be reduced to or derived from the negative relations which connect
them to what they are not. The only truly Hegelian way to answer
this challenge is to show that the very non-dialectical character of
non-dialectical difference is itself dialectical.

We begin as Hegel would with non-dialectical difference as such,
pure and unmixed, difference completely underived from negations
or relations. This is what Hegel calls pure immediacy. The immediate
is simply itself, and being itself depends on no relations or combi-
nations. To be itself is itself simply being; the immediate simply is.
The immediacy of an object is what sense certainty takes the truth
to be. Hence, sense-certainty tries to know the truth by becoming
conscious of the object as simply being. Consciousness knows it as
here and now. Being here and now is simply to be.

Consciousness finds, however, that its consciousness of here and
now refers to different heres and nows. Here and now continues to
be only by being this one as well as that one and by not being
whatever makes the one not the other. According to Vaught, this
development does not prove that the here and now is completely
dialectical, since at least some versions of the dialectic depend on

non-dialectical differences. But this is exactly Hegel's point. Because sense-certainty takes the truth to be the immediacy of the object, consciousness rejects this dialectical here and now as untrue and looks for the truth in each here and now by itself. Hence, consciousness does not turn around to confront another here. It does not refer to another consciousness of here or now, whether this consciousness is another knower or itself at another time. Consciousness focuses itself on the intuition in which it is actually engaged.[2]

However, both the singularity of the object and the intuition that knows it turn out to be mediated. The now in becoming now passes. Its being now is its becoming not now, but has been. What exists is not an isolated, unrelated point of time, but a passage of time that remains the same time—the same hour, the same day—throughout the movement from one now to another. The now is a complex time-unit resulting from the relation of different nows to each other. Similarly, the here is not an isolated point, but a position determined by the relation between front-back, right-left, above-below. A completely isolated point has no definite position. Therefore, consciousness knows a distinctive here and now only as different heres and nows determining each other to a certain space-time. Since, however, every here and now is determined by its spatio-temporal relations, consciousness would lose the immediacy of its object in a completely relational space-time continuum if it did not know the object as a plurality of heres and nows cut off from the continuum; and what isolates the object in this way cannot be anything other than the object itself. The isolation of the object would not be the object's own singularity, its independent and underived difference, if it were not derived from what the object itself independently is. Hence, the complex relations of different spatio-temporal elements which determine each other to a certain place and time must be contained within one and the same object. Consciousness knows the object's singularity, the object's absolute underived difference, by moving through different spatio-temporal elements and becoming conscious of them as belonging to each other rather than to the surrounding space-time continuum.[3] The immediacy of the object, its independent non-dialectical difference, depends on mediation and negative relations within itself. It is a mediated immediacy.

The dialectical developments of sense-certainty determine and justify the presuppositions of perception. Perception assumes that the truth of the object is its being one and the same thing in the various heres and nows which constitute it, a self-sameness that cuts it off from and makes it independent of the spatio-temporal environment in which it exists. Also, because sense-certainty has demonstrated that the object's difference can be known only as something being intuited, perception expects to know the separateness of the object by sensing its space-time determinations in the form of sense properties.[4] A property, however, refers consciousness to other properties in the space-time continuum—a color in the field of colors, a texture in the field of textures, a shape in the field of shapes. Although the property distinguishes itself within the field by opposing and excluding other properties, its determination to a certain space-time depends on its relations to the other parts of the space-time continuum, like the colors and shapes of a cosmic abstract painting. Therefore, perceptual consciousness rejects this mediation as not what the object truly is and tries to find the truth in a combination of properties determining each other within a single thing. Each property is separated from the continuum by belonging to other properties that identify the same spatio-temporal unit. Consciousness of a thing's different properties, however, turns into a series of unconnected perceptions—consciousness of color, consciousness of texture, consciousness of shape, and so forth. Hence, consciousness perceives the object not as self-same, but as a collection of unconnected, non-identical elements, and as unconnected, these elements cannot determine each other to a definite space-time and hence cannot separate themselves from the space-time continuum.[5]

If, however, perceptual consciousness detaches its knowledge of the object's self-sameness and separateness from the perception of sense properties, then it does not know what the object itself is in itself and by itself, since other things are self-same and separate and yet are not this object. In order to be itself, therefore, a thing must also be differentiated from others; and what identifies this difference is the sense properties—sense properties belonging to the continuum and distinguishing themselves within it, sense properties separated from the continuum by belonging to other properties in the self-sameness of a single thing.[6] Perceptual consciousness distinguishes, therefore, between what is unessential but necessary to a thing's difference and what is essential to it. Its essential difference is independent, a difference established by simply being itself. The many properties, which distinguish a thing from itself and relate it to others, are distinct from this essence, but necessary to it. Since, however, a thing cannot be itself without being differentiated from others, not only does the essence derive the properties from itself, it also derives itself from the properties. In order to be independently and distinctively itself, a being must negate its isolation, give itself distinctive properties by relating itself to others, then negate these relations by forming its many properties into a single character with its own independent integrity. By negation and relation, a being forms itself into what is independently different.[7] Thus the independence of non-dialectical difference shows itself to be dialectical. It is not independence by immediacy, by being aloof and unconnected. It is difference that makes itself independent by relating itself to and separating itself from what is other than itself.

According to Professor Vaught, however, a dynamic difference, even one that develops itself in relation to another, is non-dialectical if the order or direction of the process is originally, irreducibly, and independently different. If one member of the relation develops from A to B to C and the other develops from C to B to A, the difference established by the relation depends on the more fundamental difference of direction. This analysis challenges in a fundamental way the new understanding that arises from the developments of perception. Perception demonstrates that the independent identity of an object has no definite content, no difference, except as that which makes itself different by relating itself to other things and separating itself from them. What perception took to be a discrete thing turns out to be a process that has two directions—the direction outward toward the other and the direction inward away from the other. Understanding knows this process as force. But the process by which each force develops itself has no absolute, underived starting point that might give it an independently established order or direction. Perception has demonstrated that independent difference gets its independence and difference from the very process of relating and separating that develops from it. This is what understanding recognizes when it knows the object as force. Hence, force does not begin with a definite content of its own. It gets its differentiating content by relating itself to another force, the direction outward. Force becomes an independent difference by taking the content of this relation into itself as its own independent character. Only thus is its independent difference really different, i.e., identified by a definite differentiating content. Thus, every direction inward, every withdrawal into separateness and independence, follows from and depends on the direction outward.

The reverse is also true. The distinctive content derived from the direction outward expresses and characterizes the separateness and independence established by the direction inward. Otherwise, force would be absorbed by its relations; it would be a distinction within a relational system and would belong to the whole, not to itself. This is not the truth demonstrated by the developments of perception. At the end of perception, independent difference remains. It is a dynamic, mediated independence, but independence nevertheless. Therefore, the direction outward is not force itself, but its expression, a manifestation of the independent difference force gives itself by the direction inward. Within each force the direction outward follows from the direction inward, and the direction inward follows from the direction outward.

Nevertheless, there is a directional difference. Each force is the direction outward for the other's direction inward, and the direction inward for the other's direction outward. But this difference depends on the dynamics played out between the two forces. The outward movement of force, force expressed, follows a necessity imposed on it by the other's difference. Because the other is another force, not identical with this one, this one must determine its being as being differentiated, i.e., it must give itself a distinctive content by relating itself to the other. Thus, the other's direction inward, its being an independent difference not identical with this one, draws forth this one's direction outward. Since, however, the other gets the distinctive content of its difference by being in the same relation, the other must separate its content from the relation in order to maintain its non-identity. The first force, by identifying itself with the relation, drives the other inward. The same dynamic develops in reverse from the other to the first. Thus, each force gets its directional difference by negating the direction of the other and being negated by it.[8]

Vaught claims that directional difference is the non-dialectical dimension of three relations: the relation of objects to one another, the "representational" relation between subject and object, the relation of subjects to one another. We have concentrated on the relation of objects to one another because sense-certainty and perception focus primarily on what the object is. For these forms of consciousness, the subject is an object of consideration only insofar as consciousness makes possible or becomes an obstacle to knowing the object. This focus on the object follows from what distinguishes the forms of consciousness from the forms of self-consciousness, reason and spirit. The forms of consciousness assume that knowing the truth is knowing what the object is apart from and independent of its relation to consciousness. By making this assumption, they presuppose a fundamental non-identity between subject and object, what Vaught would call a non-dialectical difference; and the presupposition remains unexamined until the *Phenomenology* makes the transition from consciousness as understanding to self-consciousness. From the developments of perception alone, therefore, we can make no judgment about Hegel's claim that the difference between subject and object is dialectical; at this point in the *Phenomenology*, Hegel makes no such claim.[9]

The limits of a brief commentary make it impossible to do more than suggest how we might handle the question of dialectical differences between the subject and its other. What is other than the subject may be a world that consciousness tries to understand and explain, or a field of action that the subject adapts to its purposes, or a social order that relates the subject to other persons and to community life. In whatever form we consider it, the other and the subject differ dialectically, even in their independence and separateness, if the structure of the difference is similar to the dynamic developed for differences between objects. For example, the particular desires, interests, talents, and capacities which distinguish persons from each other and give them a distinctive personality are like properties relating a subject to the natural and social world where these inclinations find their satisfaction and fulfillment. The individual's freedom is distinct from such tendencies and independent of their connections to an independently established natural and social order. By itself, however, freedom has no differentiating content, no real difference. It makes itself concretely different by choosing to pursue certain interests, to reject others, to give some concerns priority and others a secondary role in the individual's life. In other words, the individual forms from his or her relations an integrated personality. Without the independent direction of the individual's freedom, a person simply belongs to the natural and social world, is dominated and formed by it, and has no independence. But the individual's freedom has no reality, no differentiating content, no independent character without its active engagement in the world of relations—the world of nature, other persons, society, history, religion, art. Thus, the difference of persons establishes itself in the dynamic of relating and separating, not by being given as the underived, unrelated ground of dialectical relations. The free self derives itself from its relations in the process of deriving its relations from itself.[10]

We have considered non-dialectical difference in three forms: as simply being itself, immediate and unconnected; as a difference determined by the internal dynamics of an independent thing; as a directional difference played out between two realities. In every case, what makes the difference non-dialectical turns out to be dialectical. Immediacy, independence, and directional difference establish themselves by negation and relation. What is different gets its unconnectedness from being connected. As Hegel says in the Preface to the *Phenomenology*:

> . . . that the accidental as such, separated from its circumference, that the bounded which is actual only in its connection with others should gain an existence of its own and separate freedom, this is the tremendous power of the negative; . . . Spirit gains its truth only by finding itself in absolute dismemberment."

NOTES

1. Walter Kaufmann, trans. & ed., *Hegel: Texts and Commentary* (Garden City, New York: Doubleday, 1965), p. 50. G. W. F. Hegel, *Phänomenologie des Geistes*, ed. J. Hoffmeister (Hamburg: Felix Meiner, 1952), p. 30. Hegel, *Phenomenology of Spirit*, trans. A. V. Miller (Oxford: Clarendon, 1977), §32.

2. Hegel, *Phänomenologie*, Hoffmeister, pp. 79–85; Miller, §90–91, 93–99, 102–105.

3. *Ibid.*, Hoffmeister, pp. 85–86; Miller, §107–108.

4. *Ibid.*, Hoffmeister, pp. 89–91; Miller, §111–113.

5. *Ibid.*, Hoffmeister, pp. 93–94; Miller, §117.

6. *Ibid.*, Hoffmeister, pp. 95–97; Miller, §119–121.

7. *Ibid.*, Hoffmeister, pp. 98–99; Miller, §124–128.

8. *Ibid.*, Hoffmeister, pp. 104–110; Miller, §136–139, 141.

9. *Ibid.*, Hoffmeister, pp. 80–81, 89–90, 102–03, 133–35, 175–76; Miller, §93, 111, 132–133, 166–167, 232. Cf. *Enzyklopädie der philosophischen Wissenschaften im Grundrisse*, §417.

10. Cf. Hegel, Hoffmeister, pp. 283–301; Miller, §394–418. *Enzyk.*, §471–491, 503–516. *Grundlinien der Philosophie des Rechts*, §182–183, 187, 199, 206–207, 230, 251, 260–261, 264, 268.

11. Kaufmann, *ibid.* p. 50. Hegel, Hoffmeister, p. 30; Miller, §32.

Chapter Three

HEGEL AND MARX ON THE HUMAN INDIVIDUAL

Leslie A. Mulholland

The social contract doctrines of Hobbes and Locke emphasize "mutual benefit" theory of justice and the state. According to this theory, the state and the principles of justice that it should conform to are determined by considering how the members of the community can mutually benefit one another in their pursuit of the satisfaction of selfish interests. Important contemporary theories of rights and justice developed by H.L.A. Hart[1] and John Rawls[2] are based on the mutual benefit theory. In contrast to this theory, classical political and social ethics finds the justification of political obligation and principles of rights and justice to lie in the idea of the state as what Kant calls an end in itself.[3] In accordance with classical theories the aim of political association is not merely to satisfy private interests, but also to enable man to exercise a special function different from the animal one of satisfaction of needs, i.e., allowing man to live a universal life in which he exists for the whole community and not merely himself. Here man is considered a social or political animal, or what Marx calls "a species being." In these theories, principles of justice are not only principles by which private interests are to be governed. They are also principles whereby the member of the state is able to find satisfaction of his specially human interest. Through this interest, man can transcend his private aims and experience a respect for the whole.

The works of Hegel and Marx epitomize the struggle between these two conceptions. They see the mutual benefit theory as a consequence of economic developments of capitalism. Although they commend the recognition of the equal status of all persons that comes with capitalism, their works on social ethics can be read as attempts to preserve the classical ideal in the face of growing demands of selfishness and what MacPherson calls "possessive individualism"[4] produced by the development of capitalism.

On the one hand, Hegel claims that the classical ideal can be integrated with the new economic order; on the other hand, Marx tries to show why it cannot. I want to argue that Marx's answer is conceptually a less effective answer than Hegel's, but nevertheless, that Marx, by emphasizing the practical consequences of the economic order, has exposed a flaw in Hegel's treatment of the individual sufficient to show that Hegel's aim, freedom in the state, is unachievable.

Adam Schaff, in his book *Marxism and the Human Individual*, comments that "the question that absorbed the young Marx—like the whole milieu influenced by Hegel—was the disruption of man who appears in two roles although in one and the same person: as a member of the 'civil society' (bourgeois) and of the 'political community' (citoyen)."[5] Marx's *Critique of Hegel's Philosophy of Right* develops these ideas. Elsewhere Marx expands on and clarifies his account of the disruption of the two roles which he finds lying at the root of Hegel's philosophy of right. In his penetrating essay, "Bruno Bauer, Die Judenfrage," Marx objects to the conception of man expressed by capitalist economists and identified in Hegel's account of civil society. Marx indicates that his objection is based on Kantian grounds:

> in *civil society* . . . [man] acts simply as a private individual, treats other men as means, degrades himself to the role of a mere means, and becomes the plaything of alien powers.[6]

Marx comments, however, that the degradation of man in civil society is hidden by the fact that man as a citizen is supposed to be freed from the demands of egoism. The citizen "lives in a universal human condition"[7] that is nevertheless "abstract."[8] Why the condition is universal and abstract can only be understood by contrasting it with the opposing condition within society itself. Man as citizen is opposed to man as private individual, with private interests, and pursuing his way of life for private ends. As citizen, man participates with all others in political legislation. He is expected to take the standpoint, not of his own private interests, but of the community as a whole. In this way, the life of the citizen is a "universal life." It is possessed equally by all, and it is directed at the good of the entire community.

By calling the condition of the citizen "abstract," Marx means that the rights and duties of the modern citizen do not depend on the particular biological and economic functions that individuals have in the social context. Marx clarifies his criticism by pointing out the

difference between this modern relation of private and public functions and the relation in feudalism.[9] Marx claims that in feudalism,
the relation of the individual to political rights and responsibilities
was determined by family position and economic functions. The
lord, as the economically dominant power, also had political power.
The economic power was in turn sanctioned and preserved explicitly
through the political power.

Marx strictly regards the revolution that brought civil society out
of the feudal system as serving two functions. On the one hand, it
serves the positive function of liberating "the political spirit from its
connexion with" the economic position of civil life.[10] But at the same
time, this revolution dehumanized man by producing the abstract
citizen, for while seeming to achieve the ideal of universality, it
released "the egoistic spirit" from its "political yoke" and makes
egoistic man the basis of civil society. Marx comments that egoistic
man is made the "presupposition of the political state."[11] What has
happened is not that man has been freed from the restrictions of the
feudal economic structure, but that egoistic economic activity has
been liberated from social and political control. Moreover, Marx contends, analysis shows that the actual structure of the modern state
presupposes that the state functions only as a means for the satisfaction of the selfish interests of the egoistic members.[12] The result is
that "it is man as a bourgeois and not man as a citizen who is
considered the true and authentic man."[13]

The main point of Marx's objection to Hegel is to demonstrate
that to integrate the two sides of man, it is necessary to reverse the
relation of the economic to the universal. The universal must be
made the basis of all economic activity. This requires a revolution
that eliminates not only feudal elitism, but economic egoism. The
mistake in the bourgeois ideology is the failure to recognize that the
universal character of man and not egoistic man expresses man's
true nature.[14]

From this we can find Marx's central criticism of Hegel's philosophy of right to be the following. Marx is claiming that because Hegel
begins with the egoistic man of civil society he allows no reasonable
way for the integration of the two features of man: man as seeking
personal welfare and man as citizen. For the reader of Hegel, Marx's
criticism is interesting and surprising for Hegel seems to be aware of
the problem and to have had the primary aim of resolving it. In the
following, I examine whether Hegel can meet the objection.

I

In his philosophy of right, Hegel identifies the prime problem that
the study of the good is concerned with: it is the unity of welfare

and right in the idea of the good [130].[15] Here by "right" Hegel means laws regulating the freedom of persons in movement, and in the acquisition and transfer of property. Hegel goes on to say that the right of property on the one hand or the particular aims of welfare (as private interest) on the other hand, has validity only "in so far as it accords with the good and is subordinate to it" [130]. Again, Hegel maintains,

> the idea of the state is precisely the supersession of the clash between right (i.e., empty abstract freedom) and welfare (i.e., the particular content which fills that void) [336].

Hegel's main argument in the philosophy of right can be seen as an attempt to demonstrate the conditions under which law and personal welfare can be combined so that each is achieved and furthered through the other. The specific historical problem that Hegel must resolve is that presented by the development of capitalism and the accompanying principle of personal freedom and equality.

Within a dialectical philosophy such as Hegel's, the problem can be expressed in this way: What is the mediating factor whereby the private aims and interests of the individual can be integrated with the person as a member of the political whole? Hegel is looking in effect for a structure or process through which both elements can be united. In his criticism of Hegel, Marx in effect claims that Hegel has failed to provide a convincing medium for the integration of right and welfare.

Both Marx and Hegel direct their attention to the problem of capitalism and its removal of right from dependence on economic function. Before looking at Marx's solution, let us look at Hegel's account of the mediating factor through which the general and private elements of the individual can be integrated. First, we should notice that Hegel also opposes bourgeois civil society for the way in which it makes 'self-will' and egoism the basis of the state [29]. Hegel writes:

> If the state is confused with civil society . . . then the interest of the individuals as such becomes the ultimate end of their association . . . But the state's relation to the individual is quite different from this. Unification as such . . . is the true . . . aim of the individual . . . His further particular satisfaction . . . have this . . . universally valid life as their starting point and aim [258n].

The objective of Hegel's analysis is to show that civil society contains its own negation, i.e., civil society contains a feature that compels the member of civil society to strive to transcend its limits. This self-negating element lies in the feature that Marx believes obstructs the achievement of the concrete individual: private freedom and egoism.

No less than Marx, Hegel recognizes that the classical political form, such as is characterized in part in Plato's *Republic*, expresses political rights and duties as functions of socio-economic power and position [206n]. The Platonic account of political life expresses the character of the relation of the individual to the political whole on analogy with a political organism. Hegel sees this as an important feature of the political whole. However, he finds the account insufficient. Hegel's treatment of the concept of the individual is an attempt to remove this insufficiency.

Hegel contends that the Platonic and the federal treatments of the state fail because they do not find a place for a further principle. This is the principle of individual freedom [Pref. 10] or "free infinite personality." Plato, Hegel contends, recognized the principle, but believed it to be something corruptive of the functionalist order that his *Republic* defends [Pref. 10].

The nature of the relation of each person's will to the universal (e.g., the political whole) is developed in Hegel's dialectical analysis of the structure of the will. This analysis characterizes the will teleologically, as aiming at complete freedom. It is important to see Hegel's treatment of the problem of justice and the human individual through reference to his analysis of this concept.

The goal of the dialectical analysis is to explain the features of the will as discovered from examining the logically necessary stages in the will's drive to complete freedom. Hegel identifies three main stages, each of which logically presupposes the preceding, as well as the will's drive to achieve complete freedom. As a result of the drive to freedom the will is (historically) impelled to the succeeding stage by the inability to realize the end of complete freedom. Through Hegel's analysis, moreover, we acquire a criterion of the condition in which the will can achieve complete freedom.

The first step in this dialectical structure is the moment whereby the will is separated from natural impulses and desires. Here Hegel finds the will as simple identity in relation to the content that the self reflects on [5,25].

When the will is distinguished from nature, a person is conscious of the various natural impulses, desires, and inclinations that affect the will in the course of nature [11]. Hegel indicates, however, that to the extent that the will has been separated from every particular content, it also is separated from any other will that has achieved this condition [cf. 13]. The will here is a will that is conceptually identical with other wills, a kind of "transcendental will" and so it is a universal will. Dialectically, the universality of the will is a consequence of abstraction from determinate content. But as universal the will is the potential to choose some particular object and consists initially in this potentiality.

However, the will (i.e., the person in so far as he/she engages in willing) that achieves this universality has not achieved complete freedom. The will is free, but its freedom consists in its separation from and opposition to determinate content. It conserves its freedom paradoxically only by not acting, or at least, like the stoic, refusing to commit itself to any particular activity or mode of differentiation. Here it is not free in the fullest sense, for its character depends on a negating relation to its natural impulses, which it must maintain dynamically. In this sense, the external object determines the will, and so it is not free. To be completely free, a person must incorporate the element of determination into his/her own being so that this determination is refashioned into a feature integrated with the will itself. Here the will is not determined by anything external to it. Also since the will now has specific content, it has concrete freedom.

The process toward this concrete freedom is dialectical. The will must first overcome the negative determinateness that lies in refusing to act. To do this one must choose a determinate object, i.e., set a specific end. Through this object, the will unavoidably differentiates itself from other wills [13]. But also it loses the freedom it had initially. It cancels its independent universality. Having chosen an object, it can no longer choose. So to be free a person finds he must reject this choice and posit another, ad infinitum [16]. But this never resolves the problem. In order to be fully free, then, the will must preserve itself both as universal and as having a particular, differentiating content. This dialectic of the will shows that concrete freedom is possible only in a condition where there is a unity of the universal and particular. The will is driven by the dialectic of its own nature to strive for this condition and give it a definition.

Hegel writes:

> the [free] will is the unity of both these moments. It is particularity reflected into itself and so brought back to universality, i.e., it is individuality . . . [At] one and the same time the ego posits itself as its own negative . . . and yet remains by itself, i.e., in its self-identity and universality . . . This is the freedom of the will and it constitutes the concept . . . of the will [17].

Accordingly, the will is concretely free when all its determinations are self-determinations. This occurs when it both determines itself as particular and remains universal in that self-determination. But note that to remain universal, a person must be united with all other members of the community in so far as they also achieve individuality, and the will must relate its particular difference to this unity. Hegel writes further:

> *this unity is individuality*, not individuality in its immediacy as a unit . . . but individuality in accordance with its concept; indeed individ-

uality in this sense is just precisely the concept itself [7n; my emphasis].

In this dialectical progression of the will, then, we have the structure of the will's relation to the universal. Hegel's problem in the philosophy of right is to demonstrate how the concept of the will, i.e., individuality of the member of the political whole, can be achieved. The first difficulty is to see how there can be an integration of both the universal and particular in the one subject. The second difficulty is to see how this integration can be self-determined by the subject. The Platonic state gives an explanation of the former, through the analogy of organic unity. Hegel aims to correct Plato's account by showing how individual private freedom is used to achieve the organic unity. Hegel's enterprise will fail if it can be shown that the account of the good given in the philosophy of right cannot result in concrete freedom.

II

Hegel finds the concept of the will present in all political arrangements. That is, the basic structure of political arrangements is an attempt to unite particular interests and activities with the universal common order of the state. This concept is the key to understanding such arrangements, and through it, we can assess the effectiveness of those arrangements in enabling complete freedom. History is the history of the development of political constitutions as nations strive to construct more adequate forms until the structure of the concept of the will is finally implemented in the constitution. This implementation requires the recognition of both the authority of the objective order and the personal freedom of all human beings.

In this light, Hegel's *Philosophy of Right* can be characterized as an attempt to find the passage that leads between conservativism and anarchy. On the one hand, it is a defense of the principle of individual freedom, which is the second moment in the concept of the will, against the classical conservativism of Plato. But Hegel's work can also be seen as a defense of order and tradition against the priority of private opinion.

What is not usually understood by such writers as Karl Popper,[16] and what is missed by Marx, is that Hegel attempts to defend the second moment in the concept of freedom, the exercise of particular choices, as the principle through which the universal political order and the private biological and economic order are to be mediated or combined. It is this element that the modern state has come to recognize. Hegel writes:

The principle of modern states has prodigious depth and strength because it allows the principle of subjectivity to progress to its culmination in the extreme of self-subsistent personal particularity, and yet at the same time brings it back to the substantive unity and so maintains this unity in the principle of subjectivity itself [260].

The problem is to see how the expression of the particular moment can be brought back to unity with the universal without external interference.

Hegel sees recent history as affirming two approaches to the understanding of the relation of the universal and particular. The Platonic requires that economic/political function be determined by birth, but does not allow egoism as a basis for the social whole. The social contractualist through the "mutual benefit" theory identifies individual free self-interest as the basis for political organization and order. When he is consistent (as with Hobbes) the contractualist finds political organization to be only a means to egoistic purposes.

In contrast to both these positions, Hegel writes:

. . . the question of the particular class to which an individual is to belong is one on which . . . the essential and final determining factors are subjective opinion and the individual's arbitrary will . . . Hence what happens here by inner necessity *occurs at the same time by the mediation of the arbitrary will*, and to the conscious subject it has the shape of being the work of his own will [206 (my emphasis); see also 301n for the relation of will to politics].

Hegel remarks also:

The recognition and the right that what is brought about by reason of necessity in civil society and the state shall *at the same time be effected by the mediation of the arbitrary will* is the more precise definition of what is primarily meant by 'freedom' in common parlance [206n; my emphasis].

Hegel argues that this freedom, or what he calls "subjective particularity" [206n], will function in a society as a corruptive force, hostile to the social order, unless it is "incorporated into the organization of the state as a whole" [206n].

Hegel's account of the individual posits the exercise of private choice as essential for the achievement of individuality and also essential for the stability of the social order. What must happen by "inner necessity" is that social forces be differentiated into classes. The problem with the treatment of classes in Plato and in ancient political systems was that individuals were forced into the various classes by birth. The individual could not then regard the class of which he was a member as a product of his own choice. To the extent that he felt uncomfortable with his presence in the class he would regard it as an alien and unwanted imposition. As a result he would be resentful and rebellious toward the social order. From the standpoint of the dominant members of the society, freedom would appear to be the disruptive force in the society, and the proper attitude toward it would appear to be to stamp it out.

Hegel contends, on the contrary, that if allowed to have scope particular freedom will of itself produce a condition that harmonizes with the necessary class distinctions. He claims that natural differences in capacity and interest, if left to themselves, will have the consequence that social interest groups will emerge in accordance with the established classes. He writes that "it is reason, immanent in the restless system of human needs, which articulates it into an organic whole with different members" [200n]. Hegel is contending that there is an inner principle of organization in the context in which various individuals seek to obtain the satisfaction of their various interests. This is something like Adam Smith's "invisible hand." It has the effect of producing the fundamental classes in society without having to use external, legal control to do so. Individual free choice can then be allowed to operate without interference. Contrary to Plato, and perhaps Marx, Hegel finds the organization of society to be a product of human nature in society and not a product of an order that can only be understood and imposed by authority. Hence, it is not necessary to eradicate individual freedom.

However, why should the result of the private choice be the same as the imposed organization of the earlier political/economic structures? The answer is simply that in capitalism everyone is interdependent and the choices available for the individual are determined by social needs:

> When men are . . . dependent on one another and reciprocally related to one another in their work and the satisfaction of their needs, subjective self-seeking turns into a contribution to the satisfaction of everyone else. . . . [B]y a dialectical advance, subjective self-seeking turns into the mediation of the particular by the universal . . . The compulsion which brings this about is rooted in the complex interdependence of each on all . . . [199].

What people need determines what occupations are available. When there are no jobs in one field, it is necessary to learn how to fill or create jobs in some other field that is still open. Differentiation thus depends only on social needs and itself demands that the individual adapt himself to these needs.

On the other hand, Hegel maintains, by allowing individual freedom to have its scope, the factor mediating between the universal public, and private particular can be provided. This should have as its consequence that the member of the social order will be able to combine the two features and become a concrete individual. However, does Hegel avoid Marx's objection that in his treatment, the universal becomes only a means to the satisfaction of private needs?

III

The key to understand how Hegel can respond to Marx is in the role of education. For Hegel, individual autonomy is not grasped immediately. Rather the objective order historically produced the condition in which its members are in position to opt for it autonomously. That is, individual's recognition of autonomy depends on the historical conditions that teach him about his autonomy. In the process whereby the individual adopts the objective order, we have what Hegel identifies as substance becoming subject [144].

Hegel's account of the way the unity of right and welfare is achieved in the individual depends both on the moral recognition of the autonomy of the individual and the effect on character of the relation of the individual to civil society. The effect of persons seeking their own interests in the social order is educational. This struggle teaches them that the aims of self-seeking can only be achieved by broadening their interests beyond the selfish to the more general. They find it necessary to join and support organizations that actually emphasize the priority of restrictions on private freedom of choice [184,187]. The vicissitudes of nature, competition, and generally the impossibility of any one individual having such control over the social condition that he can be permanently secured within it, teach the individual to alter his interests. Here Hegel sees the individual as being liberated from the "subjectivity of demeanor . . . the empty subjectivity of feeling . . . the caprice of inclination" [187n].

Hegel cannot simply claim that persons learn through their trials in the system of civil society to be wiser, to form corporations and not depend on private enterprise so much. The new arrangements would still be a mere means to the satisfaction of private interests. Rather, the education is to alter the individual so he finds a different basis for his daily existence and relates to the state as the foundation of his rights.

What Hegel implies but omits saying [138n] is that the individual must experience the state as an object of respect because of its support of the good. As a result, the individual must choose to be one with it as an end in itself. Indeed, Kantian language is necessary if Hegel's conception is to avoid being either chauvinistic nationalism or bourgeois ideology. Because of the individual's recognition of the dignity of the state, and the accompanying respect that he has for a just institution, instead of living for satisfaction of needs, or finding the universal a means to satisfy needs, he finds the satisfaction of needs a means to further his acting for the universal. However, he comes to this conclusion through his own experience as a free member of civil society. This idea is not imposed on him.

The main argument in Hegel's demonstration of the inadequacies of civil society depends on the claim that the insecurities of activity based only on self-dependence, whether it be economic self-reliance or a morality based on conscience, will demonstrate to the individual that the particular self cannot provide a ground for living and acting in the world. The particular ego becomes self-contradictory—that is, its activity defeats its own purposes—if made the basis of life: it cannot achieve its private aims without systematic cooperation that requires it to accept an arrangement that overrules its possessiveness. Moreover, it cannot justify its moral position over against the same competitive demands for self-assertion made by others [cf. 139n]. The practical solution to the crisis of the ego that strives for self-dependence, can only be to give up the priority of the ego and make the universal, as expressed in the objective order, the basis of its existence [cf. 149,152]. Strictly speaking though, this transition depends on the recognition that individual rights are products of the historical, objective order [152]. Without that order there can be no rights. Without the education that raises the individual to a consciousness of subjective freedom, the individual cannot identify and express that freedom.

Formally, this means that the individual recognizes that economic and moral interpersonal relations, with their potential conflicts, can be mediated only by a disinterested universal position. This position is seen by the individual to be the basis of his secular existence. The individual moves from the desire for self-achievement to the desire for justice and recognizes that justice requires a basis that is common to himself and others but by which his practical life and welfare are determined [102, 345; see also 125,126 and 220].

Such a revolution is possible, however, only if a political order actually exists that supplies the structure enabling the individual to get his private satisfaction through the reversal of priorities. Hegel writes that this depends on

> the consciousness that my interest . . . is contained and preserved in another's (i.e., the state's) interest and end . . . In this way the other is not an other in my eyes and in being conscious of this fact, I am free [268].

Hegel's remark cannot be taken as a support for the conventional.

The objective order must actually preserve the individual both as a free personality and as a being with needs. Hegel affirms:

> When the existing world of freedom has become faithless to the will of better men, that will fails to find itself in the duties there recognized and must try to find in the ideal world of the inner life alone the harmony which actuality has lost [138n].

IV

Some followers of Marx think that Marx could have consistently adopted a form of democratic socialism rather than communism. Stanley Moore writes:

> There is no more justification for describing socialist distribution as in principle bourgeois than for describing capitalist distribution as in principle socialist.[17]

Moore and other democratic socialists do not attend sufficiently to Marx's claim that he is primarily concerned with the problem of the integration of the individual at a higher level. The emphasis on how much each person gets for the work done makes the satisfaction of private rather than social ends the most important objective in the distribution. There is no economic basis here for integration. Nevertheless, the democratic socialists sense the underlying problem in Marx's thought: the individual is not recognized as having the right and power to develop private interests and determine aims and objectives through his/her choice.

It is evident from this that in the account of the human individual, the main difference between Marx and Hegel lies in the place given to the "arbitrary will" or "personal freedom" in the integration of the individual. For Marx, the integration of the individual requires the eradication of all modes of formal differentiation that allow persons to separate themselves from one another. Persons are to be "conflated" into the one social person.[18]

To explain how he believes integration is possible, Marx claims it is necessary to eradicate differentiation at the economic stage and not only at the political stage. For example, in the *Critique of the Gotha Programme* Marx writes that when the "narrow horizon of bourgeois right" has been crossed, the principle of right will be "from each according to his ability, to each according to his needs!"[19] Here Marx implies that in order to achieve the condition of integrated man, one must give up the mode of thought in which right is regarded as a means of distributing goods to each in accordance with a principle of relative distribution, i.e., equally or unequally. This mode of thinking about rights presupposes differences among persons and so is treated by Marx as a product of egoism. Indeed Marx reduces the rights to liberty, property, equality and security expressed in the Declaration of the Rights of Man and the Citizen (1793) Article 2, to man as "an individual separated from the community . . . wholly preoccupied with his private interest and in accordance with his private caprice."[20] In several passages, Marx makes it clear that he would like to eliminate rights to private property, equality and individual liberty.[21] These conflict with the true nature of man since they enable privacy and separate man from man.[22] Remarks by Marx that suggest that he is prepared to accept a kind of democratic socialism must be seen in the light of the larger goal of "true communism" and seen as stages toward it.[23] In what Marx calls "the higher phase of communist society"[24] the principle of right (from each etc . . .) is the basis of everyone's activity and the source of personal welfare. Labor in this condition furthers the principle of right, for it is aimed at the satisfaction of everyone's needs. The satisfaction of one's own private needs takes place only as a consequence of the satisfaction of the general needs of mankind and is not private satisfaction, but an expression of general human satisfaction.

Marx is claiming, however, that this condition can only be effected through the alteration of the economic basis of civil society and not, as with Hegel, through the education of the individual. The elimination of the economic conditions that allow persons to have distinct functions is to be achieved through measures determined by the dictatorship of the proletariat.[25] In part, Marx insists that this eradication of the division of labor is directed toward the division into directive mental labor, and directed, primarily physical, labor.[27]

If we refer the demand for the abolition of the division of labor to the problem that Marx has developed with regard to the integration of the individual we find that Marx is contending the following. By abolishing the separation between thinking and physical labor and also by producing a condition in which man employs free labor that extends over the totality of possible occupations, society produces a man who is universal in his real life and in whom universal labor is the means to private welfare. In this way, it seems, Marx envisaged the overcoming of the separation of universal and private interest.

The Hegelian objection to Marx must refer to the will and to the problem of abstractness. Marx opposes the universal and the differentia and affirms the priority of the former. Hence he ends up by characterizing an ideal individual who is unable to differentiate himself in practice as a distinct person, i.e., as a particular will with private aims.[28] For this (contrary to Hegel), individual private desires must be seen as obstacles to an identification with the social whole.

Nevertheless, in his account of the capitalist differentiating process, Hegel himself is forced to recognize that there is a disturbing consequence. The conditions for success presented by civil society, make it inevitable that some will fail. The conditions of freedom in the market place, with overproduction and other ills of capitalism, have the consequence that civil society will inevitably produce a rebellious rabble of paupers [245]. This rabble of paupers is unable to "feel and enjoy the broader freedoms and . . . the intellectual benefits of civil society" [243].

The consequence is that even if Hegel can provide support to the claim that there can be an integration of the universal and particular in his state, it can only be an integration for some. On the other hand, Marx proposes an account that he believes can guarantee the elimination of class conflict and produce integrated individuals, but only by excluding the condition of particular freedom through which Hegel sees the individual as ultimately able to achieve integration. Certainly, freedom has a place for Marx, but it is still not the mediating factor in the achievement of the concrete individual. In communist society the individual must regard his particular character and the capacity for an independent will as forces that tend to prevent him from achieving the freedom that lies in the universal life.[29]

For Hegel, this means that the individual does not get past the first stage in the concept of the will—where there is universality, but only in opposition to differentia that the individual may not choose as such. In this regard, Hegel would contend that Marx's integration would seem to the individual as a form of determinism. There is social integration. But the individual is compelled to regard private matters as alien to his human character. As such, Marx's society, even without functional differentiation, would not resolve the problem of Plato's republic. Moreover, the analysis of the structure of the will presents the attempt to achieve complete freedom through social universality as self-defeating; hence, the operation of the dialectic would lead members of Marx's society to react against the social whole.

Still Marx is right in seeing the proletariat as evidence of the breach between mental and physical labor. Since this disruption cannot be overcome by self-integrating freedom, Marx and Hegel can and do agree that total integration is impossible in the bourgeois state. And Marx is correct in objecting that Hegel's account at least obscures this difficulty.

Despite this impressive objection, Hegel's position can be seen as a warning against supposing that the integration of the individual can occur without individual freedom. To the extent that the individual is made to regard himself as a produce of external forces alone (either natural, as for Plato, or social, as for Marx), he can find no personal worth in his existence and must find his power of subjective freedom in him to be an alien force. As a result, the individual will must remain repressed or express itself in opposition to the status quo. On the other hand, since self-integration presupposes the possibility of the individual failing or refusing to take the step to integration, Hegel's account of the state does indeed imply the likelihood of man disrupted into two. The practical economic consequence of this is poverty, and the class of those who are so unable to satisfy their private ends through the prevailing political forms that they regard the state and their own political character as alien to themselves.

In conclusion, perhaps the main consequence of this analysis is to remind us of the limits of the political and social order. If Hegel is right, what Marx has done is not to show the way to obtain concrete individuality for all. Rather than provide a solution, Marx has achieved a critical objective. He has exposed the underlying flaw in Hegel's account of the state. The state cannot be the embodiment of concrete freedom. For Marx has demonstrated that the conceptual conditions for concrete individuality can be achieved only in a state where there is in practice class conflict, that is, where the unity of the universal and the differentia is possible only for some (so that the universal is not a true universal). As a result, a perfect social solution to the problem of concrete freedom is impossible.[30]

NOTES

1. Hart, H.L.A., "Are There Any Natural Rights," in *Political Philosophy*, ed. A. Quinton (Oxford: Oxford University Press 1967), p. 61.

2. Rawls, John, *A Theory of Justice* (Cambridge, Mass: Belknap, 1971).

3. Kant, I., "On the Common Saying: 'This May be True in Theory, But it Does not Apply in Practice'," in *Kant's Political Writings*, ed. H. Reiss (Cambridge: Cambridge University Press, 1970), p. 73. For a discussion of some of the main points of Kant's treatment of the state, see my "Kant on War and International Justice" in *Kant Studien*, vol 78, Jan. 1987. My main point there is similar to the point I make about Hegel here. More needs to be said about the relation of Kant and Hegel on the treatment of the state.

4. C.B. MacPherson, *The Political Theory of Possessive Individualism: Hobbes to Locke* (Oxford: Oxford University Press, 1962).

5. Adam Shaff, *Marxism and the Human Individual* (New York: McGraw-Hill, 1970), p. 118.

6. Karl Marx, "Bruno Bauer: Die Judenfrage," in *Karl Marx: Early Writings*, trans. and ed. T.B. Bottomore (New York: McGraw-Hill, 1963), p. 13.

7. *Ibid.*, p. 5.

8. *Ibid.*, p. 30.

9. *Ibid.*, p. 28.

10. *Ibid.*, p. 29.

11. *Ibid.*, p. 12.

12. *Ibid.*, p. 26.

13. *Ibid.*

14. *Ibid.*, p. 31.

15. Hegel, G.W.F., *The Philosophy of Right*, trans. T.M. Knox (Oxford: Oxford University Press, 1942). Most references to Hegel's text are to Hegel's paragraph numbers. 'n' indicates the addition immediately following the paragraph indicated. 'Pref': Reference to the Preface are followed by the page numbers in Knox's translation.

16. Karl Popper, *The Open Society and its Enemies*, Vol. II (London: Routledge, 1963), pp. 56ff.

17. Stanley Moore, *Marx On the Choice Between Socialism and Communism* (Cambridge, Mass: Harvard University Press, 1980), p. 82. See also Lloyd D. Easton, "Marx and Individual Freedom," in *The Philosophical Forum*, Vols. XII #3 and XIII #2 & #3.

18. This has the consequence that rights of the sort discussed by Hobbes, Locke, Kant, Mill, etc. are not allowed in Marx's ideal society.

19. Karl Marx, *Critique of the Gotha Programme* (Peking: Foreign Language Press, 1972), p. 17.

20. Marx, *Die Judenfrage*, p. 23.

21. *Ibid.*, pp. 23, 27.

22. *Ibid.*

23. See Karl Marx, "Private Property and Communism" (Economic and Philosophical Manuscripts, 3rd Manuscript) in *Early Writings*, pp. 152, 157.

24. Karl Marx, *Gotha Programme*, p. 17.

25. *Ibid.*, p. 28.

26. Karl Marx and Friedrich Engels, *The German Ideology*; the reference is found in the selection provided by E. Fromm in *Marx's Concept of Man* (New York: F. Ungar, 1961), p. 206.

27. *Ibid.*, p. 204.

28. See my "Rights, Utilitarianism and the Conflation of Persons," *Journal of Philosophy*, Vol. LXXXIII, no. 6, June 1986, pp. 323 ff. The position of Marx is another variation of the problem discussed in that paper.

29. See Marx, "Private Property and Communism," pp. 160–161.

30. The upshot of this is that we should avoid seeking a permanent social solution. Rather we should strive to balance conflicting social needs in a flexible way that allows for the changing demands of day to day reality. For a brief account of this see my "Nation, State and Consent," in *Philosophers Look at Canadian Confederation* (Montreal: Canadian Philosophical Association, 1979), pp. 129,130.

Chapter Four

HEGEL'S CRITIQUE OF MARX:
THE FETISHISM OF DIALECTICS

William Maker

Hegel has no problems to formulate. He has only dialectics.
- Karl Marx -

Karl Marx is one of the most famous, influential, and genuinely important critics of Hegel. Before I move on to the substance of this paper, to a consideration of why I believe that Marx's critique of Hegel is fundamentally wrong, let me first comment on why I nonetheless feel that this critique is of central philosophical importance.

One aspect of the importance of what Marx has to say about Hegel simply has to do with the stature of Marx in the intellectual community. Marx's thought commands considerable respect, attention, and numerous adherents, both in the larger intellectual world and in the narrower confines of philosophy.[1] In the world of ideas, Marx is a heavyweight, and what he has to say about Hegel is, and should be, taken seriously.

For philosophers in particular though, Marx's critique of Hegel has a special significance. This is not only the case because Marx and Hegel offer sweeping and comprehensive, but divergent, philosophical accounts of the human condition and of the nature and prospects for the good life. Particular differences in their views of man and the world aside, Marx's critique of Hegel is especially important to philosophers because it is the focal point for a major confrontation on metaphilosophical issues of continuing relevance. For Marx's critique is at the center of an *Auseinandersetzung* between what are closely related but nonetheless sharply contrasting views on the nature and limits of philosophy itself and on the proper understanding both of the relation between philosophical theory and reality and of the relation between the philosopher and the world of his age, issues which have always concerned philosophers and which are the subject of much philosophical discussion today.

But beyond this the importance of Marx's *Hegelkritik* is even greater, especially for philosophical students of Hegel and Marx who are particularly interested in questions about the nature and legitimacy of systematic-dialectical philosophy and the possibility of critical theory. This is the case, because unlike many other critics past and present, Marx does not dismiss the legitimacy of systematic-dialectical philosophy as such. He does not condemn Hegel's whole approach, Hegel's whole idea of a philosophical science, as irredeemably perverse and hopelessly wrongheaded.[2] Refusing to regard Hegel as a "dead dog," Marx defended Hegel against what he saw as all too prevalent unjust attacks. He forthrightly described himself as "a pupil of that mighty thinker," consistently acknowledging his indebtedness to Hegel.[3] And not only did he speak of setting Hegel aright, Marx even went so far as to conceive his own philosophy as a corrected continuation and development, an *Aufhebung*, one might say, of Hegel's.[4]

So, far from being a critic who would reject, or even simply correct Hegel, Marx seems to have understood and justified his own position in Hegelian systematic terms, as the proper, dialectically generated refinement and furtherance of Hegel's. Given this self-understanding of his position then, we can say that the overall status of Marx's philosophy, and specifically its claim to being dialectically scientific, rest at least in part on the rightness of Marx's *Hegelkritik*.

Thus, the deeper philosophical significance of Marx's critique of Hegel is twofold. On the one hand, it deserves attention from anyone interested in the general topic of the proper nature and limits of philosophical theory. This is especially the case today when so much philosophical effort is being exercised in attempts to demonstrate the aporetic character of the Western philosophical tradition to which Marx and Hegel belong.[5] On the other hand, this critique and the reconceptualization of dialectical philosophy that Marx develops in conjunction with it compels attention for some, as it is of decisive importance to students of Hegel and Marx concerned with questions about the status, the overall character and legitimacy, of systematic-dialectical philosophical theory. For what is finally at stake in this critique are the claims of this theory's two major proponents to have raised philosophy to the level of a science.

What, briefly, are the essential features of Marx's critique? How does it lead to what is allegedly a correct reconceptualization of the nature and limits of dialectical philosophy. Further, how does his critique lead to what Marx sees as a necessary and radical transformation of the relation between philosophical theory and reality and thus also to a transformation of the tasks of the philosopher, both theoretical and practical?

The leitmotif of Marx's critique of Hegel is a familiar one, and it is not original to Marx.[6] It amounts to the charge that Hegel propounds a patently metaphysical, idealistic, and pantheistic system: a system in which thought or the Absolute Idea is literally and erroneously postulated as the true essence of reality and the moving subject behind history, such that empirical actualities are regarded as the mere appearances, the products or manifestations of this Idea.[7] For Marx, however, Hegel's purported lapse into the idealistic fallacy is not a genetic flaw and an unavoidable consequence of the systematic-dialectical approach to theory which he originated. Hegel's mistake, according to Marx, is not attributable to the very nature of systematic philosophy, but rather to the particular and erroneous fashion in which Hegel understood and developed dialectics. What is wrong with Hegel's philosophy is so to speak, essentially a matter of its content as opposed to its form, although, as we shall see, correcting the error of content does have serious implications for the nature and form of dialectical philosophy.[8]

In any case, perceiving Hegel's mistake as attributable not to dialectical thought per se, but rather to a misconstrual of the proper nature of dialectics, the substance of Marx's critique is directed against what he construes as the "mystification" dialectic suffers in Hegel's hands: "With him it is standing on its head. It must be inverted in order to discover the rational kernel within the mystical shell."[9] As this mystification consists in regarding empirical actuality as a manifestation of the Absolute Idea the demystifying inversion amounts to establishing the proper priority of the material over the ideal, of reality over thought. It finally amounts to transforming what Marx takes to be a dialectical idealism into a dialectical materialism. Rather than construing dialectics fundamentally as a process or activity of thinking, dialectic for Marx must rather be seen as a process or activity in and of reality itself.[10]

Continuing this corrective inversion, seeing dialectics as a process which is discovered in reality, we come to realize then that the motor of dialectic is properly understood not as thought or the Absolute Idea, but rather as man the maker and actor: as a process taking place in and of this world and by man, the dialectic consists in man's historical self-realization and self-creation through his continual and continually creative development, enhancement, and transformation of those productive capacities that define his species being.[11] Thinking through this material, dialectical, historical process to completion, we finally come to see that it will inevitably culminate, as a consequence of human action, in a state where these capacities are capable of full realization.[12]

There are significant consequences to this effort at a critical reconceptualization of the character of dialectics and dialectical philosophy, according to which the idea or philosophy, now properly understood, is "nothing else than the material world reflected by the human mind and transformed into forms of thought" (rather than the other way around, which was Hegel's error).[13] These consequences do not pertain only to the content and substantive features of Hegel's and Marx's dialectical conceptualizations of reality. In addition, they concern their metaphilosophies, their respective understandings of the nature, limits and potential of systematic-dialectical philosophy, as well as their views on the relation between philosophical theory and reality and their positions on the tasks of the philosopher, both worldly and philosophical. As we shall see, what is finally at stake here in general is the question of the nature and possibility of a critical philosophy or theory.

From the Preface to the *Philosophy of Right* we know the views of the mature Hegel on these latter topics: philosophy cannot give "instruction," it cannot provide us with a recipe for making the world what it ought to be, and it must remain silent as to the future course of history. The task of the philosopher is not to direct action, but to provide comprehension and understanding of the real to the extent to which it is rational.[14]

Marx's view, as encapsulated in the XI Thesis on Feuerbach, could not be in sharper contrast: "The philosophers have only interpreted the world, in various ways; the point is to change it."[15] Now as Marx develops and refines this position in his philosophical project what we see emerging is a vision of the philosopher's task as involving more than just world-transforming action. What Marx presents is not merely a call for philosophers' engagement in and with the world; he also calls for, and comes to offer, a radical reformation of the character and objectives of philosophy itself and of the tasks of the philosopher as a theorist.

For as a consideration of Marx's subsequent writings and career reveals, his claim is not at all that the work of philosophy is done and that philosophers should stop philosophizing and *just* act. Rather, Marx himself continues to philosophize, and in so doing redefines the nature of philosophy itself in that he conceives a properly and thoroughly demystified systematic-dialectical philosophy as constituting not merely a call for but also a *theory* of world-transformative action as revolutionary praxis. How so?

Corrected and taken beyond Hegel, systematic-dialectical philos-

ophy, now distinctively labeled "critique," is to provide a theory of
the overcoming of philosophy; it is to present a theory of the final
transformation of philosophy qua theory into actuality through revolutionary praxis, a praxis which is itself understood specifically as
action guided by theory.[16] What this means is that the job of the
philosopher is not merely to provide an account of the manner and
extent to which the real is rational. In addition, and more importantly, his task is twofold: to make the real rational through action
and to comprehend in philosophical, systematic-dialectical theory
the character, legitimacy and necessity of this action. Put differently,
the job of the philosopher, revealed by and consequent upon the
demystification of dialectics, is to provide a dialectically scientific—a
necessary and comprehensive—account of the empirically discoverable dialectical process by which the opposition between all philosophical theory and reality is inevitably to be overcome in and
through human action.[17]

So the special and new goal of systematic-dialectical philosophy
as now understood by Marx is to give a theory of the realization of
theory, a theory of how, through dialectics, philosophy is to become
real and of how the real is to become rational or philosophical.[18]
Thus Marx's attempt to demystify dialectics reconceptualizes the
very nature and limits of dialectical philosophy. First of all it postu-
lates a dialectically necessary relation between theory as a whole,
including systematic-dialectical philosophy, and reality. (It conceives
them as at present in an opposition in need of overcoming.) Secondly, it calls for a new or further systematic-dialectical theory to
comprehend the past origins, the present state, the future movement, and the ultimate resolution of this dialectical opposition.[19]

It is just such a theory—one that claims to comprehend in dialectical terms the necessity of its own overcoming and realization qua
theory—which can then finally claim to stand as a philosophical
science of praxis in the strong sense that Hegel regards as beyond
the limits of philosophy: in the sense of a theory comprehending the
necessity of and both predicting and legitimating certain courses of
action.[20] For on the basis of its purported comprehension of the
dialectical relationship between itself as theory and reality, this transformed and expanded systematic-dialectical philosophy can claim to
speak of the future in more than a hypothetical or tentative fashion,
and it can not merely suggest, but ordain, certain courses of action.
That is, for Marx, systematic-dialectical theory offers us a *science* of
praxis in that the nature and legitimacy of certain future actions can
be philosophically demonstrated by first establishing that they follow
as a consequence of thinking through the dialectic. Dialectics, according to Marx, is a process in and of reality, discoverable by

thought; thought, having uncovered the basic workings of dialectic, can then further disclose, through dialectical reasoning, at least the general features of the dialectic's future unfolding in reality. Having disclosed this movement, theory can announce that course of action seen as in accordance with and as necessitated by the larger movement of the dialectic, thus establishing a science of praxis. Since the developmental dynamic of dialectics pertains not merely to theory, or reality, but also to the relation between the two—as demystified dialectics encompasses the emerging necessary synthesis of the ideal and the real, of the conceptual and the material—demystified dialectical theory can claim to reveal in theory what must subsequently come to be in reality.

It is important to note that this thoroughgoing reconceptualization of the nature, limits, and objectives of systematic-dialectical philosophy and the demystifying corrective inversion of dialectics involved in it seem, at least in part, to be justified by Marx in dialectical, Hegelian terms. For, according to Marx, thinking dialectically beyond Hegel entails thinking dialectically about the relation between Hegel's completed system and the contemporary world.[21] Thinking dialectically about Hegel reveals the dialectical character of Hegel's errors, as well as it reveals the need and the basis for going beyond him.[22] Thus, in provisional defense of Marx as a critic of Hegel, one might present his move beyond Hegel as one that is seemingly in agreement with Hegel's own notion of an immanent dialectical critique.[23]

What I shall now attempt to show is that in working to develop further and to transform radically the nature and limits of systematic-dialectical philosophy in the ways I have indicated, Marx has misconstrued the proper character of this philosophy and illicitly transgressed what Hegel happened to have correctly understood as the necessary limits of dialectical theory. Put in another way, what I aim to indicate is that in finally assessing Marx's claim that his is the true dialectical philosophy, we need to attend not only to Marx's explicit critique of Hegel but also equally to what I shall present as Hegel's implicit critique of Marx. In laying out Hegel's critique of Marx, I shall work to show explicitly what the limits of systematic-dialectical philosophy are through a consideration of Hegel's views on that philosophical standpoint or theoretical assumption which he sees as in need of rejection if philosophy is to be a science. I shall then claim that Marx reverts to this pre- or extra-philosophical standpoint in what he offers as his demystification of dialectics, arguing that Marx's claim that dialectics must correctly be seen as something which is first found in reality only subsequently to emerge in philosophical thinking represents not a demystification, but in fact a mystification of dialectics. Put differently, I shall argue that Marx's purported demystifying inversion of dialectics is a fundamental conceptual error, analogous to the error Marx himself diagnoses as the fetishism of commodities. I shall then argue on these grounds that Marx is also in error in attempting to develop a philosophy—a systematic-dialectical science—of praxis. Here I shall attempt to show that a proper construal of the nature and limits of systematic-dialectical philosophy precludes the attempt to construe a dialectical relation between theory and reality in Marx's sense of such a relation: namely, as a relation which can lead to an action predicting and legitimating science. Put differently, I shall argue that the limits of philosophy as sketched by Hegel in the Preface to the *Philosophy of Right* follow from the character of systematic philosophy as science and are not merely attributable to the pragmatic or genuine conservatism of a prominent Prussian philosopher and state employee. Finally, I shall consider the implications of this critique of Marx for the question of the possibility and nature of a critical philosophy.

In order to see how Marx comes to transgress the nature and limits of systematic-dialectical theory we need first of all to consider those features of such a philosophical theory that can be said to comprise its philosophically scientific character. Secondly, and of greater import, we also need to see what minimal conditions must be met such that a theory or philosophy can claim to possess these features and thus present itself as having attained the status of philosophical science. The latter is especially important because my claim is that Marx violates these conditions and thus obviates his claim that his theory is scientific in a dialectical sense and because it is the proper continuation of dialectical philosophy.

According to Hegel, systematic-dialectical philosophy is scientific thought or philosophy par excellence in that it expresses philosophical truth.[24] More specifically, it is philosophical science because it articulates what is rationally universal and necessary in a manner that is both unconditional and complete.[25] Furthermore, this philosophy can lay claim to such unconditional universality and necessity, and to completeness for what it articulates, only insofar as this philosophy is fully and exclusively self-grounding.[26]

What this idea of self-grounding means, is that this philosophy's claim to be scientific rests initially *and minimally* on the claim that nothing external to the system enters into its constitution in a determinative manner. In addition, this feature of being self-grounding itself rests further on, or amounts to, this philosophy's claim to being exclusively founded in pure and autonomous reason.[27] The connection between being self-grounding and being founded in pure and autonomous reason is this: only a mode of thought founded and developed in and through reason's radical *self*-constitution can lay claim to being a mode of thought which is genuinely and exclusively self-grounding, and thus capable of unconditionally articulating what is rationally universal and necessary. For, to be self-grounding is, minimally, to be devoid or free from anything arbitrary, assumed, or merely postulated, i.e., anything requiring further legitimation or grounding. Thus to be scientific, this philosophical discourse must be free from anything determined or justified extra-systemically or extra-rationally. And such freedom as it pertains to the nature and content of systematic philosophy—freedom from external determination—can only be attained insofar as reason is autonomous in its operations, insofar as reason is not externally or other-conditioned or determined. Thus, systematic philosophy is only fully justified or grounded and systematic philosophy can only be a science if reason is, or can be brought to be, autonomous and if reason alone can be said to have determined the form and content of the system.

I trust that it is obvious from these brief remarks that, while self-groundedness is not a sufficient condition for all the attributes of scientific philosophy, it is certainly a necessary one. The question of what other conditions must be met for systematic-dialectical philosophy to be fully scientific in all the senses mentioned above, and the question of whether Hegel's—or anyone's—version of systematic philosophy fully meets these conditions everywhere, or anywhere, cannot concern us here.

Now for Hegel, what is crucial if philosophy is to become a science in this sense, a necessary pre-condition for science, is first showing that such a standpoint of autonomous reason is attainable. And according to him this requires a prior exercise of thought in which it is systematically demonstrated that reason possesses the potential for radical autonomy and is thus in the position of generating a self-grounding science because it has been shown that reason need not necessarily be conditioned in its operations by anything external to or other than itself. Such a prior demonstration of reason's potential for autonomy involves indicating what such external conditioning amounts to or consists in and in further revealing how and why it is that the factors that constitute such conditioning—the factors which may be said to render reason heteronomous in its operations—are not endemic to these operations.

Put differently, coming to the standpoint of science requires first showing that what Hegel calls the prevailing "natural assumption . . . in philosophy"—according to which reason is always construed as in some manner necessarily conditioned—is itself an arbitrary assumption about the character of reason.[28] Revealing the arbitrary character of the assumption that reason must always be heteronomous—allegedly always conditioned by some factor or factors—is a vital condition for science because, failing such a demonstration, this philosophy's claim to autonomy would itself be, or appear, merely arbitrary: the claim to autonomy would only be a "bare assurance" unless it can be shown how it is that the contending position on reason is not a sufficient condition for science. Showing that reason can come to an awareness of and can reveal as unfounded that assumption about its own nature that allegedly establishes its necessary conditionality—its heteronomy—amounts only to an indication of the prima facie possibility of an autonomous self-constitution and self-development of reason.

More specifically, what particular assumption concerning the character of reason as necessarily conditioned must be revealed as unfounded and how, in brief, does Hegel work to do this? The governing "natural" assumption that can be said to define the necessarily heteronomous character of reason, and that is deconstructed in the *Phenomenology of Spirit*, is this: it is that preconception or understanding of reason which construes reason as always unavoidably conditioned in its operations by some given. (The *Phenomenology* is thus an attack on what Sellars calls the "myth of the given."[30]) In this prevailing assumption about the character of reason, reason is always seen as heteronomous because, according to Hegel, reason is here identified with consciousness; the conditions of all possible thought are identified with the conditions of human subjectivity. So reason is construed as necessarily conditioned—as less than autonomous, less than genuinely self-determining or self-constitutive—in that it is assumed that the operations of reason must and can only be construed in terms of that model or mode of thought in which whatever comes to be known or thought *is* always, in some sense, a *Gegenstand*, something whose determinate and knowable character is always in one way or another given to conscious awareness. And if reason can be identified with consciousness, then reason cannot be autonomous, for whatever it might come to establish or claim will always be ineluctably other-determined: it will be in some way founded in that whose determinate character is, as a "given," predetermined. But, as Hegel puts it speaking of consciousness:

> These views on the relation of subject and object to each other express the determination which constitute the nature of our ordinary, phenomenal consciousness; but when these prejudices are carried out into the sphere of reason as if the same relation obtained there, as if this relation were something true in its own self, then they are errors the refutation of which throughout every part of the spiritual and natural universe is philosophy, or rather, as they bar the entrance to philosophy, must be discarded at its portals (*Science of Logic*, p. 45).

The *Phenomenology* then comes to indicate that this is an unquestioned assumption about reason. The assumption, taken as a given, in both the pre-critical and critical philosophies, is an arbitrary assumption in the following way: it shows that when consciousness finally comes not merely to presuppose the universal validity of its mode of knowing, but actually grounds it, this radical self-grounding and self-legitimation is at the same time the dissolution of the opposition between awareness and the given that constitutes the minimal determinate character of consciousness itself. This indicates that what seemed to be a minimal and necessary assumption about the conditioned character of all thought—that whatever comes to be known or claimed must be founded in a given determinacy—is arbitrary and unfounded. Arbitrary and unfounded in that this assumption about the necessarily heteronomous character of thought cannot be legitimated without at the same time violating and transcending the very conditions held as necessary and non-transcendable.

Having arguably shown this (I cannot demonstrate here that the *Phenomenology* does demonstrate this), this preliminary exercise can then be said to have made at least possible an autonomous self-constitution by reason. For it has served to liberate reason from the tendency of lapsing into this mode of consciousness in the process of its ensuing self-constitution, thus functioning as a propadeutic exercise for systematic philosophy. (Of course, such an exercise cannot guarantee that such a lapse will not occur.)

How this preliminary exercise functions more specifically to provide a beginning point for an autonomous and self-grounding science cannot concern us here. What must concern us is appreciating that while the rejection of the standpoint and structure of consciousness allows systematic philosophy at least a plausible claim to autonomous self-grounding, it does so only at the price of establishing certain limits for this philosophy. These are limits of such a character that they cannot be transgressed if systematic-dialectical philosophy is to retain its claim to being science and which must be, and are, transgressed in Marx's attempted revision and extension of systematic-dialectical theory.

If the rejection of the standpoint of consciousness as a necessary model for philosophical thought helps to establish the scientific character of systematic philosophy as self-grounding by making it possible for reason to engage in a genuinely autonomous process of self-constitution, it does so at the price of establishing a certain kind of limitation or closure for this system as a dialectically scientific one. Insofar as part of the system's claim to autonomy rests on the claim that the categories generated in it are autonomously produced by reason alone, and as this claim to autonomy is itself based on the rejection of the form of consciousness as a determinative model for the constitution of systematic categories, this then requires that the scientific character of the system precludes an attempt within systematic-dialectical philosophy, to construe its relation to reality, *in the sense that* "reality" is conceived extra-systemically, or from the standpoint of consciousness: namely, as something that we find given in its determinacy for thought.

What does this mean, and how does it relate to Marx? To claim that the system cannot conceive reality from the standpoint of consciousness is not to say that systematic philosophy cannot speak of reality, even as an other to thought. Nor is it to say that the system cannot speak of consciousness, or of reality as a datum for consciousness. The system can and does do all of these things. It is to say that insofar as systematic-dialectical philosophy conceptualizes the real, and these and other features of it, this philosophy cannot constitute the real—as a category of systematic philosophy—in the manner of consciousness, i.e., as a category given in its determinacy.[31] Put more specifically, systematic-dialectical philosophy cannot appeal to any aspects or features of the real apprehended as a datum for consciousness, either as foundationally constitutive for its conception of the real or as evidence for the philosophical truth of its conception of the real. It cannot do this simply because, were it either to derive or to attempt to ground its categories in such a manner—by reference to what is given to conscious awareness—it would surrender to the primacy of the given and thus to a mode of thinking whose rejection as authoritative in and for the system is crucial to its claim to being scientific.

That the real is not to be conceptualized within the system in this manner is clear not only from Hegel's remarks about what conditions must be met and what position must be rejected if philosophy is to be science. It is also clear from what he has to say about the move in the system from logic to *Realphilosophie*: "The logical idea does not thereby come into possession of a content foreign to it: but by its own native action is specialized and developed to nature and mind" (*Encyclopedia*, §43). "Nature has yielded itself as the idea in the form of otherness" (*Encyclopedia*, § 247).

So to do what Hegel precisely claims he is not doing in systematic-dialectical philosophy—to look to and at the real as a given object (*Gegenstand*) and as a determinative and not merely illustrative source for the categories and determinacies of systematic philosophy—would be to resort to the pre- and extra-scientific standpoint of consciousness. And because it would necessarily involve bringing into the system merely given and not systematically and autonomously generated determinacies, it would invalidate the system's claim to being self-grounding and hence its claim to being philosophical science.

Thus, while systematic-dialectical thought can conceptualize the real and can even come to conceptualize its relation to the real, as philosophical theory and its own emergence in history—conceptual actions which are part of its working to completeness—these notions or categories ("the real," "philosophy," "history," and so forth) must be understood as categories of systematic philosophy. That is, not as categories whose determinate character and validity are established in virtue of the claim that they agree with, are "true" or "correct" descriptions of the real, history, etc., as we happen to apprehend them phenomenally, as given data for conscious thought. (Correlatively, the activities of conceptualizing the real and of conceptualizing the relation of philosophy to the real must be undertaken "systematically": without constitutive reference to the real as a datum for consciousness.) In a word, then, systematic-dialectical philosophy does not "describe" reality. According to Hegel:

> The Idea is the Truth: for Truth is the correspondence of objectivity with the notion—not of course the correspondence of external things with my conception, for these are only correct conceptions held by me, the individual person. In the Idea we have nothing to do with the individual, nor with figurate conceptions, nor with external things (*Encyclopedia*, § 213).

This then is the fulcrum of the difference between Hegel's and Marx's views, both as to the proper "method" of doing systematic-dialectical philosophy as well as on the issue of how systematic-dialectical philosophy or theory "relates" to reality. And the difference between them on these points has serious consequences for an assessment both of the nature and status of their philosophies and for the notion of a systematic-dialectical science of praxis.

First, as regards an assessment of the status of a philosophy that constitutes and presents its categories in the manner systematic philosophy must reject, on the mode of consciousness as descriptions: as we can see, and as Hegel claims, to construe the truth of philosophical categories in this way, and to proceed in philosophy in this manner, is to operate in the mode of pictorial/metaphysical thought:

> We must in the first place understand clearly what we mean by truth. In common life truth means the agreement of an object with our conception of it. We presuppose an object to which our conception must conform. In the philosophical sense of the word, on the other hand, truth may be described, in general abstract terms, as the agreement of a thought content with itself. This meaning is quite different from the one given above (*Encyclopedia*, § 24, remark).

And in metaphysics, he writes:

. . . the predicates by which the object is determined are supplied
from the resources of picture thought, and are applied in a mechan-
ical way. Whereas, if we come to have genuine cognition, the object
must characterize its own self, and not derive its predicates from
without (*Encyclopedia*, § 28, remark).

What Hegel's rejection of a foundational as well as a referential
basis for his philosophy indicates is that it is wrong—as Marx and
others do—to regard Hegel's philosophy as metaphysically idealistic.[32] This is not to deny that various things Hegel says suggest this
sort of a reading. More significantly, this is not to deny that Hegel
presents his system as, in some sense, an account of what is "true"
in reality[33] As I shall argue below, what I see as the critical force of
this system involves this latter claim. But as I shall also indicate, such
critical force hinges on the system's not being, or not being read as,
an idealistic metaphysics. In any case, to contend that Marx begins
to go awry in his *Hegelkritik* by seeing Hegel's philosophy as an
idealistic metaphysics is, for the moment, to say two things.

(1) This system is not metaphysically idealistic (or permits of a
non-metaphysical, non-idealistic reading) because it does not claim
to be an account of the real as it is phenomenally given, because it is
not meant to be a "correction" of what we know about reality from
the standpoint of consciousness. How so? How can this claim be
made for Hegel, given the tradition of Marx's misreading? As we can
now see, to hold that it is such a correction would involve making in
systematic philosophy a comparison between its account of the real
and what is purportedly a phenomenal account of the real. But just
such a comparison, if offered as a test to determine which account is
true in the sense of truth as correspondence—the sense of truth I
have just quoted Hegel as rejecting—would necessitate a return to
the standpoint of consciousness and the importation into the pur-
view of systematic philosophy of extra-systemic determinations.

(2) More generally, this system is not metaphysically idealistic,
nor is it an identity philosophy, because any metaphysical idealism
or identity philosophy presupposes as a primal given the opposition
between thought and the materially or empirically given in order to
deny the primacy of such given in favor of the primacy of thought.
The opposition between thought and the given must be taken as a
given in order to be denied or corrected: the thesis of the primacy of
thought or of the identity of thought and the given cannot be maintained without the opposition. The alleged truth of any idealism or
identity philosophy thus presupposes the opposition and is unintelligible without it. But as we have seen, for Hegel, a precondition for
systematic philosophy is the suspension in it of the opposition of
consciousness, of just that opposition between thinking awareness

and the given which must be presupposed and which cannot ultimately be eliminated if any metaphysical idealism or identity philosophy is to remain coherent.

Given these features of systematic-dialectical philosophy, and
given that in criticizing Hegel's metaphysical idealism, Marx was
attacking a straw man, how do things stand with Marx? Precisely
because of what he offers as the corrective, demystifying inversion—
the turn to material reality as an empirically given foundational datum—we can see that Marx's version of systematic-dialectical philosophy invalidates any possible claim to be scientific in a systematic-
dialectical sense of what this means. By incorporating what he claims
and insists are empirically given data, correct or true descriptions of
reality as we find it, Marx's version of systematic philosophy sacri-
fices any claim to being self-grounding, and with it any legitimate
claim for the necessity and completeness of the dialectic it postu-
lates.[34] (Whether Marx regarded it to be scientific in some other sense
is questionable. Whether it might be scientific in some other sense
cannot concern us here.)[35]

Additionally, we can also see that it is in fact Marx, and not Hegel
who propounds a mystified idealism, albeit an idealism that flies the
flag of materialistic realism. Marx's dialectical theory is a version of
idealism because it takes what is properly understood as a feature of
the relation of categories or determinacies in systematic philosophy—
the necessity of the dialectical interrelatedness and progressive co-
determination of its categories, the dialectical necessity that establishes the system's claim to completeness for what it considers—and
reads it into reality and history as an allegedly empirically discoverable feature of both. In fact, this amounts surreptitiously, and under
the guise of what is purportedly an empiricistic realism, to doing
just what Marx claims Hegel is doing: imposing the rulership of
ideas or philosophy over reality.

To put the point in another way Marx's empiricistic-materialistic
misconstrual of dialectics is analogous, as an error, to what Marx
diagnoses as the fetishism of commodities. Speaking of the "com-
modity form and its relation," Marx writes:

> It is nothing but the definite social relation between men which
> assumes here, for them, the fantastic form of a relation between
> things. In order therefore, to find an analogy, we must take flight
> into the misty realm of religion. There the products of the human
> brain appear as autonomous figures endowed with a life of their
> own, which enter into relations both with each other and with the
> human race. So it is in the world of commodities with the products
> of men's hands. I call this the fetishism which attaches itself to the
> products of labor as soon as they are produced as commodities, and

it is therefore inseparable from the production of commodities (*Capital*, vol. 1, p. 165).

I would suggest that in order to find a further analogy we must take flight, not now into the misty realm of religion, but into the equally misty realm of Marx's metaphysics. There a product of human thought—dialectics—"appears as an autonomous figure endowed with a life of its own." An "autonomous figure" that "enters into relations both with itself" (dialectics according to Marx is a cosmic process, a feature both of theory and reality and of the relation of the two) and that also enters into relations with the human race. For dialectics according to Marx is also, as found in reality, a feature of human historical relations and activities. "So it is, then, in the world" of Marx's dialectics with this "product of thought." *I* call this the *fetishism of dialectics*, which attaches itself to a product of thought as soon as it is read as a real thing. It is therefore inseparable, as I have suggested, from the production of an empirically founded systematic-dialectical philosophy.

What can we say then, finally, about the notion of a systematically dialectical science of praxis? What are we to make of Marx's claim that demystifying Hegel, and thus thinking through the dialectic between systematic-dialectical theory qua theory and reality as an empirical datum, can enable and lead us to offer a recipe for action? Can we have a theory of praxis that, on the basis of the theory's comprehension of the dialectic, is capable generally of predicting and legitimating courses of human action? Put differently, what are we to make of Marx's claim that his version of systematic-dialectical theory permits us to assume the throne of philosopher kingship? Or, taking a critical stance, just why, as I have suggested, does the proper understanding of the nature and limits of systematic-dialectical philosophy preclude such a science of praxis? How can we come to see that Hegel's views on the limits of systematic-dialectical philosophy and the worldly role of the philosopher follow from the nature of systematic-dialectical philosophy?

It is here that we need to consider and assess Hegel's claim about the "truth" of the system *vis à vis* reality, now regarding "reality" not as a categorical determination of systematic philosophy, but as an empirically given datum. Just as I have suggested that it is Marx's systematic-dialectical philosophy, and not Hegel's, that is idealistically metaphysical, I believe that it is also Hegel's systematic-dialectical philosophy that presents itself—potentially—as a truly legitimate critical philosophy.

How so? I believe that the motivation for Hegel's attempt to develop a philosophy grounded in and exclusively generated out of autonomous reason did not merely arise out of a desire to raise philosophy to the level of a science. Beyond this strictly theoretical motivation, I believe that Hegel saw that any possible worldly role for philosophy—any role that is, for a critical philosophy that can claim that reality as we find it given ought to conform to reality as we rationally conceive it—hinged on first establishing that reason has a right to claim authority over the given.[36] More specifically, Hegel felt a critical, worldly role for philosophy presupposed showing, contra Hume and even contra Kant, that reason need not submit, in what it conceptualizes, to the authority of any given. That is, if Hume, Kant—and Heidegger—are correct, if it is true that reason is and must always be in some way either externally or internally determined by a given which resists final penetration by reason, then the theoretical and pragmatic legitimacy of reason's claim to take a critical stance *vis à vis* the given is undercut. If they are correct, anything reason might claim to establish on its own as rational is and must always be arbitrary and finally unfounded, because necessarily other-determined. So if they are correct, then a consequence of reason's heteronomy is its impotence as a critical force; reason must surrender to the authority of the given. Thus, indicating that there is a legitimate critical role for reason in the world of human events requires something like a *Phenomenology*, a systematic demonstration that reason need not necessarily be determined in its operations and discoveries by some allegedly ineluctable given.

But such a demonstration has the consequence of ordaining a limited role for philosophy and the philosopher in the world of the given. For, as the philosophical account of the real as rational requires that extra-systemic, given determinancies be eliminated from the system, this further means that if the completed account of the real as rational is to have any critical force *vis à vis* the given status quo, it can only have this force extra-systemically.

Put more straightforwardly, in systematic-dialectical philosophy one cannot claim to speak in systematic-dialectical terms (with the force of unconditional, rational universality and necessity) as to whether reality as it is given, or as we think it might be, is or is not rational. Hence, one cannot claim, as Marx does to scientifically and systematically-dialectically predict or give advice as to how the world will be made rational. Why does the critical dimension of systematic-dialectical philosophy fall outside of systematic-dialectical philosophy strictly so-called? The critical dimension must fall outside simply because, in speaking as systematic philosophers, we cannot make descriptive truth claims, the sort of claims necessary for making predictions or for legitimating certain actions. We cannot do this because it ultimately undercuts not only the scientific status of the system, but also its claim to be what autonomous reason conceptualizes. To do so would undercut any legitimacy the system might have as a critical device.

So, *as* systematic-dialectical philosophers, we must remain silent about whether the world or society does or does not accord with the demands of reason as articulated by this philosophy. Or if we choose to address these questions and if we choose to claim that the world already does or that it should accord with reason, we must be careful to offer these judgments as opinions: as unavoidably involving empirical claims that are subject to challenge by non-philosophers and which are subject to challenge in a different way than the claims of systematic philosophy are. In short, if we wish systematic philosophy to have a rightful worldly impact, we must not seek to take on the role of philosopher kings.

If I am correct on these matters, it indicates that what Marx presents as the truly "critical" philosophy cannot finally have any legitimate force as critical *philosophy*. This is simply because: (1) by incorporating empirically given data it stands open to philosophically irresolvable challenges concerning its correctness. And more seriously, (2) by incorporating empirically given data as a foundation for its claims concerning the manner in which the real should be made rational, it obviates any possible claim to be speaking for autonomous reason. By acknowledging the authority of the given over what reason might establish on its own, it surrenders the basis for reason's rightful claim to critical authority and thus fundamentally and irreparably undercuts its own critical legitimacy.

The irony of this, of course, is that Marx's philosophy has given birth to so many philosopher kings, both ones who genuinely rule and ones who are pretenders to the throne. This might reinforce for us Hegel's skepticism about the worldly impact of philosophy, a skepticism I have tried to show as in agreement with his systematic philosophy. For appreciating its limits can also lead to an appreciation of the fact that, in a world that might in some ways approximate to a world of rational freedom, one cannot and does not want to try to coerce people to be rational. In any case, appreciating the limits I have spoken of can help us see how Hegel's philosophical caution, his somewhat pessimistic philosophical resignation, even his apparent conservatism, can be explained as truly philosophical in character.

NOTES

1. Klaus Hartmann's *Die Marxsche Theorie* (Berlin: Walter de Gruyter & Co., 1970) offers a thoroughgoing and important examination of Marx as a systematic philosopher. Robert Paul Wolff's *Understanding Marx* (Princeton: Princeton University Press, 1984), John Elster's *Making Sense of Marx* (Cambridge: Cambridge University Press, 1985), and Carol Gould's *Marx's Social*

Ontology (Cambridge: MIT Press, 1978) are all recent works that testify to the increased interest in Marx on the part of philosophers.

2. The most recent attempt at a wholesale condemnation of Hegel's system and its dialectic is Michael Rosen's *Hegel's Dialectic and Its Criticism* (Cambridge: Cambridge University Press, 1982).

3. Karl Marx, *Capital*, vol. 1, trans. B. Fowkes (Harmondsworth: Penguin Books, 1976), pp. 102, 103. For Marx's approving comments on Hegel see also the "Economic and Philosophical Manuscripts," p. 101 and "The Holy Family," in *Karl Marx: Selected Writings*, ed. D. McLellan (Oxford: Oxford University Press, 1977), p. 141.

4. Marx's conception of his project as an *Aufhebung* of Hegel's goes as far back as the "Notes to the Dissertation," *Selected Writings*, pp. 13–15, and is reiterated in *Capital*, vol. 1, p. 103. See also "Economic and Philosophical Manuscripts," in *Selected Writings*, pp. 104, 106.

5. Arguably, Marx himself might be said to belong to this tradition, owing to his stated objective of overcoming philosophy through its actualization, an issue I shall discuss subsequently. However, Marx still has at least one foot in the tradition, for he believes that reason is capable of attaining an adequate theoretical and critical understanding of the human condition. Thus he cannot be accurately classified with the numerous recent and contemporary philosophers who seem, at least, to deny this and who attack the traditional goals of philosophy. Major exponents of this line of thought are Nietzsche, Heidegger, Wittgenstein, Richard Rorty, and Alasdair MacIntyre.

6. Marx acknowledges his debt to Feuerbach for originating this criticism of Hegel in the "Economic and Philosophical Manuscripts," *Selected Writings*, pp. 97 and 99; and in a letter to Feuerbach, *Selected Writings*, p. 113; and in a letter to Schweitzer, reprinted in the *Poverty of Philosophy* (New York: International Publishers, 1963).

7. "My dialectical method is, in its foundations, not only different from the Hegelian, but exactly opposite to it. For Hegel, the process of thinking, which he even transforms into an independent subject, under the name of the idea, is the creator of the real world, and the real world is only the external appearance of the idea. With me the reverse is true: the ideal is nothing but the material world reflected in the mind of man, and translated into forms of thought." *Capital*, vol. 1, p. 102. See also the *Critique of Hegel's Philosophy of Right*. trans. and ed. J. O'Malley (Cambridge: Cambridge University Press, 1970), pp. 7ff., 14, 15, 17, 100, 116, 172; "Poverty of Philosophy," pp. 108,109; "Economic and Philosophical Manuscripts," *Selected Writings*, pp. 100, 109.

8. That Marx does not see the problem as lying in dialectics itself, but rather in Hegel's version of dialectics, see the quotation from *Capital* in the previous note and also the *Critique of Hegel's Philosophy of Right*, pp. 23, 24, 39, 40, 92. In a letter to Engels of the 14th of January, 1858, Marx writes: "In *the method of working* it was of great service to me that by mere accident . . . I leafed through Hegel's *Logic* again. If once again time for such work is at hand, I would have a great desire to make available for common understand-

ing on two or three sheets what is reasonable [*Rationelle*] in the method Hegel discovered and at the same time mystified."

9. *Capital*, vol. 1, p. 102. See also *Critique of Hegel's Philosophy of Right*, pp. 39, 40.

10. See "Preface To A Contribution To The Critique of Political Economy," in Karl Marx, *Selected Works* (Moscow: Progress Publishers, 1968), p. 183; also *Poverty of Philosophy*, pp. 180–181; *Critique of Hegel's Philosophy of Right*, pp. 23, 24; Karl Marx *Grundrisse: Foundations of the Critique of Political Economy*, trans. M. Nicolaus (Harmondsworth: Penguin Books, 1973), pp. 89, 102, 105, 107–108; "Towards a Critique of Hegel's' Philosophy of Right," *Selected Writings*, p. 70; "The Holy Family," *Selected Writings*, p. 134.

11. See the *Critique of Hegel's Philosophy of Right*, pp. 39, 137; *Poverty of Philosophy*, pp. 180–181, 189; "The German Ideology," *Selected Writings*, pp. 164, 171.

12. See "Preface To A Contribution To The Critique of Political Economy," *Selected Works*, p. 183; also the letter to Weydemeyer, *Selected Works*, p. 679; *Poverty of Philosophy*, pp. 174, 181, 186; "The German Ideology," *Selected Writings*, p. 178; "The Holy Family," *Selected Writings* p. 135.

13. *Capital*, vol. 1, p. 102.

14. G.W.F. Hegel, *Hegel's Philosophy of Right*, trans. T.M. Knox, (Oxford: Oxford University Press, 1967), Preface, especially pp. 10, 13.

15. "Theses on Feuerbach," *Selected Writings*, p. 158.

16. See the *Critique of Hegel's Philosophy of Right*, pp. 132, 133; "A Correspondence of 1843," *Selected Writings*, pp. 36—38,

17. See the *Critique of Hegel's Philosophy of Right*, pp. 137, 141, 142; "A Correspondence of 1843," *Selected Writings*, pp. 36–38.

18. See the *Critique of Hegel's Philosophy of Right*, pp. 136, 137, 138; "The German Ideology," *Selected Writings*, p.165; "A Correspondence of 1843," *Selected Writings*, pp. 36–38.

19. See the *Critique of Hegel's Philosophy of Right*, pp. 132, 136, 138, 139; "Economic and Philosophical Manuscripts," *Selected Writings*, pp. 77, 97.

20. See the *Critique of Hegel's Philosophy of Right*, pp. 137, 141, 132, 139; "The German Ideology," *Selected Writings*, pp. 137, 141, 132, 139; "A Correspondence of 1843," *Selected Writings*, p. 36.

21. See the "Notes to the Dissertation," *Selected Writings*, pp. 13–15; "Economic and Philosophical Manuscripts," *Selected Writings*, p. 76.

22. See *Capital*, vol. 1, p. 103; *Critique of Hegel's Philosophy of Right*, pp. 33, 39, 64, 84, 108–09, 135, 136, 137; "Economic and Philosophical Manuscripts," *Selected Writings*, p. 106.

23. "The genuine refutation must penetrate the opponent's stronghold and meet him on his own ground . . . The only possible refutation . . . must therefore consist, in the first place, in recognizing its standpoint as essential and necessary and then going on to raise that standpoint to the higher one through its own immanent dialectic." *Hegel's Science of Logic*, trans. A.V. Miller (London: George Allen & Unwin Ltd., 1969), p. 581.

24. G.W.F. Hegel, *Hegel's Logic: Being Part One of the Encyclopedia of the Philosophical Sciences*, trans. W. Wallace (Oxford: Oxford University Press, 1975), § 213.

25. See *Encyclopedia*, § 9, 12, 14 and the remark to § 41.

26. "The essential point of view is that what is involved is an altogether new concept of scientific procedure. Philosophy, if it would be science, cannot, as I have remarked elsewhere, borrow its method from a subordinate science like mathematics, any more than it can remain satisfied with categorical assurances of inner intuition, or employ arguments based on grounds adduced by external reflection. On the contrary, it can only be the nature of the content itself which spontaneously develops itself in a scientific method of knowing, since it is at the same time the reflection of the content itself which first posits and *generates* its determinate character" (*Science of Logic*, p. 27). "For reason is unconditional only in so far as its character and quality are not due to an extraneous and foreign content, only in so far as it is self-characterizing [*sich selbst bestimmt*], and thus, in point of its content, its own master" (*Encyclopedia*, § 52, remark). See also *Encyclopedia*, § 238, remark, §'s 9, 232, 4, 16, 17, 77 and G.W.F. Hegel, *Hegel's Phenomenology of Spirit*, trans. A.V. Miller (Oxford: Oxford University Press, 1977), p.44.

27. "It is by the free act of thought that it [philosophy] occupies a point of view, in which it is for its own self, and thus gives itself an object of its own production" (*Encyclopedia*, § 17).

"The most perfect method of knowledge proceeds in the pure form of thought: and here the attitude of man is one of pure freedom" (*Encyclopedia*, § 24, remark).

"Henceforth the principle of the independence of Reason, or of its absolute self-subsistence, is made a general principle of philosophy . . ." (*Encyclopedia*, § 60).

". . . the character of the rational . . . is to be unconditional, self-contained, and thus to be self-determining" (*Encyclopedia*, § 82, remark). See also *Encyclopedia*, § 3, 4, 6, 28, 60, 238, remark and the *Phenomenology of Spirit*, pp. 32, 34, 40.

28. *Phenomenology*, p. 46.

29. *Phenomenology*, p. 49.

30. Wilfred Sellars, "Empiricism and the Philosophy of Mind," in *Science, Perception and Reality* (London: Routledge & Kegan Paul, 1963).

31. See *Encyclopedia*, § 232, 1, 4, 74; *Science of Logic*, pp. 824, 826, 830.

32. See my articles "Does Hegel Have A 'Dialectical Method'?," *The Southern Journal of Philosophy*, 20:1 (Spring 1982), and "Understanding Hegel Today," *The Journal of the History of Philosophy*, 19:3 (July 1981). Also see "The Theory and Practice of the System of Freedom," by Richard D. Winfield, in *History and System*, ed. R. Perkins (Albany: SUNY Press, 1984), and "Conceiving Reality Without Foundations: Hegel's Neglected Strategy for *Realphilosophie*," *The Owl of Minerva*, 15:2 (Spring 1984).

33. "When understanding turns this 'ought' against trivial external and transitory objects, against social regulations or conditions, which very likely

possess a great relative importance for a certain time and special circles, it may often be right. In such a case the intelligent observer may meet much that fails to satisfy the general requirements of right; for who is not acute enough to see a great deal in his own surroundings which is really far from being as it ought to be? But such acuteness is mistaken in the conceit that, when it examines these objects and pronounces what they ought to be, it is dealing with questions of philosophic science" (*Encyclopedia*, § 6).

"Nothing can be more obvious than that anything we only think, or conceive is not on that account actual [*Wirklich*]; that mental representations and *even notional comprehension*, always falls short of being" (*Encyclopedia*, § 51, emphasis added).

34. See *Grundrisse*, pp. 102, 104, 105, 106; "The German Ideology," *Selected Writings*, pp. 164, 166, 171; *Critique of Hegel's Philosophy of Right*, pp. 39–40, 48; "Preface To A Contribution To The Critique of Political Economy," *Selected Works*, p. 182; *Poverty of Philosophy*, pp. 109, 173–174, 180, 183; "Economic and Philosophical Manuscripts," *Selected Writings*, p. 89; "The Holy Family," *Selected Writings*, p. 135.

35. See the "Letter to Lachatre," *Capital*, vol. 1, p. 17; *Capital*, vol. 1, p. 102; *Grundrisse*, p. 106; *Poverty of Philosophy*, p. 202; "Preface To A Contribution To The Critique of Political Economy," *Selected Works*, pp. 182, 183.

36. See Hegel's letter to Schelling, November 2, 1800, in *Hegel: The Letters*, Butler and Seiler, trans. (Bloomington: Indiana University Press, 1984), p. 63 and Joachim Ritter, *Hegel, and the French Revolution*, trans. R.D. Winfield (Cambridge: MIT Press 1982).

Chapter Five

HEGEL ON THE HUMAN AND THE DIVINE, IN THE LIGHT OF THE CRITICISMS OF KIERKEGAARD

Bernard Cullen

My modest aim in this paper is to re-examine briefly the theme in Hegel's philosophy of religion of the relation of human beings to God, in the light of the criticisms levelled against the Hegelian philosophy by Kierkegaard, especially in his main philosophical work, *Concluding Unscientific Postscript to the Philosophical Fragments*.[2] For the most part, I shall confine myself to Hegel's 1827 introductory lectures on the philosophy of religion, although of course he deals with these themes elsewhere (notably in the *Phenomenology*). I do so primarily because the 1827 lectures represent our most reliable account of his most fully developed views on the subject.[3]

My main concern is not so much to assess the validity or otherwise of Kierkegaard's criticisms, but to use them (precisely because they are so fundamental) to throw into sharp relief and hopefully to elucidate Hegel's views on this issue of perennial interest and importance, and indeed his views on the framework within which philosophy itself should be conducted. It would be silly to try to adjudicate between the two opposing views (Hegel right, Kierkegaard wrong; or vice versa). Instead, I shall confront the two positions by adopting the fiction that Hegel, in some of these lectures, is responding to Kierkegaard's criticisms. I shall both argue and try to demonstrate that Kierkegaard's jibes at "the system" of "speculative philosophy" involve either a misunderstanding or a wilful misreading of the Hegelian enterprise. Despite his ascription (not without justification) of the term "dialectic" to his own mode of reasoning and literary presentation, Kierkegaard either fails to grasp or simply refuses to accept the significance of Hegel's dialectical *Aufhebung* and the role of "mediation [*Vermittlung*]" in his dialectic.

I

The very title of Kierkegaard's *Concluding Unscientific [uvidenskabe-lig] Postscript* serves notice that the work is, in large part, a polemic against Hegel's claim that only his philosophical system is truly scientific (*wissenschaftlich*). Indeed, Hegel had often used the word *Wissenschaft* as a synonym for his own "speculative philosophy". According to Kierkegaard (alias Johannes Climacus), "the objective problem consists of an inquiry into the truth of Christianity." This is reference to the content of traditional natural theology and of Hegel's philosophy of religion. But Kierkegaard goes on to underline his chief concern: "The subjective problem concerns the relationship of the individual to Christianity. To put it quite simply: How may I, Johannes Climacus, participate in the happiness promised by Christianity?" (20). In the Appendix (545), having reiterated the claim of Christianity to bestow "eternal blessedness," he says that his book has been simply an attempt to answer the question, "How am I to become a Christian?"

A person does not become a Christian, according to Kierkegaard, by claiming "to grasp the truth of Christianity," as speculative philosophy does (200); for "Christianity is not a doctrine but an existential communication expressing an existential contradiction" (339), i.e., the incarnation of an infinite, eternal God in the finite, temporal world. Acceptance of this paradox demands not speculative philosophizing that would dissolve it but a leap of faith, "neither more nor less than the most decisive protest possible against the inverse procedure of [Hegel's] Method. . . . All Christianity is rooted in the paradoxical" (96). He contrasts this espousal of the paradoxical with Hegel's "mediation-principle, this deified and divine mediation, which performs and has performed miracles, transforming individual human beings into speculative philosophy in the abstract" (96). "Eternal happiness" can never be attained by the philosopher qua philosopher, but only by the "existing subjective thinker" who believes: "If the speculative philosopher is at the same time a believer, . . . he must long ago have perceived that philosophy can never acquire the same significance for him as faith . . . It is in faith that he is assured of [his eternal happiness]" (53).

According to Kierkegaard, Hegel subordinated the individual experience of life to the dictates of a completely abstract logical system, a fanciful construction utterly divorced from the concrete actuality it purports to conceptualize. Hegel offers nothing but "an immense building, a system, a system which embraces the whole of existence and world-history etc." But the philosopher, because he is an existing individual person, lives not in "this immense high-vaulted palace" of ideas, wherein all historical antitheses are overcome in thought, "but in an adjacent barn, or in a dog kennel, or at the most in the porter's lodge."[7] Kierkegaard reminds the speculative philosopher of his or her own inherence in history: "Is he a human being, an existing human being? Is he himself *sub specie aeterni*, even when he sleeps, eats, blows his nose, or whatever else a human being does? . . . Does he in fact exist? And if he does, is he then not in process of becoming?" (271).

For Kierkegaard, truth is only to be found in "subjectivity," in "inwardness"; and he continually charges the Hegelian speculative method and system with obliterating "subjectivity": "Speculative philosophy, as abstract and objective, entirely ignores the fact of existence and inwardness" (507); "speculative philosophy says that subjectivity is untruth, but says it in order to stimulate a movement in precisely the opposite direction, namely, in the direction of the principle that objectivity is the truth" (185). This portrayal of Hegel can be summarized by saying that Kierkegaard characterizes Hegel's speculative system as a philosophy of objectivity and identity: he insists that Hegel's much vaunted mediation of opposites (Hegel's dialectical *Aufhebung*) actually dissolves plurality in unity, particularity in universality, subjectivity in objectivity, difference in identity.

II

This is, of course, a caricature of the Hegelian enterprise of mediating and reconciling subjectivity and objectivity, difference and identity, in a higher unity. For Hegel, subjectivity is indeed untruth, but only in so far as it is merely partial truth. Kierkegaard is prepared to countenance the Hegelian *Aufhebung* and Hegel's insistence on the unity of thought and being only on the level of abstraction: on the level of existence, however, truth is subjectivity. But even a cursory reading of Hegel's lectures—on the philosophy of right, the philosophy of history, the philosophy of religion, and so on—will show that Hegel was working out his own philosophical system on the level of existence. Indeed, the whole system was elaborated primarily as a response to the bifurcation (*Entzweiung*) that permeates all aspects of the human situation. And this motivation was not simply the product of a youthful "existentialist" phase. As late as his 1822 lectures on the philosophy of right (as reported by Hotho), Hegel was emphasizing the therapeutic purpose of his systematic philosophy: "I am at home in the world [*in der Welt zu Hause*] when I know it, still more so when I have conceptualized it [*begriffen*]."[9] Kierkegaard could not be wider of the mark when he claims that the Hegelian philosopher has "forgotten, in a sort of world-historical

absentmindedness, what it means to be a human being" (109).[10] On
the contrary, the philosopher who subscribes to Hegel's philosophy
of religion seeks eternal happiness by attempting to grow in knowledge of what it is to be a human being with consciousness of and a
relationship with God. As against the Kierkegaardian insistence that
"reality itself is a system—for God; but it cannot be a system for any
existing spirit" (107), the Hegelian philosopher is confident of for-
mulating and elaborating the systematic knowledge of God and the
world that is coterminus with the philosophy of religion. Hegel emphasizes this fundamental point in his 1821 introductory lecture:

> All that proceeds from thought—all the distinctions of the arts and
> sciences and of the endless interweavings [*Verschlingungen*] of human
> relationships, habits and customs [*Gewohnheiten und Sitten*], activi-
> ties, skills, and enjoyments—find their ultimate centre [*letzten Mittel-
> punkt*] in the *one* thought of *God*. God is the beginning of all things
> and the end of all things; [everything] starts from God and returns
> to God. God is the one and only object of philosophy. [Its concern
> is] to occupy itself with God, to apprehend everything in him, to
> lead everything back to him, as well as to derive everything particu-
> lar from God and to justify everything only insofar as it stems from
> God, is sustained through its relationship with him, lives by his
> radiance and has [within itself] the mind [*Seele*] of God. Thus philos-
> ophy *is* theology, and one's occupation with Philosophy—or rather
> *in* philosophy—is of itself the service of God [*Gottesdienst*] (J 3–4,
> H 84).

This passage contains in embryo the content of Hegel's lectures,
and in particular his discussion of the relation of philosophy and
religion, his understanding of the concept of God, and of the nature,
role, and philosophical status of Christianity. It is almost as if Hegel
were explicitly rejecting the criticisms of Kierkegaard outlined above.
As he put it in this introductory lecture:

> To investigate and become cognizant of [*erkennen*] the nature [of
> religion] is the aim of these lectures. I wanted to make this cognitive
> knowledge [*Erkenntnis*] the object of my lectures because in the first
> place, I believe it has never been so important and so necessary that
> this cognition should be taken seriously once more (J 5, H 86).

I wish to claim that Hegel's conception of the dialectical relationship between human beings and God is *both* existentialist *and* speculative. The believing individual is dialectically subsumed into the
reasonable (*vernünftig*) totality that is the world in history, but remains an individual person and is not thereby obliterated in the
process. In the space remaining, I propose to examine briefly how
Hegel applies his doctrine of the mediation of opposites to the exis-

tential problem of overcoming in thought the opposition between the human and the divine.

III

Hegel's whole philosophical project was an epic attempt to overcome by the use of reason the alienating consequences of the many unresolved contradictions of modern human experience. Chief among these contradictions is the problem of the paradoxical coexistence of the human and the divine, a problem that bedevils "the unhappy consciousness."[12] Viewed from this perspective, Hegel's mature philosophical system is his answer to Kierkegaard's problem. But as early as *The Positivity of the Christian Religion*, he realized that "an examination of this question cannot be thoughtfully and thoroughly pursued without becoming in the end a metaphysical treatment of the relation between the finite and the infinite."[13]

His mature project, to conceptualize the essential inter-relatedness of all conflicting aspects of experience as moments of a single dialectical process through history, involved the reconceptualizing of religion (and specifically the fundamental doctrines of the Christian religion) in terms of an all-encompassing philosophical system, which would reveal the ultimate unity of the human and the divine.[14]

The object of the philosophy of religion, namely religion, is "the loftiest object that can occupy human beings; it is the absolute object. It is the region of eternal truth and eternal virtue, the region where all the riddles of thought, all contradictions, and all the sorrows of the heart should show themselves to be resolved, and the region of the eternal peace through which the human being is truly human" (J 61, H 149). Thus far Hegel agrees with Kierkegaard that the solution to the problem of human anguish (the problem of alienation) lies in religion. And the object of religion, says Hegel, is God, "for religion is the relation of human consciousness to God" (J 61, H 150).

God is infinite and immutable: "The object of religion [i.e. God] is simply through itself and on its own account; it is the absolutely final and in and for itself, the absolutely free being . . . God is the beginning and end of all things" (*loc. cit.*). But God is also self-positing *movement*, negating himself in the process of creating the world: "God is the sacred center, which animates and inspires all things. . . . All the endless intricacies of human activity and pleasures arise from the determination of human being as implicitly spirit" (*loc. cit.*). Spirit is designated by Hegel as the unifying element of all aspects of life. All oppositions participate in spirit, and absolute spirit is God.

But if Hegel agrees with Kierkegaard on the ubiquity and necessity of religion, he differs radically from him by insisting on philosophy as the only authentic mode of grasping the content of religion (viz. God). For to speak of "consideration" of religion and "the object" of that consideration is "to distinguish the two as freestanding, mutually independent, fixed sides that are mutually opposed" (J 63, H 151–2). This would be at variance with Hegel's basic tenet (articulated fully as early as the *Phenomenology*) that "substance," or the *object* of consciousness, must be grasped as *"subject."*[15]

Thus, "it must be said that the content of philosophy . . . is wholly in common with that of religion. The object of religion, like that of philosophy, is the eternal truth, God and nothing but God and the explication of God. Philosophy is only explicating *itself* when it explicates religion, and when it explicates itself it is explicating religion. . . . Thus religion and philosophy coincide in one. In fact philosophy is itself the service of God [*Gottesdienst*],[16] as is religion" (J 63–4, H 152–3).

Admittedly, religion and philosophy are concerned with God in quite different ways, and Hegel suggests that perhaps this is why the two have become mutually hostile since the development of Enlightenment rationality and what he calls (in 1821) *"les sciences exactes."* Hegel could almost be responding directly to Kierkegaard's charges when he remarks that "it seems, as the theologians frequently suggest, that philosophy works to corrupt the content of religion, destroying and profaning it" (J 64, H 153).[17] But he quite consciously inserts his philosophical system back into the tradition of the medieval Scholastic philosophers, back prior to the Reformation attack on the very project of Scholasticism. Referring explicitly to Anselm and Abelard, he remarks approvingly that "Scholastic philosophy is identical with theology; theology is philosophy, and philosophy is theology. So far were they from believing that thinking, conceptual knowing, might be injurious to theology that it [conceptual knowing] was regarded as necessary, as essential to theology itself" (J 65, H 154).

At this point, Hegel and Kierkegaard have diverged irreconcilably. And Hegel singles out for criticism precisely those theologians for whom "there is to be no progressing to the cognitive knowledge of God, to the divine content as this content would be divinely, or essentially, in God himself. In this sense it is further declared that we can know only our *relation* to God, not what God himself is" (J 72, H 162–3). While in Kierkegaard's terms, all we have to resort to in cementing our relation to the divine is a leap of faith, Hegel asserts that his philosophy provides the only bridge.

But why should we find Hegel's approach to the problem preferable to Kierkegaard's? Hegel finds it difficult to respond satisfactorily to those who demand a prior methodological justification for attempting to know God speculatively. He says that this is a hopelessly circular demand: "we are imposing a requirement that annuls itself," in a manner reminiscent of the notorious Greek scholastic who refused to go into the water until he had learned to swim (J 79, H 169).

There are, however, good reasons for considering religion cognitively, or speculatively, First, as Hegel claims, Christian doctrines such as the Trinity and the Incarnation are left particularly vulnerable if they can only be asserted as an expression of feeling or unthinking faith. Such an approach is unacceptably arbitrary and contingent. A leap of faith remains a matter of chance, depending on such factors as the psychology of the believer. Why should we confine ourselves, says Hegel, to such a contingent relationship to God when philosophy provides us with a secure, indeed necessary, grounding for our cognition of God in the nature of spirit itself. For Kierkegaard, the Incarnation is a paradox, an impenetrable mystery that must be embraced in faith alone, a faith that emerges out of inwardness of subjectivity. For Hegel, this dependence on whim or caprice is simply unnecessary, since the philosophical tools of cognition are available to Kierkegaard, tools that Kierkegaard is petulantly and foolishly rejecting. But when Hegel applies his philosophical categories to the process of the becoming of spirit through history, the Incarnation emerges quite naturally out of the dialectical development of human spirit: it no longer presents itself as an indissoluble paradox, a mystery that resists conceptualization.

Another reason for adopting Hegel's approach is that it works, it produces results. It does enable the believer (and he and Kierkegaard both claim to be believers) to understand the activity of God in the world: to pursue the image of the would-be swimmer, Hegel claims to show that only if you do plunge into the water before you have fully mastered the technique of swimming will you eventually learn to swim (especially if you have a good teacher).

However, the main justification for his own philosophical procedures that Hegel articulates in these lectures is that in the philosophy of religion we are dealing with "God himself absolute reason" (J 79, H 170). In investigating this absolute reason, we are inevitably behaving cognitively: "it is immediately the case that we are dealing with and investigating rational cognition, and this cognition is itself rational conceptual inquiry and knowledge" (J 79, H 170).

Hegel goes on to elaborate on this point at some length, and in the process offers a synopsis of some of the crucial elements of his logic. He reiterates his opening remarks, to the effect that religion is "the highest or ultimate sphere of human consciousness, whether [it is considered] as feeling, volition, representation, knowledge, or cognition" (*loc. cit.*). It is "the absolute result," the region of absolute truth. Kierkegaard would agree with this statement, but would disagree with respect to the attitude of the existing individual towards the object of religion, viz. God. Hegel continues: for religion to be so considered (in any of the different guises listed), "consciousness must already have elevated itself into this sphere transcending the finite generally, transcending finite existence, conditions, purposes and interests—in particular, transcending all finite thoughts and finite relationships of every sort" (*loc. cit.*). In other words, consciousness must already have effected the transition from the realm of the finite to the realm of the infinite to be in a position to consider religion as "the highest or ultimate sphere of human consciousness." Even so, this does not deter critics of philosophy (i.e. of speculative philosophy) from using what Hegel calls "finite thoughts, relationships of limitedness, and categories and forms of the finite" as arguments against the efficacy of speculation (*loc. cit.*). This is precisely what Kierkegaard does. As examples of such finite categories Hegel cites "the immediacy of knowing or the 'fact of consciousness' . . ., the antitheses of infinite and infinite and of subject and object" (J 80, H 170-1). But he dismisses these as merely "abstract forms that are no longer in place in that absolute abundance of content that religion is" (J 80, H 171).

These categories belong to the Understanding and to a stage in the development of self-consciousness that has been surpassed, the age of the Enlightenment. They are, of course, still necessary (they have been *aufgehoben*, not obliterated), but necessary only with reference to lower forms of investigation. Even Kant's *Critique of Pure Reason* had shown, he claims, "that they can serve only for the cognition of phenomena and not of the truth" (*loc. cit.*). If you want to know only about the appearances of religion, Hegel would say to Kierkegaard, then persist in the silliness of using these categories of the Understanding as sticks with which to beat the speculative form of knowing, which alone will penetrate to the truth.

Everyone *knows* that the finite is not the infinite; the interesting and important point is, however, that "these determinations are still at the same time inseparable" (J 80, H 172). He then proceeds to illustrate this fundamental Hegelian point: everyone knows that in the magnet the south pole is quite distinct from the north pole, but they are, of course, inseparable. The fact that we say colloquially that two things are as different as heaven and earth does not take away from the fact that we cannot point out earth without reference to the heavens, and vice versa. "Before one is ready to proceed to philosophy of religion," he goes on "one must be done with such one-sided forms" (*loc. cit.*).

Where there is immediate knowledge, therefore (such as Kierkegaard's claim to have immediate knowledge of God thanks to a leap of faith), it is obvious to Hegel that there is also mediated knowledge, and vice versa. Either one or the other, on its own, is one-sided and inadequate. *"The true is their unity, an immediate knowledge that likewise mediates,* a mediated knowledge that is at the same time internally simple, or is immediate reference to itself" (J 82, H 173). This is the case with Hegel's knowledge of God: it is mediated through God's creatures and other elements in the natural world; but it is immediate in so far as all those finite elements (himself included) are known as moments in the self-differentiation of absolute spirit (or God). But the unity of mediacy and immediacy, of the finite and the infinite, is achieved only in speculative thought, which itself elevates finite thinkers to the level of the infinite.

The same goes for the opposition between subject and object. According to Kierkegaard, speculative philosophy (the nefarious "system") annihilates the subject. Hegel is adamant: "the difference emphatically does not disappear, for it belongs to the pulse of its vitality, to the impetus, motion, and restlessness of spiritual as well as of natural life. Here is a unification in which the difference is not extinguished, but all the same it is *aufgehoben"* (*loc. cit.*).

Kierkegaard, however, remains unmoved. There is a kind of incommensurability between the two approaches that renders any meaningful evaluation fruitless. It is indeed ironical that for Hegel the position of Kierkegaard embodies "the unhappy consciousness," the estranged individual; while for Kierkegaard the Hegelian philosopher typifies what he calls "the reflective aesthete" who is really "the unhappiest man." According to Kierkegaard, "religiousness" must be "paradoxically dialectic" (494), and the resolution of the paradox cannot be "known" speculatively. All the same, if real comparative assessment is ultimately pointless, it has to be said that Hegel can accommodate Kierkegaard, as a moment in the dialectic of self-consciousness (much to the annoyance of the latter), while Kierkegaard cannot, of course, accommodate Hegel. My own view, for what it is worth, is that there's something more satisfying, both intellectually and existentially, in a philosophical approach that endeavours to accommodate and integrate in a totality the various conflicting aspects of human experience. But then again, that is probably just a reflection of my own accommodating temperament.[18]

NOTES

1. Among the many earlier studies of this topic, I have found most helpful the following: Stephen Crites, *In the Twilight of Christendom: Hegel vs. Kierkegaard on Faith and History* (Chambersburg, Pa.: American Academy of Religion, 1972); Mark C. Taylor, *Journeys to Selfhood: Hegel and Kierkegaard* (Berke-

ley: University of California Press, 1980); Niels Thulstrup, *Kierkegaard's Relation to Hegel*, trans. George L. Stengren (Princeton: Princeton University Press, 1980).

2. To remind ourselves of the chronology, Hegel lectured in Berlin on the philosophy of religion in 1821, 1824, 1827, and 1831. Kierkegaard was born in 1813. He entered the University of Copenhagen in 1830, was exposed to the Hegelianism dominant there, and rejected it. He attended the inaugural lecture of Schelling's course on "The Philosophy of Revelation" in Berlin in November 1841, and made further brief visits to Berlin in the spring of 1843, 1845, and 1846. The *Postscript* was finished in early 1846, when Kierkegaard was not yet 33 years old.

3. I have been able to take advantage of the marvellous new collaborative edition of the several sets of Hegel's lectures on the philosophy of religion. References in this article are to *Vorlesungen über die Philosophie der Religion, Teil 1: Enleitung und Der Begriff der Religion*, ed. Walter Jaeschke (Hamburg: Felix Meiner Verlag, 1983), and *Lectures on the Philosophy of Religion, Volume 1: Introduction and The Concept of Religion*, ed. Peter C. Hodgson, trans. R.F. Brown *et al.* (Berkeley, Los Angeles, London: University of California Press, 1984). The texts are henceforth referred to as J and H respectively.

4. Although the evidence presented by Thulstrup shows clearly that Kierkegaard was confronted with Hegel's works (especially his *Logic* and the *Philosophy of Right*) from his early student years at Copenhagen, it is still quite plausible to claim (*pace* Mark Taylor) that Kierkegaard just did not fully understand Hegel's dialectic; on the other hand, there is also plenty of evidence (especially in Kierkegaard's *Journal*) to suggest that he thought he did grasp the force of Hegel's project and acknowledged his intellectual achievement, but simply rejected it.

5. *Kierkegaard's Concluding Unscientific Postscript*, ed. Walter Lowrie, trans. David F. Swenson (Princeton: Princeton University Press, 1941), p. 20. Numbers in the text refer to pages in this edition.

6. At the very beginning of his first lecture (1821) on the philosophy of religion, Hegel declared: "The object of these lectures is the philosophy of religion, which in general has the same purpose as the earlier type of metaphysical science that was called *theologia naturalis*. This term included everything that could be known of God by reason alone. . . ." (J 3, H 83).

7. *Fear and Trembling and The Sickness unto Death*, trans. Walter Lowrie (Princeton: Princeton University Press, 1954), pp. 176–77.

8. See my *Hegel's Social and Political Thought* (Dublin: Gill and MacMillan and New York: St. Martin's Press 1979), especially pp. 52–55.

9. See T.M. Knox's translation of the *Philosophy of Right* (Oxford: Oxford University Press, 1942), the "addition" to §4.

10. Kierkegaard was particularly scandalized by the notorious dictum in the Preface of Hegel's *Philosophy of Right* that "what is rational [*vernünftig*] is actual [*wirklich*] and what is actual is rational": this demonstrated to his complete satisfaction that Hegel's dialectical reconciliation of subject and object amounts to no more than the quietistic resignation of the cowed

individual before the established powers that be. His serious misinterpretation of Hegel's political philosophy (a misinterpretation he shares, moreover, with many others) stems from his failure to distinguish, as Hegel does, between genuine "actuality" (Hegel's *Wirklichkeit*) and mere empirical factuality (*Tatsätlichkeit*): everything that happens to exist does not warrant the philosophical description *wirklich*. Philosophy articulates those aspects of modern states that are in accordance with reason (*vernünftig*) and those that are not. Only those that are developing in accordance with reason are *wirklich*. Philosophy, for Hegel, is certainly not prescriptive in the sense that he does not indulge in wishful thinking; but neither does it merely describe (and tell us to accept) what exists. A quick comparison between the institutions described in the *Philosophy of Right* and those in place in the Prussia of the 1820's is sufficient to illustrate the point. Philosophy demonstrates the *Vernünftigkeit* of the institutions that have emerged and are emerging (to the extent that they are indeed *vernünftig*), which very demonstration will hasten the process whereby reason becomes fully realized in the institutions of the modern state. And those states which are not developing such *vernünftige* institutions *ought* to be doing so. Far from being a quietistic document, the *Philosophy of Right* is a progressive (and in some respects subversive) document: its message is that "reason will prevail!"

11. Hegel here provocatively uses a word also meaning "worship": that is to say, philosophy is itself a form of worship.

12. The *locus classicus* for Hegel's portrayal of "the unhappy consciousness" is in his *Phenomenology of Spirit*, trans. A.V. Miller (Oxford: Oxford University Press, 1977), pp. 126–138.

13. *Early Theological Writings*, trans. T.M. Knox (Chicago: University of Chicago Press, 1948), p. 176.

14. It is suggestive to think of Hegel's system as the philosophical retelling of the first eighteen verses of St John's Gospel, which is regarded by many as a synopsis of the basic truths of Christianity.

15. See my "Hegel's Historical Phenomenology and Social Analysis," in *Hegel Today*, ed. David Lamb (London: Croom Helm, 1987).

16. See note 11 above.

17. Hegel explicitly refers to theologians "of the last thirty to fifty years" (probably Schleiermacher and F.A.G. Tholuck) who have wreaked much greater havoc on traditional Christian doctrines such as the Incarnation and the Trinity by practically ignoring them (J 66–7, H 156–8).

18. I wish to record with gratitude that my participation in the Emory conference of the Hegel Society of America was made possible by a generous grant from the British Academy.

Commentary on "Hegel and Kierkegaard"
Robert L. Perkins

Professor Cullen says that his "main concern is not to assess the validity or otherwise of Kierkegaard's criticisms" of Hegel. However, before the paper is over, he has said that Kierkegaard is petulant and foolish to disregard the "tools of cognition" available to him. After reflecting on the paper at length it is clear to me that Cullen has not succeeded in assessing the validity of a single one of Kierkegaard's arguments, though he does succeed in repeating the old misunderstandings as well as making a number of puzzling and unsupported judgments.

Professor Cullen asks us to entertain the ancient "fiction" that some of Hegel's lectures are a reply to Kierkegaard. Then apparently not willing to spare us a single tired cliché he urges in his last paragraph that "for Hegel the position of Kierkegaard embodies 'the unhappy consciousness,' the estranged individual . . .'" The problem with such an approach to the issues between Kierkegaard and Hegel is that it affirms, whether it intends to or not, the criticism of Hegel to the effect that the distinction between yes and no is finally lost in Hegel's system. Hegel thus suffers that fate of Heraclitus who had a student, we all recall, who said that one could not even step into the same river once.

If I may, I will offer at the beginning a sugar stick from Kierkegaard's journals. I want to suggest that Kierkegaard does not go beyond Hegel, amending, improving, correcting, defending or even filling out the system, and so forth. Many an academic career amounts to no more than going beyond Hegel in a manner satirized by Kierkegaard in his journals: "Those who have gone beyond Hegel are," he writes, "like country people who must always give their address as *via* a larger city; thus the address in this case must read—

John Doe *via* Hegel" (JP 1, 1571).[1] Kierkegaard thinks Hegel's achievements far too great to be surpassed (i.e. gone beyond) by second rate thinkers such as the persons who introduced Hegel into provincial Copenhagan, whose capacity is exhausted by recognizing Hegel's greatness but who then attempt to guarantee their own world historical significance by going beyond Hegel, amending, improving, and so forth (JP 2, 1572).

Kierkegaard, on the other hand, is so overpowered by Hegel's philosophy that he had, mistakenly or unmistakenly, to struggle against it for the integrity of his own existence. He pays Hegel the highest compliment one philosopher can pay another. Kierkegaard takes Hegel's philosophy with the utmost seriousness and addresses it. Whether or not Kierkegaard is correct in his assessment will be debated for some time still, but Kierkegaard is never so condescending as to say, "Yes, but. . . ." He is audacious and respectful enough to say "No" (JP 2, 1608).

Likewise, Kierkegaard did not write scholarly commentaries and exegesis on the texts of Hegel, full of footnotes and erudition. Rather, he engaged Hegel as a philosopher. Professor Cullen suggests that Kierkegaard deliberately misunderstood or wilfully misread Hegel. I suggest a third alternative: Kierkegaard understood the fundamental import of Hegel's system and rejected it for philosophic reasons. Kierkegaard may not have grasped this detail or that, but I would argue that he understood the fundamental import of Hegel's system.

Is Kierkegaard fair to Hegel? Kierkegaard satirizes Hegel, to be sure, but the issue is philosophic. The answer to this question cannot be given in a paragraph, but let it suffice for now that Kierkegaard satirizes only those aspects of Hegel's thought where Hegel is apparently oblivious to his presumption to divine knowledge and where Hegel at best misunderstands, or at worst assaults the integrity of the individual. Kierkegaard learned much from Hegel, and he may have disagreed with much more, but these are the primary issues which provoked his irony and satire.

Professor Cullen lays hold of a crucial text on this issue when he refers to *The Philosophy of Right*, where Hegel writes, "I am at home in the world when I know it, still more when I have conceptualized it" (PR, Z to #4). Kierkegaard in his journals uses the same figure: "Insofar as Hegel was fructified by Christianity he sought to eliminate the humorous element which is in Christianity and consequently reconciled himself completely with the world, with quietism as the result" (JP 2, 1586). Kierkegaard objects to this being at home in the world. He marvels that anyone could be at home in this world, even if one has conceptualized it. More radically, how could one be at home in the world if one has conceptualized it?

Kierkegaard suggests that quietism is the result of Hegel's being at home. The issues between Kierkegaard and Hegel are fundamental and reflect two opposed views of the world. It should be noted in passing that Marx and Kierkegaard are in agreement about the quietistic meaning of Hegel's philosophy. The convergence of Marx and Kierkegaard on this issue does not prove they are correct, but it does not follow that counter assertion resolves the issue in Hegel's favor.

How are these opposed views manifest in Professor Cullen's paper? First, he charges that "Kierkegaard characterized Hegel's speculative system as a philosophy of objectivity and identity; he insists that Hegel's much vaunted mediation of opposites (Hegel's dialectical *Aufhebung*) actually dissolves plurality in unity, particularity in universality, subjectivity in objectivity, difference in identity." Unfortunately, Professor Cullen does not elaborate on this interpretation.

Second, Professor Cullen says that "Kierkegaard either fails to understand or refuses to accept the significance of Hegel's *Aufhebung* and the role of mediation (*Vermittlung*) in Hegel's dialectic." This interpretation is also left unsupported.

Third, Cullen shows no comprehension of Kierkegaard's concept of subjectivity and faith. "For Kierkegaard," Cullen writes, "the Incarnation is a paradox, and impenetrable mystery that must be embraced in faith alone, a faith that emerges out of inwardness of subjectivity. For Hegel, this dependence on whim or caprice is simply unnecessary . . ." "A leap of faith," Cullen further explains, "remains a matter of chance, depending on such factors as the psychology of the believer."

In order to reply to the first interpretation we must ascertain what Kierkegaard meant by Hegelian identity. He certainly does not mean the resolution of all distinctions into the night in which all cows are black. Kierkegaard, though he did hear Schelling in Berlin in 1841, was finally convinced, after an initial enthusiasm, that Schelling had little, if any, grasp on the contours of human existence in the world. Thus if Kierkegaard perceives Hegel's philosophy as a philosophy of identity, it is assuredly not an identity of a Schellingian type. With that given, then we still have to determine what Kierkegaard thinks of Hegelian identity.

Kierkegaard discusses the issue of Hegelian identity in the context of the distinctions between thought, existence and being in the *Concluding Unscientific Postscript*. Without elaborating in any detail, let me assert that a great deal of Hegel's meaning of these terms is contained in Kierkegaard's concepts, but with some interesting differences. Kierkegaard read Hegel's philosophy as an attempt to overcome the distinction between thought and being characteristic of some philosophical traditions stemming from Aristotle, the Greek skeptics, Ockham, the empirical tradition, and Kant, to name a few. Kierkegaard's treatment of the issues is singularly original and surprising in view of his reputed anti-Hegelianism.

First Kierkegaard agrees with Hegel's comment in the *Encyclopedia* that identity must not be understood as applying to an imperfect order. "It is this fact alone," Hegel writes, "which marks everything finite—its being in space and time is discrepant from its notion" (*Logic*, 108).

In the case of ideas the unity of thought and being is actualized. Kierkegaard uses as examples the ideas of the good and the beautiful to suggest that as abstractions these can and must be identical with being in the sense that they are equally ideas. "The good, the beautiful, and the other ideas are in themselves so abstract that they are indifferent to existence, indifferent to any other than a conceptual existence. The reason why the principle of identity holds in this connection is because being in this case means the same thing as thought" (CUP, 293). Both the good, being and the beautiful, as ideas, are equally *ens mente*. Thought and being are identical in such instances and at that level of abstraction. If I understand Kierkegaard correctly, this is what he takes the identity of thought and being to mean in Hegel. Whether Kierkegaard rightly understands the Hegelian unity of thought and being is a different question, but he thinks he has and he agrees with Hegel about the unity at that level of abstraction, if something of what I have sketched is what Hegel thinks.

However, this is not the perspective of the existing human being. If an existing individual asks about the unity of thought and being, whether they are the same, then an answer has to be given at the same level that the question was asked, at the level of existence. Recall Kant's illustration of the real and imaginary one-hundred dollars. An affirmative answer, that being and thought are one, however, rests on the assumptions of a gradation of being, assumptions made by thought for thought. The existing individual, on the other hand, has to deal with up and down, right and left, and other such immediate and existential matters. This discrepant world, with its multiple contradictions, is what the existing individual has to deal with. For Kierkegaard, existence breaks up the ideal unity of thought and being. "Hegel is absolutely right," Kierkegaard writes, "in asserting that viewed eternally, *sub specie aeterni*, in the language of abstraction, in pure thought and pure being, there is no either/or." Kierkegaard and Hegel never agreed more.

However, the difference between them is made crystal clear in a quotation from Kierkegaard: "Existence is always something partic-

ular, the abstract does not exist" (CUP, 294). However, Kierkegaard
is far from concluding that abstract thought is without validity. Kierkegaard does not explain the validity of abstract thought in this
context, but its validity lies in its existence as a thought experiment.
Being does not exist, for it is an abstract, a product of thought and a
tool for thought. The only being it has is *in mente*, and as such it
does not exist at all.

This longish explanation of what Kierkegaard means by identity
is necessary to lay hold of the significance of Professor Cullen's first
remark, previously quoted. It is true that Kierkegaard thinks of Hegel's system as a philosophy of identity, and that within it the distinctions between thought and being, plurality and unity, particularity and universality, and subjectivity and objectivity are overcome.
As Kierkegaard sees the issue, the unities of the system are all well
and good, but they do not bear on existence. The unities in the
system are conceptual. The system does not grasp existence; it grasps
only its own creations. Nothing in existence is changed when it is
taken up into Hegel's system.

Kierkegaard recognizes that "the Hegelians distinguish between
existence and reality: the external phenomenon exists; insofar as it is
taken up into the idea, it is real. This is quite correct, but the Hegelians do not define the boundary, [that is] to what extent each phenomenon can become real in this way . . ." (JP 2, 1587).

My comment on Professor Cullen's second remark that Kierkegaard does not "accept the significance of Hegel's *Aufhebung* and the
role of mediation (*Vermittlung*) in Hegel's dialectic" follows from my
first comment.

First let us note that Kierkegaard has no problem with the philosophic procedure of mediation as Hegel uses it in his system, and
for the reasons as stated above regarding the identity of thought and
being. However, regarding existence, he thinks Hegel and the Hegelians fudge. "On paper," Kierkegaard writes, "the proposal to mediate looks plausible enough. First we posit the finite and then the
infinite; thereupon we set it down on paper that there must be a
mediation. And it is incontrovertible that here has been found the
secure foothold outside of existence an existing individual may mediate—on paper" (CUP, 375). This devastating irony goes to the heart
of the issue between Hegel and Kierkegaard. For Kierkegaard, the
mediation of the categories in the system does not touch existence.

Kierkegaard, on the other hand, thinks the finite and the infinite
are related in existence. The unity will not have to be created in the
future or structured into a system. Rather, the unity of the finite in
existence is simply given. The existing individual is finite and infinite
(SUD, 29–35; CUP, 376). As composed of these two, the task of the

individual is to become one of these existentially. "It is impossible to become both at the same time, as one *is* both by *being* an existing individual" (CUP, 376). Kierkegaard's concept and practice of dialectic arises from this task of becoming, and it is in this sphere of existential becoming that Kierkegaard rejects the principle of mediation.

It is at this point that Kierkegaard's critique of Hegel becomes quite polemical, and for ethical reasons. The life of the individual is always caught up in the dilemma, either/or, either the finite or the infinite. "Personality will for all eternity," he writes, "protest against the idea that absolute contrasts can be mediated (and this protest is incommensurable with the assertion of mediation); for all eternity will repeat the *immortal* dilemma: to be or not to be—that is the question (Hamlet)" (JP 2, 1587).

Rightly or wrongly, Kierkegaard saw the Hegelian mediation as "failing to define its relation to the existing individual, and by ignoring the ethical [it] confounds existence" (CUP, 275). As Kierkegaard understands the social, political and ethical implications of mediation, especially as he sees it applied in *The Philosophy of Right*, it is a complex rationalization of and justification for bourgeois existence. There Hegel dialectically transmutes the political and social arrangements of Europe into the rational idea. Kierkegaard, considerably less impressed with the rationality of the bourgeois world and entirely convinced, as a good Platonist, of the reality of a transcendent and absolute good, wrote: "Mediation is a rebellion of the relative ends against the majesty of the absolute, an attempt to bring the absolute down to the level of everything else, an attack upon the dignity of human life, seeking to make a man a mere servant of relative ends" (CUP, 375). One can scarcely read the section on civil society, with its stress on rectitude for instance, and not agree that such an understanding of Hegel is justified if one is a Platonist, a Christian in the orthodox sense of believing in a God whose thoughts are not our thoughts, or is one who worked from the concept of existence. The difference between Hegel and Kierkegaard rests finally in Hegel's feeling at home in the bourgeois world. Kierkegaard's view of the world is scarcely homey.

My comments on Cullen's views that Kierkegaard's concept of faith is whim and caprice will be quite brief. Kierkegaard spend his whole effort to define faith with reference to the Socratic in the *Philosophical Fragments* and with reference to subjectivity in the *Concluding Unscientific Postscript* in order to rebut the idea that faith was either the product of reason on the one hand or mere caprice on the other. He textures the concept of faith through the categories of guilt, suffering, paradox, being absolutely related to the absolute and relatively to the relative, the Socratic, objectivity, subjectivity, dialectic, and so forth, precisely to avoid such off-the-cuff misunderstandings of faith and subjectivity.

To put the shoe on the other foot, while denying that Cullen's view of Kierkegaard is correct, one still wonders whether Cullen has not made it at all clear what his notion of faith is. What is the status of the ordinary person's faith for Cullen? I am not satisfied with Hegel's treatment of faith as the act of the ordinary person, and I wish Cullen had told us more of his own view of these matters. In the face of Cullen's silence I have to think Hegel did better, but that cannot be reported here.

Except to say of Hegel, apparently approvingly, "the Incarnation emerges quite naturally out of the dialectical development of human spirit . . ." Cullen has not declared for us his own view of the content of faith. This rendition of Hegel's view is said to be continuous with the project of pre-Reformation Scholasticism. That is certainly a surprise, for even the most emanationist of Scholastics held that the Incarnation was an act of God, emanating from his own life, and not the emanation on the human spirit. Cullen does not develop this point, but it would have been more than interesting to determine just who these Scholastics were who thought that the Incarnation emerges from the human spirit.

It is quite safe to agree with Professor Cullen's remark that "Kierkegaard did not accept the significance of Hegel's *Aufhebung*," but there are deep philosophic and existential reasons for this lack of acceptance that require further analysis along the lines suggested here.

NOTE

1. I will use the following sigla in the text itself:

CUP: Sören Kierkegaard, *Concluding Unscientific Postscript*, trans. David F. Swenson and Walter Lowrie (Princeton: Princeton University Press, 1941).

JP: *Sören Kierkegaard's Journals and Papers*, ed. & trans. Howard V. and Edna H. Hong, 7 vols. (Bloomington: Indiana University Press, 1967–1978).

PR: *Hegel's Philosophy of Right*, trans. T.M. Knox (Oxford: Clarendon Press, 1958).

Logic: The Logic of Hegel, trans. William Wallace (London: Oxford University Press, 1950).

Chapter Six

HEGEL'S REVENGE ON RUSSELL: THE "IS" OF IDENTITY VERSUS THE "IS" OF PREDICATION

Katharina Dulckeit

Hegel occupies a unique place in the history of philosophy. Although often uncritically adored by his followers, he has perhaps been subject to more scorn and criticism than any other philosopher. This is particularly true in the case of contemporary analytic philosophy. Since the tools of the analysts are those of formal logic, it is hardly surprising that they regard Hegel's onto-logic with suspicion. Moreover, since one's logic, in any case, is intimately involved with one's metaphysics, there seems little, if anything, the analytic and Hegelian philosophers can say to each other that does not ultimately boil down to a difference in basic assumptions. It appears, then, that we are faced with a most un-Hegelian opposition. This, it seems to me, is quite unfortunate. Analytic philosophy would undoubtedly benefit from the philosophical riches Hegel can offer. And some Hegel scholarship, surely, could use a bit of the rigor insisted upon in analytic circles without having to give up the dialectic.

In this spirit I want to consider a philosophical puzzle today that has given rise to a number of different philosophical theories: the informativeness of statements of identity. Frege used it to show that there must be a difference between sense and reference, Russell appeals to it to prove his contention that names behave logically differently from descriptions, and, most recently, Kripke has argued that the informativeness of identity statements (together with his notion of rigid designation) shows that there must be necessary *a posteriori* truths. To Hegel, finally, it reveals the dialectical relation between the subject and the predicate in a judgment, which he calls "identity-in-difference."

The notion of "identity-in-difference" has been subject to much scorn and ridicule. One of Hegel's foremost critics was Bertrand Russell, who made the following remarks:

> Hegel's argument . . . depends . . . upon confusing the "is" of predication, as in "Socrates is mortal," with the "is" of identity, as in "Socrates is the philosopher who drank the hemlock." Owing to this confusion, he thinks that "Socrates" and "mortal" must be identical. Seeing that they are different, he does not infer, as others would, that there is a mistake somewhere, but that they exhibit "identity-in-difference." Again, Socrates is particular, "mortal" is universal. Therefore, he says, since Socrates is mortal, it follows that the particular is the universal—taking the "is" to be throughout expressive of identity. But to say "the particular is the universal" is self-contradictory. Again Hegel does not suspect a mistake but proceeds to synthesize particular and universal in the individual, or concrete universal. This is an example of how, for want of care at the start, vast and imposing systems of philosophy are built upon stupid and trivial confusions, which, but for the almost incredible fact that they are unintentional, one would be tempted to characterize as puns.[1]

In what follows, I shall examine how Hegel arrives at the notion of identity-in-difference in judgment. With Pippin, I shall argue that Hegel not only does not overlook the distinction between one kind of "is" and the other, but actually devotes his entire analysis to a consideration of the issues involved in such a distinction.[2] Moreover, I shall turn the tables on Russell and argue that Hegel's theory can account for the informativeness of certain kinds of statements of identity which Russell, ironically, is unable to explain by appeal to his famous Theory of Descriptions. His lack of charity toward Hegel may therefore come back to haunt him. After all, according to Russell himself, the adequacy of a theory is judged by the number of puzzles it can solve.

I

In its most abstract terms a judgment, according to Hegel, is expressible in the proposition "The individual is the universal" (a is F) or, more definitely, "The subject is the predicate" (s is P).[3] There are two terms in a judgment, then, and they are connected by the copula "is." It follows that an adequate theory of judgment must at least account for the nature of the relationship between subject and predicate.[4]

The relation between s and P is expressed by the copula. Just what does it mean to say "the subject 'is' the predicate?" On the one hand the subject or individual seems utterly different from, even opposed to, the predicate, yet on the other hand the copula appears to assert precisely that they are one and the same. Says Hegel:

> No doubt there is . . . a *distinction* between terms like individual and universal, subject and predicate, but it is nonetheless the universal fact that every judgment takes them to be *identical* (LL, § 166, emphasis added).

The suggestion seems to be that, somehow s and P are both (1) *distinct* from each other, and also (2) *identical*. *Formally*, that is, the judgment announces the identity of s and P, but since in fact P does not *exhaust* s, there is a tension between what the form of the judgment posits and what the content delivers. In fact, (1) and (2) appear to be mutually exclusive alternatives. In Hegel's words:

> What the judgment enunciates to begin with is that *the subject is the predicate*; but since the predicate is supposed to be *not* what the subject is, we are faced with a *contradiction* which must resolve itself (WL, p. 74; SL, p. 630).

Let us use an example. In the judgment "The rose is red," subject and predicate appear to be entirely independent from one another. For the subject as an object exists whether or not it possesses this particular predicate, and the universal determination exists in other subjects even if it does not belong to *this* one. From this subjective vantage point, says Hegel, the act of judging merely involves the reflection of whether a given predicate located "in someone's head" ought to be attached to an object existing "outside" that person, an object which is what it is, regardless of whether or not the judgment is made. The independence of the two extremes suggest that s and P are distinct and opposed to each other, and consequently, are related merely *externally* (WL, pp. 68–69; SL, pp. 625–656). Just as from a grammatical point of view, the copula is a device by which two separate words are connected. Insofar as the copula asserts the nature of their relation, therefore, it at once expresses their differences. In short, alternative (1)—that they are different—seems to be the correct choice.

On the other hand, however, when the judgment is viewed *objectively*, says Hegel, it appears that the very attachment of P to s expresses that their relation cannot be merely external. In the judgment "This action is good," for instance, the copula clearly expresses that the predicate belongs to the *being* of the subject and is "in and for itself identical with it" (WL, p. 69; SL, p. 626). In this sense the copula expresses the unity of s and P, for "the subject . . . becomes determined only in its predicate, or only in the predicate is it a subject" (WL, p. 72; SL, p. 628). What is more, the original meaning of the German word "judgment" (*Urteil*) even suggests a diremption (*teilen*) of an original unity which, at the same time as it determines the individual as universal, also determines the universal as actual (WL, p. 71; SL, p. 628). Seen this way, then, the two parts of the judgment constitute and reflect a unity. Thus, although a judgment uses two terms, in expressing that the individual *is* the universal, the copula mirrors and announces the unity of the concrete object of experience, of *this* rose, for instance, which is red. It appears, therefore, that (2) is the right alternative after all.

At this point, however, another difficulty arises. This actually existing rose may be red, but there are many roses that are red, and no rose is red only. The simple fact that several individuals may fall under a universal and that the individual is the seat of many universals, implies that finite individuals cannot *possibly* be identical with the universals which are predicated of them.[6] So we are back to square one.

But since (1) and (2) are in conflict, the implication for the understanding is that a choice must be made between them. This, however, not only seems difficult, as we have just seen, but—as Pippin has noted[7]—appears to confront us with a genuine dilemma, because alternative (1) will generate a contradiction, while (2) will yield a tautology. Suppose, for instance, that (1) is correct and the individual is in fact distinct from the universal, and hence *s* from *P*. On this assumption, any attempt to say *what* a thing is appears to lead us directly into the following contradiction: While we may correctly assert with respect to the rose that "The individual is the universal" or "*s* is *P*," we would be just as correct in asserting, on the basis of (1), that "The individual *is not* the universal" or "*s* is not *P*." According to our previous example, we would then get (a) "The rose is red" and (b) "The rose is not red," since other things are red and are not this rose (WL, pp. 76–89; SL, pp. 631–641). But again (a) and (b) clearly conflict. Oddly Hegel not only seems undisturbed by this, but appears to be urging just such an interpretation. In his analysis of sense-certainty in the *Phenomenology*, he had already established that saying what a thing is must also involve saying what this particular thing *is not*. This implies that the positive judgment "*s* is *P*" cannot be made apart from the negative judgment "*s* is not *P*." Or: unless it is the case that both (a) and (b) are correct, nothing *informative* could ever be said about what a thing is, such that alternative (2) would always yield some empty version of "*s* is *s*" or (c) "The rose is a rose." The identity would be *formal*, in other words, and, as Hegel has already shown, formal identity is always tautologous.[8] Apparently, then, Hegel can avoid the empty (c) only by embracing the seemingly contradictory (a) and (b).

This, precisely, is what distresses Bertrand Russell, according to whom no one can reasonably be expected to accept a contradiction. But fortunately he thinks we need not do so in this case, since the problem arises in the first place only due to a confusion which persists throughout Hegel's treatment of logic: a confusion, in other words, of the "is" of predication with the "is" of identity.

Russell appears to have a point, for when we apply this distinction to the case at hand, the problem vanishes. We simply say that "is" in alternative (1)—claiming that s is *different* from P—is the "is" of predication, while the "is" in alternative (2)—claiming *identity*— would be just that, the "is" of identity. Now (a) and (b) are no longer contradictory, for (b) simply denies that s is *identical* with P, although the latter may certainly be *predicated* of the former, as in (a). Consequently (a) and (b) are no longer read as simultaneously predicating P of s and then denying that predication.[9] Thus the offensive contradiction has vanished.

From Hegel's point of view, however, this Russellian rescue has little to recommend itself. For the alleged mix-up has now turned into a distinction which, according to Hegel, lands us in as much difficulty as the "stupid and trivial" confusion which gave rise to it.

II

In order to see why Hegel must reject the Russellian approach it must be remembered that his analysis of the forms of judgment in the *Logic* is motivated by his interest in *essential* judgment. There are two conditions for such judgments. To begin with, a judgment is an essential judgment only if P tells us precisely and exclusively what s is; no less and no more. But merely predicating universals of particulars is insufficient for this, *unless* the term in the predicate position at once expresses the essential nature of the subject. This, in turn, argues Hegel, *is possible only if the "is" expresses some identity between s and P*. For if essential determination were possible exclusively via predication, the subject and predicate would remain separate and the relation between them expressed by the copula would remain *external*. As a consequence, s would refer to one thing, namely an individual, while P would designate something distinct from s, namely a *universal*. But the truth of sense-certainty in the *Phenomenology* has already shown that qua individual, an individual is grasped only through the mediation of universals. It follows that divorced from these, it would then have to be an individual without a universal nature, i.e., a bare individual. This applies equally, if the individual is the subject of a judgment, as Hegel points out in the *Logic*: The subject without the predicate, he explains, is just what the thing is without its qualities, namely *bare* (WL, p. 72; SL, p. 628). Thus, if *s* and *P* are utterly distinct they must be mutually exclusive, which means that *s* will necessarily be bare, and *P* necessarily abstract.[10] And this is precisely why we cannot appeal to the Aristotelian notion of class inclusion which maintains that although *s* and *P* are different, the predicate is nevertheless *in* the subject. A class is an *abstract* universal or "what is merely held in common." In Hegel's *onto*-logic concepts cannot be merely abstract but always involve being.[11] Clearly then, where judgments of essence are concerned, the "is" of predication will not do because it entails the distinction between *s* and *P* which would commit us to a metaphysical thesis already overcome in the *Phenomenology.*[12]

Secondly, according to Hegel, an essential judgment must also be *informative.* The "is" of identity as Russell conceives it, however, would result in a mere tautology, since the identity it would express between the two terms of the judgment would be a merely abstract or formal identity. Hegel's whole point, then, is to show that neither the "is" of predication nor the "is" of identity are capable *on their own* to yield an informative judgment about what something is essentially. Again Hegel's own example serves to illustrate this nicely: "The rose is red" may be *informative*, but fails to tell us about *what it is* that is red. And, according to Hegel's view, *s* must already be a particular before we can predicate of it a property, such as "red." And while "The rose is a rose" exhibits the form of an *identity* statement, it hardly provides information about the essential character or nature of whatever is asserted to be identical with itself.[13] Unless we want to deny that judgments about essences (which must express identity) can also be informative, argues Hegel, what we need is neither the "is" of predication nor the "is" of identity, but a *dialectical* unity of the two which we might call the "is" of "identity-in-difference." According to Hegel, Russell's example for the "is" of identity is really an example for the notion of identity-in-difference as Hegel conceives of it, although it does not yet constitute a perfect instance of it. The same applies to Hegel's own example. In the judgment "The rose is red," the difference between *s* and *P* is still very great and the "is" only *minimally* mediates between the two terms. Because they depend in part on the content, the degrees of mediation cannot be spelled out explicitly. But in Hegel's view, judgments progress from this still largely "immediate" or "qualitative" judgment in which the "is" closely parallels Russell's "is" of predication, through a long series of progressively more adequate judgments in which *s* and *P* become increasingly more congruous until they are finally "identical."[14] But even here, the identity retains an inner distinction and, consequently, is unlike Russell's own conception of formal identity (i.e., identity which does not consider content). It is clear, then, that, for Hegel any absolute distinction between the "is" of predication and identity *ultimately* vanishes. But surely, this is not to say that Hegel cannot tell the difference between them where it does exist,[15] particularly since his entire treatment of judgment clearly consists of a careful working out of this very difference, culminating in "identity-in-difference." Since difference is preserved in even the most perfect case of identity, Hegel can hardly be accused of *denying* the distinction between s and P. Quite clearly, he insists on it. Insofar, however, as the distinction is *internal*, what is distinguished at once remains a unity or "identity." Or, to put it even more strongly, the identity *is* an identity *only by virtue of* the (internal) distinction. Surely, discovering the inadequacy of two philosophical notions in isolation (i.e., in abstraction) is not the same as overlooking their difference.

At this point, however, at least three objections might be raised. First, suppose we grant that Hegel in fact did not confuse the two senses of "is." Is it not true, nevertheless, that by appealing to his notion of "identity-in-difference" all *merely* "different" (i.e., predicative) judgments such as "The rose is red" must, by comparison, necessarily be found wanting? For it is rather obvious that these do not tell us what s is essentially, but simply inform us about a property s happens to have. But what is wrong with that? Why should anyone insist that such judgments, that *all* judgments, tell us what a thing is essentially? Judgments such as "The rose is red" are simply different yet plainly useful and important sorts of judgments. This, in fact, seems precisely to be Russell's point. By demanding that all judgments define the essence of the subject concept, Hegel seems unfairly to stack the cards against certain kinds of judgments from the start.

But this criticism misses the point. Given Hegel's interest in essential judgments, it is entirely legitimate and reasonable that he begin by identifying and examining qualitative judgments containing what parallels the "is" of predication and noting in what way they differ from essential judgments. Ironically, therefore, he is doing precisely what Russell alleges he fails to do, except that he finds that what distinguishes the two kinds of judgment is not an *absolute* difference. Hence, Hegel is perfectly aware that common qualitative or predicative judgments are important, in fact, crucial to ordinary language, as his own examples show. By no means, therefore, does he wish to condemn them as inferior or useless. Nor is he denying that they can be, and often are, *correct*.[16] And he definitely *does not* argue that all judgments "ought" to be essential judgments, or that they really are disguised essential judgments. He is simply pointing out that if one wishes to know the essential nature or identity of the subject, qualitative judgments will not suffice, since even the longest list of properties will not enlighten us in that regard *unless* the term in the predicated place expresses the essential character of the subject. And this, he argues, is possible only if *s* and *P* are identical in their difference.

Secondly, given the above, it might be thought that perhaps the gulf dividing Hegel and Russell is less wide than it first appeared, or that the difference between them, on this score, is merely one of degree. Russell, one might say accordingly, just makes a *strict* or absolute distinction between the "is" of predication and identity, while for Hegel, a developmental process of some sort leads from one to the other.

To think in this way, however, would be seriously to misunderstand Hegel's central point. For *identifying a thing's essence necessarily involves difference*. Without difference there would be only one term, and the assertion of identity would be impossible. This means that Russell could never get an "is" of identity from which to distinguish that of predication in the first place, unless he admits their interdependence. But this is just what he wants to deny when he asserts their radical difference. From this it also follows that Russell is mistaken when he thinks that "Socrates is the philosopher who drank the hemlock" is an example of an identity statement which excludes all difference. In sense-certainty, Hegel had shown that saying *what* something is is possible *only* by saying what it is not. His point he takes to have been established both in the *Phenomenology* and in the *Logic* where he criticizes the law of identity. Now he merely applies this insight to his analysis of judgments. The inadequacy of the "is" of identity *by itself* stems precisely from its exclusion of difference. If all difference is eliminated the judgment will no longer be informative but tautologous, for it is the "identity-in-difference" alone which allows identity judgments to be informative. Russell's own example of an identity statement, however, is clearly an informative judgment. Consequently, it is actually an instance of Hegel's "identity-in-difference."

Finally, if it is true that "identity-in-difference" explains how identity statements can be informative, then asserting the identity between *s* and *P* no longer results in a tautology. But how is such identity possible? If it is accomplished only by virtue of the difference contained in the identity, will not this difference generate all over again the contradiction associated with the first alternative which asserts *s* is distinct from *P*? Whatever our strategy, in other words, will it not remain true that, as Russell laments, "The particular is the universal" is a self-contradictory proposition? We will now examine these questions respectively, a task that involves an assessment of Hegel's critique of formal identity as well as the Law of the Excluded Middle.

III

The Law of Identity, which Hegel takes up in the "Doctrine of Essence"[17] says that "everything is identical with itself." But if we wish to *express* the fact that something is self-identical we must put it in the form A = A, a proposition which clearly uses *two* terms, not one. So while the object o is *one*, to understand and state that fact requires *two* terms "$o = o$." According to Hegel, this is consistent with Leibniz's Law of the Identity of Indiscernibles. Implicit in the Law of Identity, then, is something which simply eludes the logic of the understanding: the idea that identity makes sense only as self-identity which, in turn, implies self-relation and, therefore, contains *essentially* the idea of difference (LL, § 116). Difference is the necessary condition for grasping (as well as expressing) the notion of identity. What is more, as is the case for all opposites for Hegel, identity and difference are interdependent, or mediated, such that either one makes sense only in terms of the other.

Now it might be objected (as one of my non-Hegelian colleagues did) that Hegel's argument works only because it ignores hierarchies of language. Thus one could claim that "$o = o$" employs two tokens of the same term and that the difference, consequently, is only metalinguistic.

This approach, however, fails to explain how statements of identity can be *informative*. Taken abstractly, an identity of the form A = A (where the terms on either side of the identity sign are repeated) must remain tautologous. Suppose, for instance, we are asked "what is a rose?" and reply "A rose is a rose," then we obviously have said nothing informative.[18] The propositional form, however, e.g., "A rose is . . ." clearly promises some information, and hence, argues Hegel, a *distinction* between s and P (LL, § 172, *Zusatz*). In his words

> . . . instead of being a true law of thought [the Law of Identity] is nothing but the law of abstract understanding. The propositional form itself contradicts it: for a proposition always promises a distinction between a subject and object, while the present one does not fulfill what its form requires (LL, § 115).

But my analytic friend, not being the sort who is easily dissuaded, promptly tried another strategy, making the same point in a slightly different way which, ironically, echoes an objection Hegel himself considers.

Look, he said, Hegel takes refuge with the notion of identity-in-difference in order to avoid the contradiction supposedly entailed by the claim that one and the same entity is both identical and different. But even while it is true that it is only *qua* self-identical that anything can be judged to be different, this need not entail a contradiction if matters are viewed as follows: Things simply are what they are, they are self-identical, while difference falls *outside* them into an externally reflecting subject. If identity is an *internal* relation and difference an *external* one, then something can be both identical and different without conflict. Thus, assigning identity and difference to two different, mutually exclusive spheres, or levels, seems to get us *out of*, not into the problem Hegel laments.[19]

Hegel has two responses, one specific and one general. First, he argues that if the notion of an internal identity and an external difference is pushed, then the difference between them would become so radical that all comparison between them would become impossible.[20] We would end up with something Hegel terms a "simple variety" of things, which is to say that things will remain utterly indifferent to, and unaffected by, one another:

> If we follow the so-called law of identity, and say—The sea is the sea, the air is the air, the moon is the moon, these objects have no bearing on one another (LL, § 117, *Zusatz*).

The point is that if we begin with the notion of abstract identity, we inevitably end up with an absolute difference. But the latter notion cannot explain experience: we do not regard things as merely different, but rather *compare* them with one another and discover features of *likeness* and *unlikeness*. And whereas abstractly identical things remain utterly different from all other things, likeness and unlikeness enjoy a reciprocal relationship. Comparison, argues Hegel, makes sense only on the hypothesis of an existing difference, and distinguishing makes sense only on the hypothesis of an existing similarity (LL, § 118, *Zusatz*).[21] To say that two things are alike *in certain respects* is meaningful only on the assumption that they also differ in certain other respects, and *vice versa*.[22]

But Hegel has a second, perhaps more important, argument against the strategy as such of assigning conflicting notions to different levels. While this may seem like a convenient device by which to extricate oneself from contradiction, *in and of itself*, he would claim, it is ultimately ineffective. For this trivial maneuvering (which frequently, it seems to me, amounts to an exercise in intellectual dishonesty) explains absolutely nothing *unless* we can justify this move. (It will not do, that is to say, merely to point out that this tactic will get us out of a contradiction in which otherwise we would be caught.) Hegel's point is that the necessary justification remains impossible as long as we take these different levels as *mutually exclusive*. The burden is on us, rather, to account for how they are connected. Hegel attempts to do just that.

Clearly, then, Hegel's solution agrees with the notion of hierarchies insofar as he acknowledges that identity and difference occur on two different levels. But he goes much further. His dialectic shows how such opposites are nevertheless related, thus explaining how it is possible that the same entity can be both self-identical and different, one and many, and so forth. Generally speaking, the unity of opposites never occurs on the same level but on a higher one (hence it is *aufgehoben*). However, since it is one and the same thing which is also many, or different, the level on which it is one, and so forth, cannot be utterly divorced from that on which it is many. Hegel, therefore, does not deny hierarchies but rather explains what they mean or how they are possible.

Hegel's onto-logic also motivates his criticism of the Law of the Excluded Middle, a law which, as Hegel puts it, "would feign avoid contradiction, but in doing so falls into it" (LL, § 119).[23] As formulated in the two Logics, the law states: "Something is either A or not A, there is no third" (WL, p. 544; SL, p. 438) and "A is B or A is not B" (LL, § 119).

The crucial point in saying that there cannot be anything that is not either A or not A, is the claim that there can be no third possibility which is indifferent to the opposition because the difference between the opposites is absolute. Thus the Law of the Excluded Middle ordinarily is taken to mean something like the following: "Of all predicates, either this particular predicate or its 'non-being' (i.e., the lack of the predicate) belongs to a thing." More specifically, explains Hegel:

> The opposite means here merely the lack (of a predicate), or rather *indeterminateness*; and the proposition is so trivial that it is not worth the trouble of saying it. When the determinations sweet, green, square are taken . . . and then it is said that spirit is either sweet or not sweet, green or not green, and so on, this is a triviality leading nowhere (WL, p. 544; SL, p. 438).

In abstract logic *P* and *not-P* simply cancel each other out. According to Hegel, however, true opposition should not lead from one determination to its non-being or indeterminateness, which is clear from the principle of determinate negation. After all, Hegel continues:

The determinateness, the predicate, is referred *to something;* the proposition asserts that *something is determined* (WL, p. 544; SL, p. 438, emphasis added).

For Hegel, therefore, "A is B or A is not-B" can be an important proposition, if and only if it is taken to express that everything must be *determined* either positively or negatively.[24] Thus *P* and *not-P* do not constitute an *absolute* or *essential* difference but are opposite determinations *of something;* the latter being the third that the law seeks to exclude. One is invariably reminded of the Greeks here for whom the idea of change was hard to grasp until they hit upon the idea of an unchanging substratum which remained identical through the change. Hegel argues that opposite determinations presuppose *a ground* which is neither yet both of them, and hence contains identity as well as difference (LL, § 119, *Zusatz*). This ground, or essence, is the (*dialectical,* not abstract) unity of identity and difference (LL, § 121).[25] Thus, he concludes:

Instead of speaking by the maxim of the Excluded Middle (which is the maxim of abstract understanding) we should rather say: Everything is opposite. Neither in heaven nor in earth, neither in the world of mind nor of nature, is there anywhere such an abstract "Either-or" as the understanding maintains. Whatever exists is concrete, with difference and opposition in itself (LL, § 119, *Zusatz* 2).

Perhaps it bears repeating that Hegel's argument—including the statement just quoted—must not be taken to mean that he wishes to deny the principle of contradiction. In fact, "contradiction is the very moving principle of the world" he says (in § 119, *Zusatz* 2) and certainly, we might add, of his philosophical system. Due to its tremendous importance he insists "it is ridiculous to say that contradiction is unthinkable." But this remark is not intended to suggest that, for the understanding, a self-contradictory statement can be true. The philosophical error does not consist in self-contradiction per se but rather in the persistence in such contradiction. In Hegel's words:

The only thing correct in that statement [that contradiction is unthinkable] is that contradiction is not the end of the matter, but cancels itself. But contradiction, when canceled, does not leave abstract identity; for that is itself only one side of the contrarity. The proximate result of opposition (when realized as contradiction) is the Ground, which contains the identity as well as difference (LL, § 119, *Zusatz*).

The opposites are not essential opposites (to use the term in a non-Hegelian fashion) but opposite *determinations* of essence. Their identity or unity is *dialectical* which, in contemporary terms, is best (if not entirely accurately) expressed by saying that it occurs on a level which is other than that on which they are different. There is no contradiction in holding that the ground has opposite determinations, or that identity is upheld in difference.

In this way Hegel has answered the final problem we considered: since identity is achieved by virtue of difference, we had asked, will it not generate a contradiction all over again? The answer is "yes," of course new opposition is generated, but only to pass to another level of self-reconciliation, more adequate than the previous one. Thus contradiction is the moving principle of the dialectical process which finally results in the concrete universal or, which is the same thing, the determined particular.

Let us pause here for a moment and reflect on what Hegel's interpretation of the Law of the Excluded Middle has delivered with respect to the issue under consideration. According to this law, identity and difference in non-dialectic logics are mutually exclusive notions when applied to the same term and in the same sense. This is obviously appropriate for a logic that abstracts from content. On this view it follows that if *s* and *P* in a judgment are not identical they must be different. In the latter case their relation is explained in terms of class inclusion and the "is" of predication which is strictly distinguished from the "is" of identity. But as we have seen, based on such a radical distinction neither notion can be made intelligible. The result is a kind of logical Catch-22: the distinction is possible only on the condition of the very interdependence it denies. As it turns out, however, the dilemma exists just for the logic of the understanding, which is not to say that it is false but that it constitutes a phase which is *aufgehoben* from the point of view of reason. Hegel's dialectical slip through the horns of the dilemma reveals a third alternative not available to the understanding: subject and object, argues Hegel, are neither identical nor different but constitute an identity-in-difference. Thus essential judgments which must express identity also exhibit difference which is precisely what accounts for the fact that they can also be informative.

And this brings us to the final twist of irony in this story, which is surely a case of poetic justice: Russell, I submit, cannot on his own theory account for the informativeness of certain kinds of statements of identity which Hegel handles without effort. It is this matter to which I shall now turn my attention.

IV

For Russell, a logically proper name is a term whose meaning just *is* the object for which it stands. But if the meaning of a word really is its denotation, it seems we cannot explain how it is possible to have a meaningful, informative identity statement. As Frege had already pointed out, if "a = b" asserts the identity of whatever is denoted by "a" and "b," then, (provided it is true) "a = b" would not differ from "a = a" which simply asserts the identity of an object with itself. Nevertheless, statements of identity often do express important information. "The morning star is the evening star," for example, is clearly informative in a way "The morning star is the morning star" or "Venus is Venus" is not. The implication for Frege was that all terms in a language have a sense distinguishable from their reference. But because of his theory of meaning, this strategy, obviously, did not appeal to Russell. For if the meaning of a name just is its denotation, that precludes it from having any independent "sense." Thus Russell concludes that there is something wrong with the notion that all terms function as names. Now, it is obviously inappropriate to go into his Theory of Descriptions here, and, at any rate, it is well trodden territory. But the upshot is that, from a logical point of view, general names, descriptions and even ordinary proper names do not really *name* anything but actually function as descriptions.[26] Russell's claim that descriptions and ordinary names are incomplete symbols is a *reductio ad absurdum* from the assumption that they are logically proper names.[27] To prove his contention, he must show not just that names and descriptions behave differently, but that his theory solves certain persistent problems. "A logical theory," he says, "may be tested by its capacity for dealing with puzzles . . . and I shall show . . . that my theory solves them."[28]

I want to test it against only one puzzle: the informativeness of identity statements. Take, for example, the following proposition: "Scott is the author of *Waverly*." What is being asserted here, according to Russell, is that an entity named "Scott" is identical with an entity called "the author of *Waverly*." Hence, says Russell, the "is" is that of *identity*, not predication (a point we must obviously grant him for the sake of the argument). Now let us suppose, he continues, "the author of Waverly" is a *name*, a name, say, for entity *c*. Then our proposition would read: "Scott is *c*." Now, according to Russell, *there are only two alternatives*: (i) either Scott *is not* identical with *c* or (ii) he is identical with *c*. In the first case "Scott is *c*" would be *false* and in the second case it would be *tautologous*, i.e., equivalent to "Scott is Scott."

> For the name itself is merely a means of pointing to the thing, and does not occur in what you are asserting, so that if one thing has two names, you make exactly the same assertion whichever of the two names you use, provided they are really names and not truncated descriptions" (LK, 245).

The point, of course, is that "Scott is the author of *Waverly*" is neither false nor tautologous and hence it is not the form "Scott is c" where "c" is a name. According to Russell, the problem lies in mistaking the denoting phrase for a name. The solution lies in the recognition that "c" is a disguised description.

However, there are several problems with this solution. First of all, according to Russell himself, ordinary proper names such as "Scott" *are* truncated descriptions. It follows that the example fails entirely unless we grant Russell the use of "Scott" on the model of a genuine name.[29] But that done, a problem remains. For Russell can explain the informativeness of identity statements only in cases in which one term is a name and the other a description. He cannot, it seems to me, explain the case using two names (having already given up the right to say they are both disguised descriptions): "Cicero is Tully" for instance, or, to use his own example, "Scott is Sir Walter." According to Russell's theory of naming, such propositions must be tautologous, they must be on par with "Scott is Scott" (LK, 246), but clearly they are not. The Theory of Descriptions may or may not be correct, but it can hardly be recommended on the basis of solving this puzzle.

Hegel, on the other hand, has no problem whatsoever with identity statements of this sort. The logic of the dialectic, which does not exclude content, can explain why "Scott is c" may be informative, even if "c" is a name. As we have seen, this involves a unique notion of identity and his denial of the Law of the Excluded Middle. What lands Russell in his difficulty is precisely his appeal to the latter. There are only two mutually exclusive alternatives: either "Scott" is identical with "c" or he is not identical with "c." And again, given his theory of meaning "Scott is Sir Walter" must be *either* true and tautologous *or* meaningful and false. Russell's celebrated Theory of Descriptions thus fails to account for what is obvious to any user of ordinary language. Hegel's onto-logic, however, his unique interpretation of the Law of the Excluded Middle and the notion of identity in difference can explain how "Scott is Sir Walter" can be both true and informative.

If it is true, then Scott, indeed, is none other than Sir Walter and the "is" expresses this identity. But difference is retained at the heart of identity and this difference is expressed logically by the copula. Thus Hegel can account for cases in which propositions expressive of identity, as a matter of fact, impart information.

I want to conclude with a final thought. The Hegelian answer to the problems we have considered here, is clearly one of which the formal logician cannot avail himself because he thinks of these logical laws as merely abstract laws of thought.[30] Thus it might be objected that the solution is effective only because, ultimately, it assumes an Hegelian point of view. If it is assumed that Hegel's onto-logic is superior to formal logic then Russell's entire philosophy must obviously be located on the level of the understanding with all the inadequacies that entails. If, however, one assumes the Russellian point of view, according to which the notion of a logic which includes content is mistaken, then the distinction between the two kinds of "is" is not only possible but solves the problem *without* getting us into another one. Thus, it might be argued, while perhaps I have shown that Hegel is not oblivious to the distinction as Russell alleges, and therefore that Russell is wrong about *Hegel*, I certainly have not shown that *Russell* is wrong. Perhaps. But my goal was to defend Hegel against Russell's accusations, and I believe I have accomplished that. I have shown that Hegel is guilty neither of confusion, stupidity, or triviality. His account, instead, is sophisticated, consistent, elegant and, above all, effective.

With that granted, an opponent might still be inclined to shrug off this entire discussion by saying that more than one road leads to Rome, and that the answers differ appropriately given the difference of the philosophical frameworks within which they operate. But the rub, it seems to me, is that given each system, Hegel's answer in this case clearly is more satisfactory than that of the formal logician. This is because the latter's recourse to hierarchies, as so often is the case, remains unjustified. And the reason for this, I take it, is that he must explain the thinking of the understanding without going beyond the level of that thinking. The question at issue, therefore, is precisely the status of the understanding itself.[31] The dialectic moving from the understanding to reason, accomplished what the logic of the understanding cannot achieve. Seen this way, it is arguable at least, that perhaps Hegel's logic is superior to that of his analytic rivals after all.

Such lofty topics, however, I leave to others. But let me say something about the relatively tiny problem of how to account for the linguistic phenomenon just discussed: in settling a score one must take care to appeal to the proper criterion and for Russell, as we know, the adequacy of a theory turns on its explanatory power. So one can hardly fail to appreciate the irony in the fact that while perhaps we will never know who won the war, according to Russell's own criterion, he lost the battle.

NOTES

1. Bertrand Russell, *Our Knowledge of the External World as a Field for Scientific Method in Philosophy* (London: G. Allen & Unwin, 1914, rpt. 1961), pp. 48–49.

2. Robert Pippin, "Hegel's Metaphysics and the Problem of Contradiction," *Journal of the History of Philosophy*, vol. XVI, Number 3 (1978), pp. 301–312. I have also benefited greatly from the excellent article by Richard Aquila, "Predication and Hegel's Metaphysics," *Kant-Studien*, 64 (1973), pp. 231–245.

3. Hegel's theory of judgment can be found in the "Doctrine of the Notion" in the Logic. See *Wissenschaft der Logik*, 1812–16, pp. 65–116, in Hegel's *Sämmtliche Werke*, 26 vols. (Jubilee edition), ed. Hermann Glockner (Stuttgart 1927–1940); hereafter cited as WL. All quotations are from A.V. Miller's translation, *The Science of Logic* (New York: Humanities Press, 1969), pp. 622–661 (cited as SL with references to WL). Also see Hegel, *Enzyklopädie der philosophischen Wissenschaften im Grundrisse (1830)*, ed. by Friedhelm Nicolin and Otto Pöggeler (Hamburg: Meiner, 1969), Teil I, *Logik*, translated by William Wallace as, *The Logic of Hegel*, 2nd edition, 1892, §'s 166–180; hereafter cited as LL. With respect to the formulations of a judgment just given, please keep in mind that, from an Hegelian point of view, it is not only unnecessary, but impossible, to distinguish strictly between these metaphysical and linguistic notions because they are, for Hegel, two expressions of the same relation.

4. In Hegel's words: "We have to examine . . . how the relation of subject and predicate in a judgment is determined, and how subject and predicate themselves are at first determined through this very relation" (WL, p. 68; SL, p. 625). This is not to suggest, of course, that accounting for this relation would constitute a sufficient condition for any theory of judgment even in Hegel's day (consider hypothetical judgments, for instance, disjunctions, and so forth). The relation between subject and predicate is, however, one necessary condition for an adequate theory, and for our purposes the interesting one.

5. Hegel calls this a "qualitative" judgment. See LL, § 172 and WL, pp. 75–91; SL, pp. 630–643.

6. "To say 'The rose is red' involves (by virtue of the copula 'is') the coincidence of subject and predicate. The rose however is a concrete thing and so is not red only . . . The predicate on its part is an abstract universal, and does not apply to the rose alone. There are other flowers and other objects which are red, too. The subject and predicate in the immediate judgment touch, as it were, only in a single point, but do not cover each other" (LL, § 172, *Zusatz*).

7. Pippin, pp. 309–310.

8. Hegel's critique of the Law of Identity will be discussed below.

9. Pippin, pp. 309–310.

10. "[T]he subject is immediately an *abstract individual* which *simply is*," says Hegel, "and the predicate is an *immediate determinateness* or property of the subject, an abstract universal" (WL, pp. 74–75; SL, p. 630). I agree here with Richard Aquila. I am at odds, however, with another of his arguments. He claims that Hegel denies immediate reference on the ground that it commits us to the existence of bare particulars which are intolerable for Hegel. But I take the failure of immediate reference to lie in the *nature of the referring act itself*. Accordingly, this failure cannot result from a dogmatic denial of an

undesirable sort of object. Thus, while it is indeed true that the nature of the referent is conditioned by the nature of the referring act, such that immediate reference would entail an immediate or bare referent, the reverse is not necessarily the case. Strictly speaking, the characteristics or nature of the referent, in and of itself, does not imply anything about the nature of the referring act. Thus a denial of the existence of bare particulars is not sufficient to establish that reference cannot be immediate. For it leaves open the possibility that if there were such things as bare particulars, then reference to them might succeed immediately. Hegel's whole point, however, is that all possible reference is *necessarily* mediated. Immediate reference fails because as a relation between subject and object it presupposes that the referring subject individuate its object, and that is possibly only via the dialectic of determination, negation and mediation. That the individuated object is not a bare object is a result of the mediated nature of reference, and thus cannot be the ground on which immediate reference fails. See Aquila, p. 234. Aquila also claims that Hegel's metaphysics results from his views on predication, an interpretation with which I differ as well. Also see Dulckeit "Can Hegel refer to Particulars?," *The Owl of Minerva*, 17:2 (Spring 1986), pp. 181–194.

11. Hegel's notion of universal, particular and individual is much closer to the (dynamic) Spinozistic notion of substance, attribute, and mode.

12. This is also Pippin's view. See Pippin, p. 310.

13. For Hegel, in fact, all identity statements of the form a = a (where the terms on either side of the identity side are repeated) are formal, empty and uninformative. We shall return to this issue later.

14. To follow this progress, which continues throughout the Logic, is obviously beyond the scope of this work.

15. In non-Hegelian terms we might say that it can be found on the level of the understanding, the surface structure of experience, but it collapses when we probe the surface to uncover the deep structure.

16. Correct, in fact, is precisely what they are. Hegel distinguishes "truth" from "correctness" (see LL, § 172 with *Zusatz*, § 213, *Zusatz*, and § 24, *Zusatz* 2). According to this distinction "truth" should be reserved to describe a situation in which the distinction between s and P has been overcome, viz., fully internalized. Strictly speaking, then, predicative judgments are at best correct or, which is to say the same thing, contain only limited truth. All empirical judgments would fall into this category.

17. WL, pp. 510–515; SL, pp. 411–416.

18. This is why "utterances after the fashion of this pretended law (a planet is—a planet, magnetism is—magnetism, mind is—mind) are, as they deserve to be, reputed silly" (LL, § 115).

19. In fact, it explains why the "maxim of diversity" as Hegel calls it, which states that "there are no two things completely like each other," does not contradict the Law of Identity, as Hegel himself notes. See LL, § 117: "the . . . diversity is supposed due only to external comparison, anything taken per se is expected and understood always to be identical with itself."

20. Of course this would also contradict Hegel's conclusion in sense-certainty, viz., that what a thing is essentially, is established precisely by its relation to others.

21. "Hence," he continues, "if the problem be the discovery of a difference, we attribute no great cleverness to the man who only distinguishes those objects, of which the difference is palpable, e.g., a pen and a camel: and similarly, it implies no very advanced faculty of comparison, when the objects compared, e.g., a beech and an oak, a temple and a church, are near akin."

22. "The two, therefore, do not fall on different aspects or points of view in the thing, *without any mutual affinity*: but one throws light on the other. Variety thus comes to reflective difference, or difference (distinction) implicit and *essential, determinate* or *specific difference*" (LL, § 118).

23. The understanding appeals to this law in order to extricate itself from the problem engendered by two apparently true maxims that clearly conflict with each other: The Law of Identity that claims that "Everything is essentially identical" and the maxim of essential difference stating that "Everything is essentially different." The two maxims are obviously at odds with each other, as one expresses that a thing must be, essentially, *self-relation*, while the other claims that it must also be, essentially, an *opposite* or a relation to its *other*. But if identity and difference, self-relation and relation to the other, are viewed as *mutually exclusive* it is clear that everything cannot *essentially* be both.

24. In this way it would express the fact that identity passes over into difference, and difference into opposition. Ironically, the "naive intelligence of abstraction" which clings to the idea that opposition must express *absolute* difference, cannot grasp that the very third it seeks to deny, is implicit in the law itself. In Hegel's words: ". . . the third that is indifferent to the opposition *is given* in the law itself, namely, A itself is present in it. This A is neither +A nor −A, and is equally well +A as A" (WL, p. 545; SL, p. 438). Note that Hegel uses the same symbols for subject and predicate because he is considering *essential* opposition.

25. I cannot pursue this new dialectic, but would at least like to note that, for Hegel, "the Law of Sufficient Ground" as he calls it, implies that everything is essentially mediated. He argues, however, that this mediation cannot merely be *assumed*, but must be *explained*, because the substrate is not merely "indifferent" to its determination. Otherwise we would be in the same camp as Spinoza, for whom the substance/attribute/mode distinction is left inexplicable. "Absolute indifference," says Hegel, "may seem to be the fundamental determination of Spinoza's substance . . ." (WL, p. 396; SL, p. 382). And formal logic simply lays down this law without ever deducing it or exhibiting its mediation. But if we want to know why Y happened to X, it is not satisfactory to be told simply that it is in the nature of X for Y to happen to it. As Hegel remarks in LL: "With the same justice as the logician maintains our faculty of thought to be so constituted that we must ask for the ground of everything, might the physicist, when asked why a man who falls into water is drowned, reply that man happens to be so organized that

he cannot live under water; or the jurist, when asked why a criminal is punished, reply that civil society happens to be so constituted that crimes cannot be left unpunished" (§ 121).

26. Descriptions, according to Russell, are "incomplete symbols" in that, contrary to what their grammatical form suggests, they do not denote, refer to, mean or stand for any objects, but rather are empty and vacuous, requiring "definition in use" because they have no meaning in isolation. See Bertrand Russell, "On Denoting," in *Logic and Knowledge*, ed. by R.C. Marsh (London: G. Allen & Unwin, 1956), pp. 39–56 (cited as LK), and "Description and Incomplete Symbols," LK, pp. 241–253.

27. Leonard Linsky, *Names and Descriptions* (Chicago: University of Chicago Press, 1977), pp. 20–21. Based on this Linsky argues that it is not the case— as sometimes alleged—that Russell confuses meaning and reference. While that may be correct, it can hardly be denied that he *conflates* them in his theory of logically proper names.

28. LK, p. 47.

29. Unfortunately Russell is inconsistent, even within the Logical Atomism papers, with respect to what is to count as a particular object of acqaintance and, consequently, what counts as an appropriate bearer of a logically proper name. Although he specifically identifies them with sense-data, he often depicts sense-data as the appearance of ordinary objects, such as desks, or even persons. For example, in *The Problems of Philosophy* (London 1912, rpt. 1952) he implies that it would be possible for him to be acquainted with the Emperor of China but, as it happens, he is not (see pp. 44–45, also p. 54). Elsewhere, having just insisted that we must be acquainted with a particular before we can name it, he illustrates this thusly: "You remember, when Adam named the beasts, they came before him one by one, and he became acquainted with them and names them" (LK, p. 201). Both cases are surely inconsistent with the sense-data theory, according to which the body (and still more the mind) of an individual (like Bismarck) is a complex entity and can only be known by description (see pp. 54–55). Only Bismarck himself, says Russell in *Mysticism and Logic* (London 1918, rpt. New York 1921, p. 216) might have used his name to designate the particular of his acquaintance, "assuming," that is, "that there is such a thing as acquaintance with one-self," a question on which he wavered as well, going from "probably" to "probably not." For a good discussion on the career of "particulars" see Ronald Jager, *The Development of Bertrand Russell's Philosophy* (New York: Humanities Press, 1972), pp. 310–312, also p. 319. By the time Russell wrote *An Inquiry into Meaning and Truth* (London 1940, rpt. 1961), "this," even as a logically proper name, no longer picks out *simples*, but actually designates something *complex*. Whatever interpretation of "particular" we choose from among Russell's generous offerings, the crucial point for our purposes is that they are bearer of logically proper names, and that despite Russell's official position, in this example "Scott" is meant to play the role of a genuine name.

30. For Kant, for example, identity (*Einerleiheit*) and diversity (*Verschieden-heit*) are not categories, but subjective concepts of reflection, and as such

not determinant of objects (*Kritik der Reinen Vernunft*, B 317 ff.). But as Mure reminds us, Hegel's is an idealist doctrine that depends on the active nature of the real and therefore cannot be adopted by the realist. Says Mure: "From such a realist position identity and difference prove an insoluble contradiction if their significance is honestly pressed. A *modus vivendi* can only be achieved by the short-term policy of relying on the immediacy of sense, and taking things to be simply identical in some respects with other things, simply different from them in others. This is to assume in each thing a miraculous power of retaining its self identity and resisting logical dissolution. That this miracle cannot be explained is supposed not to matter because it is a matter of fact." G.R.G. Mure, *A Study of Hegel's Logic* (Oxford: Clarendon, 1950), p. 99. As we know, Hegel believes that "matters of fact" and the way we experience them must be rendered intelligible.

31. The whole matter has been put very well by Mure: ". . . the context in which 'A is B' is correct, and 'A is not B' necessarily incorrect because contradicting it, is just the context of arrested movement of 'detached' inactive 'real' things, which forms the proper object-world of the Understanding so far as it is *not* Reason. The question at issue, however, touches the status of the Understanding itself. And that is a philosophical context where truth and not correctness is concerned. Truth is not the avoidance of contradiction, but the passage through it to self-reconciliation . . . [Hegel's treatment] shows precisely and importantly the clash between his logic and logics of the Understanding, which attempt to interpret the thinking of the Understanding without rising above the level of that thinking" (p. 105 and p. 104).

Commentary on Katharina Dulckeit's
"Hegel's Revenge on Russell"
John N. Findlay

I was very happy to be asked to comment on Miss Dulckeit's paper on Hegel's revenge on Russell. Like herself, I am an admirer of both Russell and Hegel, and like herself, I tend to admire Hegel as the greatest, if also the most difficult of all philosophers. Miss Dulckeit's paper is persuasive because it makes clear that in Hegelianism we go beyond the mere symbolic form of our assertions, and the way they lead on to other symbolical assertions, and explore differences in the thought that lies behind them and beneath them.

In this connection, I believe that one of the most important turning points in the history of philosophy and psychology was the work of the Würzburg school of psychologists under Oswald Kulpe and many others who held that thought is possible as a pure gist without any accompaniment of verbal or other pictures, and that it may in complete purification from pictures and symbols have the most definite and detailed structure, contrary to Aristotle's view that all thought needed to found itself in phantasm of some sort, including imaginal pictures and verbal images. I often imagine a final blissful escape into the intelligible world where I shall simply pull the chain and see all words and images go down the pipe and all language games come to a close. It is because thought is travestied when it is too closely bound up with illustrations or images or customary words that we must somehow learn to do without them. Hegel, though not a member of the Würzburg school, which flowered long after his death, did press on to many pure thoughts that range beyond pictures and language games.

It is in the light of such unencumbered thinking that we may consider Miss Dulckeit's treatment of Hegel's treatment of Identity in Difference. When we think of or perceive any object, except the most artificially simple, we think of it or perceive it as a unity of many parts, aspects and determinations, and though we see or conceive it in a single glance, we are aware at the same time of its vast many-sidedness and articulation of aspects and determinations of structure. What then is mistaken in saying that the object of our thinking is in all such thought-references a single embracingly total object, but which is also in all such references a number of distinct partial or aspectival objects? And what is wrong in saying that what we have before us is at once a set of different and aspectival objects, which are at the same time, owing to their close and perhaps necessary compresence and correlations, a single object differentiated in them all? And if this common place situation is expressed in terms of Identity in Difference, what is there so dangerously wrong about it? It does not imply that the partial and aspectival objects are all the same partial or aspectival objects, but only that they are aspects of one and the same total object, which, for a thought interested in wholes, is in a plain sense present in them all. They may in fact be incapable of existing, or being correctly thought of outside an embracing whole or wholes. To be thus holistic in one's thought is what for Hegel it means to be reasonable, just as to refuse to integrate partial aspects into wholes is for Hegel the mark of the wretched *Verstand* or understanding, which despite its partiality for the partial is in truth incapable of understanding anything at all.

In Hegel of course thought moves towards a holism in which there are really no wholly independent objects: not only is every distinct object a part or moment or aspect of some whole, but every such whole becomes a part of a more embracing whole, until at length we arrive at an ultimately embracing whole, of which everything else is a part, moment or aspect. In Hegel of course this tracking down of wholes goes much further than in ordinary systems of thought, and has moreover a note of ineluctable necessity which ordinary thought cannot stomach. Thus thoughts as empty as pure Being or mere Nothing necessarily lead to the thought of a plurality of determinately different wholes and sets and series of objects, and lead on to the thought of measures or ratios which give continuity and order to such sets and series. We are led on by the dialectical impulse of our thought to the thought of an infinite series of variously qualified and quantified objects and classes of objects whose governing measures and ratios lead on to the idea of unchanging essences or natures which lie beneath the outer manifestation of objects. These essences or natures further require a field in which they can display themselves, and thus lead thought on to a world of objects and appearances in space and time, and their manifold manifestations and the forces and laws that govern them. Hegel is so far from being a mere idealist, that for him a material universe in space and time is an absolute necessity of thought. Only in such a world is it possible for us to think or to be.

But the unthinking, mechanically ordered material world has to be thought of as providing a home for the activities of teleologically developing living creatures and ultimately for creatures capable of thought and other spiritual activities. It is by a necessary process that the being of thinking being develops all the foundations of ordered societies, and thence into a long development through varied historic forms of society until at length we arrive at the fullest self-conscious flowering of conscious Spirit in Art, Religion and Philosophy. I am not going to do more than refer to the universal consciousness which Hegel offers us in these fields.

But what I wish to maintain is that a developmental teleology such as Hegel offers us can defensively be regarded as a key to the cosmos that we live in. And it is a systematic teleology leading to the full development and flowering of all the higher powers of theoretical and practical understandings characteristic of the thinking subject. I do not know exactly how far Miss Dulckeit will agree with me in welcoming all these intellectual perspectives. But we are in agreement in believing in thought that is embracingly holistic and in seeing Hegel as the most glorious example of such thought. Russell, Wittgenstein, etc., were wonderful products of certain historic drifts in modern western thought, but we may hold that Hegel is the most compellingly articulated product of the motives underlying our whole historic, human effort to understand ourselves and our world.

Chapter Seven

HEGEL AND HEIDEGGER

Robert R. Williams

At first glance, Heidegger seems to fall within the circle of Hegel's critics. Heidegger's call for a deconstruction of the metaphysical tradition is so sweeping that it is difficult to imagine who might be left out. Most of what Heidegger has written about Hegel is polemical and critical.[1] Much of the criticism turns on the twin, interrelated themes of phenomenology and ontology. Both Heidegger and Hegel see phenomenology as an introductory corrective philosophical method, preparatory to ontology. Both interpret phenomenology as a necessary preliminary to ontology, making ontological reconstruction both possible and inevitable. The ontology which phenomenology makes possible is both a critique of and departure from the Cartesian transcendental tradition. In re-opening the *Seinsfrage*, Heidegger advances a critique of the metaphysical tradition as a forgetting of Being and the ontological difference between Being and beings.[2] Hegel is included in Heidegger's critique because he is considered as not revising, but rather completing the traditional *Seinsbegriff*. Heidegger's complaint is that Hegel is insufficiently radical, and so prisoner to the metaphysical tradition.

However, as Hegel would remind us, matters are never so simple and may be the very opposite of their initial appearance. Thus, Gadamer explains away many of Heidegger's anti-Hegel pronouncements as due to the polemical situation in which he found himself. Gadamer notes that Heidegger was attacked from essentially Hegelian premises. Faced with Hegelian objections, Heidegger had to define his views over and against these objections, if not over and against Hegel himself.[3] Moreover, Heidegger's colleague at Marburg, Nicolai Hartmann, interpreted Hegel's *Phenomenology* and *Logik* as important contributions to the incipient phenomenological move-

135

ment. In such a situation the question was whether Hegel had not already done what Heidegger wanted to do. The criticism of Heidegger was that he was not sufficiently aware of his own proximity and indebtedness to Hegel. Gadamer formulates the interpretive issue in the following terms:

> Is Heidegger's thinking to be placed within the borders of Hegel's empire of thought, as are, for instance . . . Feuerbach, Kierkegaard . . . and Jaspers? Or do all the correspondences to Hegel which Heidegger's thought indisputably displays prove precisely the opposite—namely that his questioning is radical and comprehensive enough to have left out nothing which Hegel asks, and . . . to have asked more deeply than Hegel did, and thus to have gotten behind him?[4]

If one somehow manages to see beyond the polemical smoke, Heidegger's convergence with Hegel is considerable: both are critical of foundationalism, both turn away from a search for foundations to a phenomenological description of the life-world, both are critical of a transcendental philosophy that imposes on the world its demands and requirements of intelligibility. Finally, Heidegger's so-called "*Kehre*" from the fundamental ontology of *Dasein* to the self-disclosure of Being is parallel to Hegel's move from so-called subjective to objective idealism. In view of such deep convergence, Heidegger acknowledges that his relation to Hegel is not one of simple opposition or either/or.[5] Rather his relation to Hegel is ambiguous: it is possible to say that in view of his "existential polemics" Heidegger is a critic of Hegel, and that in view of his so-called later development Heidegger is adding some footnotes to Hegel's project of philosophical reconstruction.

In what follows we shall explore Heidegger's ambiguous relation to Hegel, beginning by examining Heidegger's case for undermining Hegel as representative of the tradition. The core of this attack is the portrayal of Hegel as a Cartesian and metaphysician. The reply to this attack is to ask whether Hegel is not better interpreted as correcting and breaking with the primacy of subjectivity, and the foundationalism of Descartes.[6] Second we shall examine Heidegger's rejection of Hegel's *Phenomenology* as genuine phenomenology, and his claim that Hegel's *Phenomenology* is the *parousia* of the absolute. Then we take up the issue whether the identification of the task of ontology as categorical analysis blurs or passes over the ontological difference.

I. Heidegger's Critique of the Tradition

Heidegger's claims to have undermined Hegel rest in large part on Heidegger's reading of Hegel as a Cartesian, as bringing to fulfillment the Cartesian project of developing philosophy as a self-justifying autonomous science (*Wissenschaft*).[7] Heidegger's critique of Descartes is extended to include Hegel. Descartes breaks with the tradition by turning to the subject as the foundation of knowledge. At the center of philosophy as a representational system is the subject which must accompany all representations. The turn to the subject inaugurated by Descartes, continues in both empiricism and rationalism, through Kant's Copernican revolution and critical philosophy. But the turn to the subject, although apparently inverting the classical Greek metaphysical tradition by granting priority to the subject, does not, in Heidegger's view, really signify a fundamental departure from classical metaphysics. For despite the transcendental turn, the traditional categories of substance (Aristotle) are retained. If the categories of substance are retained, so is the concept of substance as the underlying substratum, the *hypokeimenon*, even in such transcendental philosophers as Kant, Fichte, and Schelling. Thus Heidegger complains that there is no real advance in logic in reference to the fundamental ontological question—the *Seinsfrage*—from Aristotle through Kant and Hegel.[8] All that has been done is to shift the *hypokeimenon* from the world to the subject.[9] Hegel's famous slogan that substance is subject appears to Heidegger as instance of and not an alternative to metaphysics. The "real break" with Cartesianism does not occur in Hegel; rather it is Heidegger who effects the breakthrough to genuinely new premises. Thus Heidegger sharply distinguishes *Dasein*, the human subject in its facticity, from the transcendental subject (*hypokeimenon*). Unlike the subject of idealist metaphysics *Dasein* is not the foundation of the world, rather *Dasein* is being-in-the-world. This distinction is at the basis of Heidegger's claim that the metaphysical tradition, including Hegel, has obscured the *Seinsfrage*.

In *Being and Time* Heidegger pressed for a re-opening of the question of Being. It is necessary to re-open the *Seinsfrage* because of the obscurity and contradictions surrounding the concept of Being. For example, Being is understood as the most universal concept, but yet not as a genus. How then can Being underlie the traditional logical categories? If Being is not really a genus, how can it be claimed that the categories are *instances* or modes of Being? Despite such problems, Being is held to be self-evident. Yet if anything is evident it is rather that Being is not self-evident. Heidegger flirts with Nietzsche's suspicion that Being is nothing but vapor and smoke.[10] The fact that such doubts have been raised shows that the meaning of Being has become obscure and hardly understood. However, the question of Being cannot be pursued in traditional ways, for it is precisely the tradition that has obscured the question. The question of Being, in other words, reaches deeper than a categorical analysis, for the question is in part what do the categories of Being mean? What are the categories categories *of*?

Heidegger's pursuit of the *Seinsfrage* leads him to the analysis of *Dasein*. Since Being is indeterminate and problematic, and since *Dasein* finds its own being at stake, *Dasein* is the origin of the question of Being. Hence the existential analytic of *Dasein* precedes ontology in the sense of an elaboration of categories. This analytic is not just a new region of Being to which the traditional categories may be applied. *Dasein* has its own, unique mode of existing which is to be distinguished from mundane entities present at hand (*Vorhandensein*): "*Das Wesen des Daseins liegt in seiner Existenz.*"[11] Unlike entities present at hand, *Dasein* is characterized by possibility, i.e., the possibility of existing. For this reason the traditional categories of being do not apply to *Dasein*, and traditional ontology is unable to do justice to *Dasein* in its freedom. The existential analytic of *Dasein* generates not mundane general categories, but existentials, i.e., structures of existential possibilities.[12]

In *Being and Time* Heidegger holds that Being presences in the two basic modalities of categories and existentials. However, in his *Introduction to Metaphysics* Heidegger takes a more critical stance towards the ontological tradition. Traditional categorical ontology is no longer merely one possible mode of Being's presencing, rather categorical ontology is a symptom of decline and forgetfulness of Being. The identification of the task of ontology as elaboration of categories presupposes a prior identification of Being with Idea. Heidegger writes:

> . . . as soon as the essence of Being resides in whatness (Idea), whatness, as the Being of the essent, becomes that which is most beingful in the essent . . . Being as Idea is exalted, it becomes true being, while Being itself, previously dominant, is degraded to what Plato calls *me on*, what really should not be and really is not, because in the realization it always deforms the Idea . . . by incorporating it in matter. The Idea now becomes a *paradeigma*, a model. At the same time the Idea necessarily becomes an Ideal . . . The *chorismos*, the cleft, has opened between the Idea as what really is, the prototype and archetype, and what actually is not, the copy and the image.[13]

In Platonic Idealism, what is originary, namely the event of presencing itself, is regarded as derivative, degraded to mere becoming and regarded as having ontological status derivative from the Idea. In Husserlian language, the life-world is displaced, regarded as subjective-relative. The inversion of the life-world consists in a shift of attention from *Being as event of presencing* to *Being as presence*, and from truth as disclosure (*aletheia*) to truth as correspondence (*homoiosis*). Granted such an identification of Being with Idea, the way to identifying ontology with categorical explication is now open: for categories are universal predicates that explicate the Idea, the stable present. The prime example of the resulting categories is mathematics, and ontology, particularly modern ontology, is a *mathesis universalis*.

The exact meaning of this shift of attention, the passing over of the ontological difference, is far from clear. On the one hand, Heidegger thinks it amounts to an error. This "error" is due to "philosophy" or metaphysics, viz., the passing over of the event of Being as disclosure, and the surpassing of the world towards transcendent Ideas which are identified as "true being."[14] But this error, if it be such, is not simply a methodological mistake. It has deeper reasons. For as Heidegger observes, "the essence of truth as disclosure could not be maintained in its original force. Unconcealment . . . broke down. 'Idea' and 'statement,' *ousia* and *kategoria* were saved from the ruins."[15] But what does it mean to say that truth as unconcealment or disclosure cannot be "maintained," or that it "broke down"? Is the event of Being's presencing dependent on *Dasein*? Heidegger saw that an affirmative answer would implicate *Being and Time* in the transcendental philosophy and metaphysical foundationalism that it seeks to overcome. In contrast, the later Heidegger traces the breakdown in the presencing of Being as due to Being's own historicality, i.e., Being can withhold itself, as well as grant itself.

Our discussion has brought to light two critical issues Heidegger raises against Hegel, which we formulate as questions: (1) Does Hegelian phenomenology cover and obscure the world of the natural attitude, the life-world, even as it directs philosophical attention towards that world? (2) Does Hegel obscure the ontological difference when he identifies the task of transcendental ontology as categorical analysis and logic? Specifically, if identity and difference are categories, does this eliminate or obscure the ontological difference?

II. Heidegger on Hegel's *Phenomenology*

In both his treatments of the *Phänomenologie des Geistes*, Heidegger flatly denies that Hegel's *Phenomenology* is phenomenology in the Husserlian sense.[16] According to Heidegger, phenomenology for Hegel does not signify a method, or an introductory discipline. The title, *Phenomenology of Geist* does not employ an objective genitive which would make *Geist* into a theme or object of inquiry, i.e., a phenomenology of———. Instead it employs a subjective genitive, i.e., the *Phenomenology of Geist* is the *Dasein* of *Geist*, the *parousia* of the absolute, or the absolute self-presentation of *Vernunft* (*absolute Selbstdarstellung der Vernunft*). The *Phenomenology of Geist* thus displays the absolute's appearance to itself, which in turn grounds its decision to abide with us in pure presence. With such a prejudging of Hegel's *Phenomenology* and its procedure as "metaphysics," it comes as no surprise that Heidegger rejects Hegel's claims to a description and immanent critique of ordinary consciousness which leads ordinary consciousness to the standpoint of science. Stated otherwise, the *Phenomenology* does not really introduce the central thesis of the *Logic*, namely the identity of thought and being, it rather presupposes that thesis, and so presupposes the *Logic*.

Heidegger interprets the "phenomenological We" not as neutral observers of ordinary consciousness, but as the possessors of absolute knowledge, the knowledge of the *parousia* of the absolute.[17] Without the presupposition of absolute knowledge, Hegel's *Phenomenology* could not begin at all.[18] The *Phenomenology* is possible only because it begins absolutely with the Absolute.[19] Hegel's *Phenomenology* is not a neutral description in Husserl's sense. Rather it is description "with the eye of absolute knowledge."[20] What does this mean? Heidegger interprets the term "absolute" from its Latin root (*absolvere*), to loose, absolve or release. Absolute knowledge therefore means a knowledge "absolved" from dependence on objects in assuring itself of truth.[21] There can be no "givens" for absolute (absolvent) knowledge; there is nothing prior to transcendental subjectivity, which qua transcendental, absolves itself completely from all givens. Consequently the task of the *Phenomenology* is to deconstruct the myth of the given, to banish the naivete that objects are given to natural consciousness. With the collapse of the transcendent thing-in-itself into immanence as prepared by Fichte's critique, transcendental knowing is totally productive of the object, and has therefore absolved itself from any reference to or dependence on any given. The *Phenomenology* therefore deconstructs all forms of otherness and shows them to be immanent aspects or elements in a single overreaching thought, or absolute knowledge. The *Phenomenology* demonstrates that transcendental philosophy has no givens. Nothing can be "prior" to absolute autonomy and freedom. Thus the *Phenomenology* introduces the *Logic* as a pure autonomous transcendental ontology, a doctrine of categories of pure Being. Being is identified with Idea, pure presence, obscuring the ontological difference.

III. Critique of Heidegger

Heidegger construes the *Phenomenology* as an introduction to transcendental philosophy. According to his interpretation, transcendental philosophy, which begins with the final *Gestalt des Bewusstseins*, and continues in the *Logic*, is pure knowledge absolved from all givens. If all givens are thus constituted in and by pure transcendental knowledge, then Hegel must identify Being with Idea, and ultimately with transcendental subjectivity. Hence Heidegger interprets Hegel as completing Cartesian Idealism by reconstructing it as consistently transcendental. Truth is no longer a question of correspondence between idea and reality. Rather, since Being is wholly identified with Idea, truth becomes identified with the self-certainty and consistent self-constitution of transcendental subjectivity. Hegel's project requires the identification of Being with Idea that for Heidegger is a symptom of decline, of forgetfulness of Being, life-world, and the ontological difference.

Heidegger's picture of Hegel is close enough to have some plausibility; nevertheless it remains a distortion. Heidegger refuses to see or acknowledge Hegel's criticism of and break with Descartes, or to entertain the possibility that Hegel's concept of *Geist* includes but goes beyond transcendental subjectivity. Elsewhere I have tried to show that Hegel's concept of *Geist* transforms the traditional concept of subjectivity into intersubjectivity, while at the same time historicising the transcendental.[22] This interpretation implies that Hegel does not reduce the truth question to correspondence or to mere correctness. Rather, since Hegel like Husserl and Heidegger turns to the *Lebenswelt* and describes ordinary consciousness, he too has a version of truth as a historical process of disclosure of being. Moreover, Werner Marx—who has made the most complete study to date of Heidegger's relation to Hegel and moreover sides with Heidegger—explicitly repudiates Heidegger's reading of Hegel as a Cartesian.[23] Included in this repudiation is Heidegger's interpretation of absolvent knowledge, although Marx thinks that this interpretation is justified in part by Hegel's *Phenomenology*. Marx's point is that the issue of Hegel's theory of truth cannot be settled on the basis of the *Phenomenology*, which is the sole text on which Heidegger comments. Hence Marx turns to the *Logic* to show that Hegel has his own version of truth as process of disclosure.

However, Reinhold Aschenberg shows that Heidegger's claim that Hegel holds a Cartesian conception of truth as representation, correctness etc., cannot be sustained even as an interpretation of the *Phenomenology*.[24] Aschenberg identifies four distinct conceptions of truth in Hegel's *Phenomenology*, only one of which is the traditional correspondence theory, and that is subject to Hegel's philosophical critique. Hegel has his own criticism of the reduction of truth from disclosure to mere correctness. According to Aschenberg, Hegel develops a categorical theory of truth, not the traditional view of correspondence that Heidegger complains about and attributes to him. However, the truth question is not reduced entirely to categoricality, for Aschenberg thinks that Hegel's *Phenomenology* is a pre-categorical ontology. Thus he supports the view that Hegel's philosophy includes both a version of truth as disclosure and a speculative or categorical theory of truth. In Hegel's language, truth involves both immediacy and mediation. The categories are reconstructions in thought of what is. However, the *Logic* presupposes but does not demonstrate that the categories have instantiation. For this reason the *Logic* depends on the *Phenomenology* to show the existential presuppositions or conditions of the categories. But the *Logic* shows that the important truth question is whether a "reality" corresponds to its concept and so is genuine.

In what follows, I first want to discuss Heidegger's misreading of Hegel's *Phenomenology*. Contrary to Heidegger, Hegel's intent is genuinely phenomenological in Heidegger's sense. Hegel's speculative philosophy does not absolve itself from, but rather presupposes experience and ordinary consciousness, which it reconstructs. The task of speculative philosophy is to transform *Vorstellungen* into *Begriffe*, but not to displace the former by the latter. Second, I will examine a critique of Hegel's alleged reduction of the ontological difference to the category of difference. It is claimed that Hegel levels the ontological difference by reducing it to a form of categorical identity. On the other hand Marx finds that, contrary to Heidegger, Hegel conceives truth as process of disclosure in which hiddenness is not simply eliminated, but is an essential condition of disclosure.

A. The *Phenomenology* of Hegel

Heidegger's interpretation of Hegel as a transcendental philosopher conceals an important point, namely that Hegel is equally opposed to the above account of transcendental philosophy as *absolvent Wissen*. Kant's version of transcendental philosophy stands in the tradition of legislating the a priori structure to which the world must conform in order to be experienced. But Hegel is an anti-transcendental philosopher in the Kantian sense of transcendental, in which transcendental subjectivity is conceived as legislating and imposing a priori the conditions of being and knowledge on unformed materials. Although Heidegger's phrase "absolvent knowledge" is intended to identify Hegel with Kant's transcendental philosophy, neither Hegel's *Phenomenology* nor his *Logic* are transcendental philosophy in the Kantian sense.

In the introduction to the *Phenomenology*, Hegel offers a critical hermeneutics of the traditional metaphor of knowledge as an instrument for laying hold of the absolute. The point of this hermeneutics is to deconstruct the knowledge-as-instrument metaphor which has held the tradition, including Kant, in thrall, and to liberate philoso-

phy from the task of adjusting the instrument to the given, or imposing it on the given. To be sure Hegel elsewhere speaks about
thought overreaching (*Übergreifen*) its object, its other. But what does
it mean to say transcendental thought overreaches its other? At first
glance it might mean that the *Begriff* has a notorious "boarding house
reach," thus encroaching on and dominating its other. However, this
is the view which Hegel rejects. Overreaching does not mean domination, but rather a being at home with self in the object. *Übergreifen*
does not have the connotation of bringing an independent object or
given into immanence, but rather the sense of transcendence towards the object. In other words, Hegel's *Übergreifen* is close to
Eckhart's *Gelassenheit*, a letting the other be, allowing it to appear
without foisting pre-conceived criteria upon the object. This "letting
be" has the sense of disclosure, creating space for the object to show
itself and generate its own categories, criteria and so forth,[25] which
speculative thought must respect and reconstruct. To be sure, *Übergreifen* has other connotations as well, namely "encroachment." But
the speculative meaning is frequently the opposite of the ordinary
meaning, as Hegel and Heidegger like to point out. In the context of
Hegel's philosophy of identity, thought is at once one member of a
polar opposition, and the consciousness of the whole. Heidegger
does not even take up these issues.

However, given Heidegger's willful reading, even caricature of
Hegel as *absolvent knowledge*, it comes as no surprise that Heidegger
finds sense-certainty is prejudged in advance as science (*Wissenschaft*), albeit the poorest sort.[26] "Real" sense-certainty is never allowed to speak for itself, but is spoken for. Experience is metaphysically predetermined; from beginning to end Hegel's *Phenomenology*
is the *parousia* of the absolute.[27]

Heidegger focuses on Hegel's claim that sense-certainty itself distinguishes between instance, or example (*Beispiel*) on the one hand,
and universal (*Wesen*) on the other. Heidegger rejects Hegel's careful
distinction between the standpoint of the phenomenological We and
the standpoint of ordinary consciousness. What Hegel says about
the distinction between essence and instance, claims Heidegger, does
not mean "that we don't make this distinction [viz., between essence
and example] at all, but merely find it like we find a knife lying in
the street . . . Hegel does not say that we do not make this distinction but merely find it; rather he says it is not *only* we who make this
distinction. Of course 'We' make this distinction. We have to make
it; We have to have already made it in order to find it."[28] The implication is that real sense-certainty does not make the distinction between essence and instance at all; rather the distinction is imposed
by Hegel on sense-certainty. Absolute knowledge so illumines and

144 Robert R. Williams

pervades sense-certainty that the latter can only confirm what is said about it a priori (*vorgreifend*).[29] Hegel violates phenomenological neutrality by reading theoretical categories into his descriptions.

Thus Heidegger "finds" Hegel's account of sense-certainty a circular tour de force. Hegel does not take sense-certainty as it comes, as a given; rather determining it in advance as a mode of knowledge, he reads into it all the standard categories and epistemological distinctions of the tradition. Hegel's analysis of sense-certainty shows that "an actual sense-certainty is not only this pure immediacy, but rather an example or instance of such."[30] It comes as no surprise therefore that Hegel "discovers" the truth of sense- certainty to be the universal. The universal "Now" is what remains the same throughout alteration and the disappearance of particular "Nows," and is indifferent to the passing/perishing of particular nows. This means that the universal is the true being of sense-certainty. Thus Hegel is antiphenomenological because of the inversion that occurs in his account of sense-certainty. Heidegger's point here is similar to his critique of Plato in his *Introduction to Metaphysics*, specifically the inversion and displacement of *physis* by *eidos*. For Plato, the idea or universal comes to be identified with real being, while *physis* or the concrete particular is displaced and downgraded to mere inexact appearance.[31] If this is Heidegger's point and intended as a criticism of Hegel, it is made in obliviousness to Hegel's own oft reiterated critique of Platonic dualism, abstract transcendence, and his critique of abstract universality: an infinite opposed to the finite is itself finite.

Heidegger's denial that Hegel's *Phenomenology* is phenomenology is a case of tendentious argument and interpretation. Hegel contends that the major distinction running throughout the section on sense-certainty, namely between example and universal, is not a distinction made only by philosophy, it is made by ordinary consciousness itself. Hegel distinguishes carefully between "our" view (i.e., the views of the phenomenologist and the speculative philosopher) of sense-certainty, and sense-certainty's view of itself. He writes: "It is not only "we" who make this distinction between *Wesen* and *Beispiel*, between immediacy and mediation, but we also find it in sense-certainty itself. It is in this latter form, and not in the form "we" have already determined, in which it is to be taken up."[32] The point of this distinction is that Hegel claims to be deriving the criteria of his examination from ordinary consciousness itself. The criteria must emerge from ordinary consciousness and its experience, and not be imposed on the latter. Hegel maintains that the *Phenomenology* must take up the distinction between essence and example in its original pre-theoretical form, not the theoretical version of this distinction known to the philosophical we. This is surely a phenomenological intent, even if it could be demonstrated that Hegel fails to observe his own stricture. For this reason his discussion of space and time—the "here" and the "now"—however limited, is entirely appropriate here, rather than being completely out of place in a "purely conceptual-categorical dialectic." It is the embodied life-world subject or *Dasein*, not a Cartesian pure *ego cogito*, who turns around and sees a house instead of a tree, and so forth. Hegel's distinction between the lived form and the philosophical form of the essence/instance contrast points to the presence of both in the *Phenomenology*, and to the relevance of philosophical categories in clarifying the self-subversion of ordinary consciousness.

In fact Hegel anticipates Husserl's distinction between the life-world "essence" (*morphe*) which is typical, true for the most part, and the exact formal-mathematical essence (*eidos*).[33] The latter is a construct that presupposes abstract homogeneous space; the former is not a construct, but embodied in lived space. If Heidegger were correct in his interpretation, then Hegel must identify the life-world with a set of formal categories, i.e., lived space and time must be identified and/or confused with abstract homogenous space and time, or with a purely logical conceptual dialectic. The chapters on Self-Consciousness, Spirit and Religion as structures of historical life-world consciousness, would be entirely out of place in such a logically-structured and ordered work of "pure thought." While some interpreters might agree with this interpretation of the *Phenomenology*, Heidegger does not bother to render it plausible, much less defend it by careful analysis of the text. He fails to do justice to Hegel's complex intentions and problems in the work.

Hegel's view of the relation between ordinary consciousness and the philosophical standpoint is complex and elusive. Hegel does not identify the *Gestalten des Bewusstseins* with or collapse them into the logical *Begriffe* or categories. Instead there is a correspondence between the concrete *Gestalten des Bewusstseins* and the abstract concepts of science. The distinction between ordinary consciousness and science is not one of content, but rather one of form. The content, the *Inhalt* is the same: The existing *Geist* is not richer than science, but neither is it poorer in content.[34] Although the exact import of the correspondence is not clear, the correspondence between *Gestalten* and *Begriffe* means that the former cannot be regarded as simply eliminated by the latter. The *Begriffe* are not "absolved" from the *Gestalten des Bewusstseins* as Heidegger would have us believe.

Hegel makes this point in the preface to the *Phenomenology*, in his discussion of the relation between the ordinary consciousness and the philosophical standpoint. Philosophical science presupposes that the individual consciousness elevate itself to its standpoint, the aether of pure self-knowledge in absolute otherness. However Hegel goes on to grant to ordinary consciousness a right to be educated by science:

> Conversely, the individual has the right to demand that science at least hand him a ladder to its standpoint, or show him the latter standpoint in himself. *This right is grounded in the absolute independence which it knows itself to possess in each Gestalt of its experience . . . for in each Gestalt it has the immediate self-certainty . . .*[35] (emphasis added)

According to this passage, Hegel ascribes to pre-theoretical ordinary consciousness an independence and priority over philosophical reflection. In what does this independence consist? Does it mean that immediate self-certainty of ordinary consciousness does not require certification or justification from philosophical reflection? That possibility cannot be excluded. Perhaps Hegel approximates Husserl's account of the general thesis of the natural attitude, or belief in the world. Since belief in the world does not arise from experience of particular objects, but rather makes such possible, Husserl described it as transcendental, i.e., *Urglaube* in the world, that the world out there is as it shows itself to be. There may be doubts and errors about this or that aspect of the world, but such partial doubtings presuppose and are carried out on the basis of the general thesis.

Hegel appears to anticipate Husserl when he writes, "In this belief (*Glaube*) thought goes straightway to the things themselves (*an die Gegenstände*) . . . All incipient philosophy, all sciences, even the everyday action and praxis of consciousness lives in this faith."[36] Although Hegel is critical of the claims of immediate knowledge, he nevertheless holds that philosophy would not dream of setting aside this faith since philosophy itself lives this faith.[37] Whatever the "grounding" of the natural attitude by *Wissenschaft* may mean, it does not and cannot displace this immediate openness to the world. The sole difference between philosophy and immediate knowledge is that the latter takes up a parochial attitude on behalf of immediate knowledge. Hence Hegel regards this attitude towards thought and objectivity as certainty but not yet truth in the form of truth. Truth involves mediation as well as immediacy.

Next we should consider an important but puzzling statement Hegel makes concerning the relation of philosophy and religion. Both have truth as their concern and content. But religion is a form of immediate consciousness. If the natural immediacy were simply cancelled and eliminated, then it would follow that religion is *aufgehoben* in philosophy, and that it would have no independence from philosophy. However, Hegel denies this. Instead Hegel asserts that "religion can exist without philosophy, but philosophy cannot exist without religion."[38] This statement confers upon religion, a form of immediate consciousness, an existence independent of philosophy. Since religion is a form of immediate consciousness, this statement implies that even though the path to absolute knowledge may be experienced by ordinary consciousness as the highway of despair, immediate consciousness is nevertheless not simply teleologically suspended and cancelled by the speculative *Begriff*. Religious consciousness and praxis are independent of the speculative comprehension and transformation. The latter can interpret the former but it does not provide the sole key to its intelligibility. Hegel makes the same point about the priority and independence of immediate forms of life *vis-à-vis* philosophical reflection in the famous preface to the *Philosophy of Right*.[39] Philosophy is its own time comprehended in thought. Philosophical reflection is retrospective, it can understand, but it cannot rejuvenate a form of life (*Gestalt des Lebens*) grown old.

It is crucial for Hegel that the correspondence between concrete forms of life and consciousness (*Gestalten des Bewusstseins*) on the one hand, and philosophical consciousness, logical *Begriffe* on the other, not be collapsed into sheer identity. The priority and independence of the natural attitude should not be undermined by Hegel's teleological holism. If this correspondence between *Gestalten des Bewusstseins* and the elements of the system (*Begriffe*) is integral and necessary to Hegel's system, then it cannot be maintained that Hegel is guilty of misplaced concreteness, displacing the life-world in favor of theoretical redescriptions, mathematizations, and so forth, or vulnerable to this line of Heidegger's critique. It should be noted that Hegel never abandoned his distinction between *Logic* and *Realphilosophie*. Although there is dispute about the precise meaning of this distinction, the fact that Hegel makes such a distinction at all shows that the system is not simply to be identified with the *Logic*. Moreover, the central systematic problem is precisely the correspondence and correlation between the *Logic* and *Realphilosophie*, of which the *Phenomenology of Spirit* is one instance. In short, Hegel's *Phenomenology* deserves to be regarded as genuine phenomenology. So interpreted, Hegel's *Phenomenology* could be regarded as "true" in Heidegger's sense of truth as disclosure. If so, then it is more and other than absolvent knowledge.

B. Categorical Logic and the Ontological Difference

Does Hegel obscure or eliminate the ontological difference when he identifies the task of transcendental ontology as categorical analysis and logic? Clearly much depends on what is meant by category

and categorical analysis. It is misleading to claim that Hegel follows
the tradition in interpreting the problem of Being simply as a category problem in the classical Aristotelian sense. Hegel's concept of
category, precisely because it is an identity of thought and being,
essentially includes subjectivity. For this reason, the unique Hegelian
category does not forget the ontological difference, but rather rein-
terprets it. The dispute concerns the adequacy of this
reinterpretation.

Hegel maintains that traditional objectifying thought obscures the
fundamental problems of ontology, which lie deeper than a list or
collection of categories. Kant is correct to have undertaken a transcendental deduction of the categories, but Kant is insufficiently
radical. Hegel complains that Kant takes over the traditional Aristotelian categories historically as givens, and confines his concerns to
the question whether the categories are subjective or objective. Despite the transcendental turn and deduction according to which categories are categories of transcendental subjectivity, Kant produces
another life-less list or table of categories. Hegel thinks that the
fundamental problems of ontology lie deeper. Hegel shares the post-
Kantian concern to make critical transcendental philosophy self-con-
sistent and systematic. Following Fichte, but also hearkening back to
Aristotle, the task is to show the unity and interconnection of the
categories as synthetic forms of the identity of thought and being.
They are phases in the self-constitution of rational thought. But
rational thought is more than abstract empty formal thought. Not
even Kant was interested in the categories merely as empty thought
forms, he was after the categories as concrete filled forms of the
identity of thought and being. What Kant failed to do was to penetrate to the vital unity and connection of the categories and show the
self-constitution by which thought progressively apprehends and
pervades being. Hegel thinks that the telos of such a process is not
idealism which eliminates, but a holism that articulates while preserving the difference between thought and being. Hegel's holism is
not immediate, but discursive and articulated. For this reason Hegel
is a foe of all identifications of truth with immediacy, intuition or
simple disclosure. Without denying immediacy, he defends discur-
sivity and mediation as equally co-constitutive of truth.

Hegel's contention is challenged by Jacques Taminiaux, who is
critical of Hegel's identification of the philosophical task with providing a "doctrine of categories." Taminiaux specifically rejects Hegel's
treatment of identity and difference as categories. When difference
becomes a category, it is no longer "original," i.e., belonging to the
disclosure of Being. Rather, difference "is wholly submerged in the
different once it is defined as self-generation of the Concept . . . the

common foundation for all beings . . ."[40] According to Taminiaux, Hegel raises the issue of ontological difference, only to eliminate it by reducing it to a counterpart of identity. If identity and difference are categorically homogeneous, then Hegel's dialectical logic levels the ontological difference. What is an event disposing thought, cannot itself be made over into a formal structure of thought, or something which thought disposes. And that is what occurs when difference is reduced to a moment in the dialectic. Moreover, difference is eliminated when, as a category, difference has been comprehended, rendered transparent to thought. Is difference comprehended still difference? Taminiaux believes not.

There are several points to be noted concerning Taminiaux's evaluation of the issue. The first is that Taminiaux's discussion of the so-called reduction of difference to the different, cites only Hegel's early work, *Glauben und Wissen*. This is unfortunate, because the question which Taminiaux raises concerning difference and categorical homogeneity are addressed by Hegel primarily in the *Logic*. Taminiaux apparently attributes to Hegel the traditional conception of a category as a given, which Hegel rejects. This understanding of the categories is subject to criticism and correction in Hegel's *Logic*, specifically the so-called "subjective logic" or doctrine of the *Begriff*. Second, it is significant that the dialectical development is characterized by Taminiaux as a *step away from the origin* and for this reason objectionable. This critique shows that Taminiaux tacitly appeals to some form of immediate knowing, or truth as disclosure, and intends to play off truth as disclosure against truth in a mediated conceptual sense. Such a view would not be unfamiliar to Hegel, for he had encountered a version of it in Jacobi's immediate knowledge. Hegel maintains that what is immediate is categorically the poorest, least developed form of truth, while what is mediated is the concrete, explicit and developed form of truth. The point is Hegel thinks truth involves both immediacy and mediation.

Does dialectical-discursive mediation eliminate the ontological difference as Taminiaux suggests? Is difference rendered transparent to thought and immanent, still difference? If difference is interpreted categorically, then isn't the contingent event of disclosure levelled off and forced into a conceptual straightjacket? The ontological difference is a difference constitutive of the process/event of disclosure. This difference cannot be *aufgehoben*, for it precedes and conditions the dialectical transitions. But the difference of disclosure is passed over and ignored if and when difference is identified with a category that is homogeneous with other categories, e.g., sameness (or identity). Yet without such categorical homogeneity, no transition from one category to another is possible. There are two questions here:

does difference belong to the event of disclosure of being, and how is the difference of disclosure related to difference as a category? Does the move to a categorical treatment of difference eliminate difference by comprehending it and rendering it transparent to reason, or does categorical comprehension of difference mean rather that difference is categorically necessary? In the latter case it would be incorrect to charge Hegel with simply eliminating difference, for what is categorically necessary cannot be eliminated.

Werner Marx sides with Taminiaux in thinking that a categorical interpretation in Hegel's sense eliminates the difference. According to Marx, Heidegger pits the notion of the ontological difference as a difference which accompanies and remains an aspect of the disclosure of Being against Hegel's self-conceiving concept. Difference here means not something which is thought, but rather something unthought, the unthought background and horizon of thought. If difference cannot be thought, then it cannot be *aufgehoben* in thought, and Hegel's self-conceiving concept cannot rediscover itself in this other, this difference. This difference remains alien, opaque to thought, and is not the dialectical negation or other of thought.[41]

However in his earlier book, *Heidegger and the Tradition*, Marx persuasively shows that the issue of truth in Hegel needs to be addressed in the context of Hegel's *Logic*. Marx advances this point as an objection against Heidegger's reading of Hegel's concept of truth on which the above noted objections, including his own, depend. He writes "The crucial objection against Heidegger's determination of the essence of truth in Hegel . . . is that the essence of truth is shown in its pure form not in the *Phenomenology* but only in the *Science of Logic*."[42] Marx concedes that Heidegger's reading of Hegel does him violence. Heidegger is wrong to understand Hegel as a Cartesian who reduces truth to certainty or to correspondence, or who reduces Being to what is merely present at hand.[43] Significantly, when Marx turns to the *Logic*, he discovers there an account of truth as a process, an event of disclosure. According to Marx, Hegel's conception of truth as a process of disclosure is a decisive break with the traditional concept of truth. This "locates" Hegel closer to Heidegger than to Aristotle.

Marx develops this point in a discussion of the metaphor of light and darkness which, following Heidegger, he finds running throughout the philosophical tradition from Plato and Aristotle onwards. The various metaphysical positions were developed in terms of the metaphoric image of light and darkness. In some darkness preceded light; in others light and darkness both held sway in dualism. But the most influential positions of Western metaphysics were the ontologically optimistic ones in which light possessed complete mastery over darkness and thus guaranteed the total intelligibility of Being. How is Hegel related to this tradition? In view of the complexity of the issues and Hegel's thought, Marx is not sure, although he wants to say that Hegel ultimately belongs to the third in which light overcomes darkness, while Heidegger breaks with this tradition. Let us examine some of the complexity.

To begin with, Marx credits Hegel with breaking with the philosophies which interpreted light as having complete unbroken mastery over darkness. Indeed, Hegel is one of the first of his generation to realize the impossibility of returning to ancient classical conceptions, however tempting and desirable it might be. Hegel grasped more profoundly and formulated more explicitly than any of his contemporaries the historical breach and gulf which separated his age from that of Aristotle. In the *Differenzschrift*, historical reality is not one uninterrupted stream of light, it is broken, rent asunder and this fact of brokenness and alienation is the reason why philosophy is necessary.[44] If light simply mastered the darkness or eliminated it, philosophy in Hegel's sense would not be necessary. Thus Hegel's philosophy thematizes no shallow optimistic metaphysics of light, but rather darkness in the forms of negativity and alienation. For the alienation creating the presupposition of philosophy is not merely contingent, or an historical accident. It is rooted in reason, in life itself.

Second, Marx contends that Hegel shares with Aristotle the conviction that reason, *Nous*, has the power to heal all wounds, to overcome and reconcile every breach and sundering of Being, every alienation and diremption. Does this mean that Hegel is to be classed together with Aristotle? Marx thinks not. Such an assessment

> would overlook the essential distinction that for Hegel, unlike Aristotle, Being and essence are not purely and simply disclosed. For this reason there is not in Hegel the *noesis*, the intuitive inspection which on sheer contact is able without possibility of error to grasp the truth of Being . . . And the "absolute intuition" of Schelling is not in Hegel; rather there is only the "strenuous toil of the rational reflection" which can only grasp the truth as the whole . . .[45]

Again,

> Though reason is stronger than the sundering of Being, the light of reason does not come in one burst. This is shown in the *Science of Logic* inasmuch as "activity," subjectivity must bring itself forth; it has to unveil the blindness of the categories of the objective logic. Since this unfolding of the truth is consummated as a coming forth into light, it must take place in relation to the not yet luminous.[46]

Marx explains that for Hegel there is an essential connection between light and darkness in truth as event of disclosure. Darkness, negativity is co-constitutive of the disclosure of being. This is Hegel's version of truth as *aletheia*, and is the common ground which he shares with Heidegger. In other words, Heidegger's insistence upon truth as disclosure may "get underneath" Plato and Aristotle, but it does not undermine Hegel, for this insight is already Hegel's insight.

Nevertheless, despite the obvious importance of such a conception of truth as disclosure involving untruth and concealment as its condition, background and horizon, Marx holds that Hegel ultimately awards the palm to light over darkness, to truth over untruth. Despite Hegel's appreciation of history and negativity, in his thought "light retains predominance," and he remains ontologically too optimistic.[47] Marx points to Hegel's teleological conception of negation and *Aufhebung*, and concept of dialectic as an orderly process of transitions towards perfection. Marx claims that Hegel's ultimate view is the complete victory of light which overcomes darkness, untruth and so forth. Thus Marx writes concerning the absolute Idea: "Although this highest stage, the absolute Idea, the full truth, contains in Hegel's words, 'even the harshest opposition,' nevertheless it 'eternally overcomes' it. The dialectical order guarantees the conclusive victory to the light, to the truth undisguised by untruth."[48]

However Marx derives such an interpretation only by selectively quoting Hegel out of context. Specifically, Marx bases his interpretation on the following passage of the *Logic*, from which he quotes selectively. The full passage reads:

> The identity of the Idea with itself is one with the process; the thought which liberates actuality (*Wirklichkeit*) from the appearance of purposeless change and transfigures it into the Idea, must not represent this truth of actuality as a dead repose, as a mere picture, lifeless without impulse and movement, as a genus or number or an abstract thought. For the sake of the Freedom which the concept (*Begriff*) attains in the Idea, the Idea contains the most stubborn opposition within itself. Its repose consists in the security and certainty with which the Idea eternally generates and eternally overcomes that opposition, for in such opposition it coincides with itself.[49]

It is evident that the passage which Marx claims to assert the eternal overcoming of darkness by light, of opposition by identity, does not really say this, or better, it says this but not only this. Marx can obtain his interpretation only by suppressing the crucial point that the Idea eternally engenders opposition as well as eternally overcomes opposition. Marx oversimplifies Hegel, and thus caricatures the position by claiming that it ultimately ends up being the very idealism which Hegel himself so trenchantly criticized and rejected in the *Phenomenology*. It is by no means clear as Marx contends that Hegel's dialectical conception of truth as a process inclusive of untruth, guarantees a 'conclusive victory' to light, to truth undisguised by untruth.

Otherness and idea, identity and difference are equiprimordial, and not as Marx suggests, related such that identity swallows up difference or that difference is subordinate to identity. In other words, difference is not derivative from Hegel's identity, but is "essential" to it. This is illustrated in the initial discussion of Being and Nothing in the *Logic*. Nothing, or difference, is not a second category deriving from or instantiating Being as the first category. Rather the move to Nothing is an immediate transition of Being itself: it shows that pure Being cannot be fixed or grasped. The attempt to grasp Being pure or as such, ends in failure. The determinate feature of Being is its indeterminacy. Hence when thought tries to think such utter indeterminacy, it fails, and winds up immediately thinking of nothing. Here is a transition, not merely conceptual but immediate, and transition implies difference. Difference therefore belongs to the process whereby Being is disclosed. It is these immediate transitions which the first category of the *Logic* formulates. However, this means that the first and fundamental category of Hegel's *Logic* is not Being in the ontic sense, or Being as a genus, but rather becoming, or process (*Werden*). Thus, while Hegel's categories are idealizations, they are not abstract formal idealizations that are simply homogeneous and so exclude difference. For it is a requirement of categorical idealization in Hegel's sense that it cannot relinquish the moment of difference, because difference is immediately co-present in the disclosure of Being: the determinacy of Being is its indeterminacy. Dialectic as a method does not create, but preserves and exemplifies the difference.

Marx's and Taminiaux's interpretation do violence to Hegel. Hegel's point can be stated thus: It is a requirement of spirit that the world be opaque to spirit. J.N. Findlay formulates Hegel's position concerning light and darkness, otherness and difference in the following way:

> Spirit, the principle of unity and universality, can only fully understand the world by regarding that world as being no more than the material for its own activity, as being opaque to such activity merely to the extent that such opacity is a necessary condition for the process of removing it, of rendering the world transparent.[50]

Findlay's formulation probably comes closer to the position Marx is criticizing than Hegel's. For opacity is a much weaker term than Hegel's hiddenness, negativity or historical alienation. Nevertheless,

Findlay has succeeded where Taminiaux and Werner Marx fail, in capturing what Hegel is after. To be sure, there is no doubt that Hegel's project of absolute knowledge that removes opacity, is fundamentally different from Heidegger's. The question however is whether the removal of opacity is to be interpreted non-dialectically as done by Marx and Taminiaux, or rather as Findlay formulates it. Findlay's formulation is felicitous in bringing out the crucial point that opacity, otherness and so forth is a necessary condition of its own removal. Hence if removal is meant as simple elimination or exclusion of difference, otherness and so forth, then the conditions for Spirit's self-realization are likewise removed. Hegel's position collapses into the abstract idealism, immediate knowledge and so forth that he rejects. The alternative is to interpret otherness ontologically as a permanent requirement of Spirit's self-realization. The Other of thought is not superfluous, but rather a necessary condition of Spirit and the realization of Spirit and of the Logical Idea. Such is the fundamental point of Hegel's distinctive formulation of identity. If thought simply eliminated otherness, its very project of comprehending and knowing the world and itself would fail.

NOTES

1. Heidegger writes critically about Hegel; however, his interpretation and critique of Hegel is not based upon a full study of a single Hegelian text, much less an account/interpretation of Hegel's thought as a whole. Instead of a book like *Kant and the Problem of Metaphysics*, we have Heidegger's lectures on the *Phenomenology* (1930), which treat sense-certainty and the initial sections of self-consciousness, his *Hegels Begriff der Erfahrung* (1942) which is a commentary on the introduction to the *Phenomenology*, and finally his essay *Identity and Difference* (1957) which deals with the *Logic* and which seeks to pin on Hegel the polemical label of "onto-theological concept of Being." The absence of a book length study of Hegel's thought as a whole is a serious gap, a failure to make good on his sweeping critical charges levelled at Hegel.

2. Martin Heidegger, *Sein und Zeit*, 15th ed. (Tübingen: Niemayer Verlag, 1984), paragraph 6, pp. 19ff, hereafter SZ; *Being and Time*, trans. MacQuarrie & Robinson (New York: Harper Brothers, 1962); cf. also Martin Heidegger, *Basic Writings*, ed. David Farrell Krell (New York: Harper & Row, 1977), pp. 64ff. For a discussion of the ontological difference, see Heidegger, *Grundprobleme der Phänomenologie* in *Gesamtausgabe*, Band 24 (Frankfurt am Main: Klostermann, 1975), pp. 321ff. English Translation: *Basic Problems of Phenomenology*, trans. A. Hofstadter (Bloomington: Indiana University Press 1982); see also Joseph Kockelmans, *On the Truth of Being* (Bloomington: Indiana University Press, 1984), pp. 73ff.

3. Hans-Georg Gadamer, *Philosophical Hermeneutics*, trans. & ed. David Linge (Los Angeles: University of California Press, 1977), pp. 230ff. Hereafter cited PH.

4. Hans-Georg Gadamer, *Hegel's Dialectic*, trans. P. Christopher Smith (New Haven: Yale University Press, 1976), p. 103. For a similar formulation, cf. PH, 230ff. Gadamer points out and supports the standard German criticism of Heidegger that he is not sufficiently aware of his own proximity and indebtedness to Hegel. The present writer also concurs with this assessment. However it is virtually a contemporary dogma that Heidegger has undermined metaphysics if not "philosophy," and so has taken the full measure of Hegel. For recent challenges to the above dogma, cf. Jacques Taminiaux, *Dialectic and Difference: Finitude in Modern Thought*, ed. Crease & Decker (New Jersey: Humanities Press, 1985), p. 86; Dennis Schmidt, "Between Hegel and Heidegger," *Man and World*, Vol. 15, No. 1, 1982, pp. 17ff.

5. Martin Heidegger, *Hegels Phänomenologie des Geistes*, Gesamtausgabe, II. Abteilung, Vorlesungen 1923–1944, Band 32, hrsg. von Ingtraud Goerland, (Frankfurt: Klostermann, 1980), pp. 56, 92, 145. Hereafter cited as HPHG.

6. For a discussion of Hegel's departure from Cartesian-transcendental philosophy, see my "Hegel's Concept of Geist," in *Hegel's Philosophy of Spirit*, ed. Peter Stillman (Albany: SUNY Press, 1986), and "Hegel and Transcendental Philosophy," *Journal of Philosophy* Vol. LXXXII, No. 11, November 1985, pp. 595ff.

7. For Heidegger's reading of Hegel as Cartesian, cf. his *Hegels Begriff der Erfahrung*, in *Holzwege* (Frankfurt: Klostermann 1950), pp. 128ff, hereafter HBE; *Hegel's Concept of Experience*, trans. K.R. Dove (New York: Harper & Row, 1970), pp. 27ff. The major study of Heidegger in English, William J. Richardson, *Heidegger: Through Phenomenology to Thought* (The Hague: Martinus Nijhoff, 1963) repeats and embellishes Heidegger's Cartesian reading of Hegel (see pp. 331–361). Another reading of Hegel as Cartesian is to be found in Tom Rockmore, *Hegel's Circular Epistemology* (Bloomington: Indiana University Press, 1986).

8. Martin Heidegger, *An Introduction to Metaphysics*, trans. Ralph Manheim (New Haven: Yale University Press, 1959), p. 188. Hereafter cited as IM.

9. Heidegger, HPhG, pp. 107ff. Cf. also *Die Zeit des Weltbildes*, especially the Zusätze 4 & 9 in *Holzwege*. "The Age of the World as Picture," in *The Question Concerning Technology*, trans. William Lovitt (New York: Harper, 1977).

10. Heidegger, SZ, pp. 3ff.; IM, pp. 35ff.

11. SZ, p. 42.

12. SZ, p. 44.

13. IM, p. 184.

14. *Ibid*.

15. *Ibid.*, p. 190.

16. HPHG, pp. 29, 34, 40, 42; HBE (*Holzwege*), pp. 197ff.

17. HPHG, p. 67. For a study of the "We," cf. K.R. Dove, "Toward An Interpretation of Hegel's *Phänomenologie des Geistes*," PhD. dissertation, Yale University, 1965.

18. *Ibid.*, p. 71.

19. *Ibid.*, p. 54.

20. *Ibid.*, p. 75.

21. *Ibid.*, pp. 69ff.; cf. also Richardson, pp. 332ff.

22. See note 6 above.

23. Werner Marx, *Heidegger and the Tradition*, trans. Theodore Kisiel and Murray Greene (Evanston: Northwestern University Press, 1971), p. 53. Hereafter cited as HT.

24. Reinhold Aschenberg, *Der Wahrheitsbegriff in Hegels Phänomenologie des Geistes*, in *Die ontologische Option*, hrsg. Klaus Hartmann (Berlin: Walter de Gruyter, 1976), pp. 220ff.

25. Hegel, *Wissenschaft der Logik*, in *Theorie Werkausgabe* (Frankfurt: Suhrkamp Verlag, 1970), 6:277, hereafter cited as SK, followed by Volume and page reference. See also *Enzyklopädie*, SK, 6:159; see also Reiner Schürmann, *Meister Eckhart* (Bloomington: Indiana University Press, 1978), p. 245, note 111: Hegel upon discovering Eckhart exclaimed, "Here we have found at last what we were seeking." Cf. also John Caputo's study, *The Mystical Element in Heidegger's Thought* (Athens, Ohio: Ohio University Press, 1978), which brings out themes common to Heidegger and Eckhart. The fact that both Hegel and Heidegger can appeal to Eckhart in itself proves little; but it provides excellent grounds to be suspicious about Heidegger's claims that Hegel's dialectic is oriented simply on the Greek *logos* problem, and is a supreme exemplification of metaphysics as the will to power.

26. HPHG, p. 75.

27. HBE, *Holzwege*, pp. 125ff.; 190ff.; ET, pp. 50ff., 102–112.

28. HPHG, p. 85.

29. *Ibid.*

30. Hegel, *Phänomenologie des Geistes*, ed. J. Hoffmeister (Hamburg: Meiner Verlag, 1952), p. 80. Hereafter cited as PhG.

31. See above note 13.

32. Hegel, PhG, p. 80.

33. Edmund Husserl introduced this distinction in his book *Ideas* (1913), trans. Boyce Gibson (New York: Collier MacMillan, 1962), and developed the distinction in his later philosophy, in his *Experience and Judgement*, trans. J. Churchill and K. Ameriks (Evanston: Northwestern University Press, 1973), and *The Crisis of European Sciences*, trans. David Carr (Evanston: Northwestern University Press, 1970); for a discussion see Alfred Schutz, "Type and Eidos in Husserl's Late Philosophy," Alfred Schutz, *Collected Papers*, Vol. III, ed. I. Schutz (The Hague: Martinus Nijhoff, 1966).

34. Hegel, PhG, p. 562.

35. Hegel, PhG, p 25 (emphasis added).

36. Hegel, *Enzyklopädie der philosophischen Wissenschaften* (1830), hrsg. Nicolin & Pöggeler (Hamburg: Meiner, 1969), §26, p. 60; *The Logic of Hegel*, trans. W. Wallace (Oxford: Oxford University Press, 1873).

37. *Ibid.*, §64.

38. *Ibid.*, *Vorrede zur zweiten Ausgabe*, p. 12.

39. Hegel, *Rechtsphilosophie*, in *Theorie Werkausgabe*, Vol.7; *Philosophy of Right*, trans. T.M. Knox (London: Oxford University Press 1952).

40. Taminiaux, *op. cit.*, pp. 88, 75.

41. Marx, *Hegel's Phenomenology of Spirit*, pp. 106–7.

42. Marx, HT 53. While Marx is surely correct to stress the importance of Hegel's *Logic* on this issue, the points to which Marx directs attention—the discussion of light and darkness—Hegel had already made in his first publication, the *Differenzschrift* (1800). See note 44.

43. HT, pp. 99, 136.

44. Hegel, *Differenz des Fichteschen und Schellingschen Systems der Philosophie*, in *Theorie Werkausgabe*, SK, 2: 22ff.; *The Difference Between Fichte's and Schelling's System of Philosophy*, trans. W. Cerf & H.S. Harris (Albany: State University of New York Press, 1977), pp. 91ff.

45. HT, p. 56.

46. HT, p. 57.

47. *Ibid.*

48. *Ibid.*

49. Hegel, *Wissenschaft der Logik*, in *Theorie Werkausgabe*, SK, 6:467–68, my translation. *Hegel's Science of Logic*, trans. A.V. Miller (New York: Humanities Press, 1969), p. 759.

50. J.N. Findlay, *Hegel. A Re-examination* (New York: Collier Books, 1962), p. 54; cf. also p. 253.

Commentary on Robert R. Williams' "Hegel and Heidegger"
Eric von der Luft

Professor Williams seems to see the history of modern metaphysics as a sort of chess game between its two giants, Hegel and Heidegger. Has Hegel (white) correctly anticipated all of Heidegger's moves? Or does Heidegger (black) yet have one devastating move that undermines Hegel's strategy? The game is fascinating and deserves our scrutiny.

I disagree with very little in Williams' paper. (That may surprise those who are familiar with the history of public exchanges between Professor Williams and myself.[1] But apparently we have found common ground with regard to Heidegger where we did not find it with regard to Schleiermacher.) I shall accordingly direct my remarks not toward criticism, but only toward elaborating and clarifying one key point.

Heidegger claims that Hegel represents the culmination of the systematic western metaphysical tradition rather than a breaking away from it. He makes this claim partially on the basis of his belief that Hegel is a Cartesian, i.e., a foundationalist and rationalist who has failed to discover any truly new principles of ontology. In order to make such a claim for Hegel as the culmination of this tradition, Heidegger could just as easily have called him an Aristotelian, a Platonist, a Parmenidean, a Leibnizian, a Spinozist, or—well, you name it. There seems little justification to specify Descartes in particular as Hegel's philosophical ancestor if Heidegger is only going to identify Cartesian subjectivism with Aristotelian substance metaphysics anyway. Yet, as Williams rightly points out, this is just what Heidegger does.

To see Hegel as the culmination of this tradition (or, for that matter, to see any single figure as the culmination of any tradition) is in effect to define the tradition, i.e., to act in the place of the historian by setting arbitrary limits on the tradition. In this case Heidegger seems to be specifying the corpus of metaphysical speculation that went on under the influence of Aristotle up to and including Hegel. Although Descartes is his paradigm (and thus his whipping boy), it is clear, on the evidence of his various critiques of Hegel, his discussion of Descartes in §§ 19–21 of *Being and Time*, and his contrast of pre-Socratic and post-Socratic views of Being, beings, and language in *Introduction to Metaphysics*, that he means substance metaphysics in general. Having thus defined the "tradition," he includes Hegel and excludes himself. The question then becomes: Is it fair to include Hegel among substance metaphysicians? The answer must be no, in spite of Hegel's professed reverence for Aristotle.

Several times in his paper Williams criticizes Heidegger's interpretation of Hegel as continuing traditional metaphysics rather than breaking away from it, as Heidegger believed he himself had done. Williams is quite correct to do this. However, in an earlier version of his paper, he put this criticism in much more blunt language (which I wish he had kept): "Hegel is better understood as breaking with transcendental philosophy from Descartes to Kant, than as a continuation of it." Thus, as Williams emphasizes, Heidegger's labeling of Hegel as a Cartesian is not only misleading, and unfair to Hegel, but also an error. Moreover, if it is subjective idealism which Heidegger sees as the transcendental philosophy that, in Cartesian fashion, seeks to be the new ground of a rigorous science, then it is Fichte, not Hegel, whom he should appoint as the true successor of Descartes.

But what is this so-called "tradition" and what would a "culmination" of it or a "breaking away" from it involve? Isn't what we actually have in the history of western metaphysics not a unified "tradition" *per se*, but instead just a 25-century-long sequence of intelligent suggestions about metaphysics, a sequence whose discontinuity is mitigated only by the fact that most of the later thinkers have read the works of the earlier? To call that sequence, or any portion thereof, a "tradition" is only a historian's device, at best a convenience, at worst a contrivance. It is certainly not a "tradition" in the strong sense that, for example, rabbinic teaching is. Every new thinker in the western metaphysical "tradition" is both its "culmination,"—insofar as he or she puts the most recent material into it— and at the same time a genuine "breaking away" from it—to whatever extent he or she is not just some predecessor's epigone. Thus Aristotle, in his time, was both the culmination of Platonism and a breaking away from it and in the same way Plotinus, in his time, was both its new culmination and new breaking away from it, etc., etc.

Analogously, we might discern a "tradition" in the policies of British monarchs, and in so doing we might regard the accession of James I as both the "culmination" of the reign of Elizabeth I and a "breaking away" from it. But again, that would only be a historian's device, and not really a valuable designation.[2]

Does Heidegger then delude himself by pretending to stand outside of the tradition he has defined?

By claiming to be outside of the metaphysical tradition Heidegger is not trying to avoid or eliminate metaphysics, as did, for example, A.J. Ayer in *Language, Truth, and Logic*. He is not so naive. He knows full well that what he is doing is metaphysics and that this cannot be avoided. Yet Heidegger still fails to recognize that he stands in quite the same relationship to western metaphysics in the mid–20th century that Hegel stood to it in the early 19th, Kant in the late 18th, Descartes in the early 17th, etc., i.e., as something new and different, a change of direction, just another simultaneous "culmination" and "breaking away." And even though Heidegger himself refuses to see his deconstruction project as in the same historical framework with regard to previous speculation as were once Hegel's dialectic, Kant's Copernican revolution, or Descartes' *cogito*, present and future historians of philosophy will surely see it that way, i.e., they will place Heidegger, *malgré lui*, squarely within the so-called "tradition."

It is important for us to recognize that, for Heidegger, the "tradition" of which Hegel is called the culmination is not the *totality* of western philosophical thought, but only the post-Socratic portion of it. Heidegger is thus not claiming to be starting philosophy anew, but rather only to be returning to pre-Socratic modes of awareness. In other words, he intends to do a sort of "end run" around the post-Socratic tradition (especially from Aristotle to Hegel), deconstruct *that*, and thereby disclose the truth of Being which the pre-Socratics (he believes) knew and which the systematic categorizing of post-Socratic philosophy has hidden, lost, and forgotten. Heidegger's philosophy is an attempt to recover the past glories of metaphysical speculation such as he imagines were current among the earliest pre-Socratics. His project is thus a sort of philosophical nostalgia, a romantic yearning for a lost paradise, a quest to return to a "Golden Age," a "Pure Land," a speculative Garden of Eden.

At the risk of sounding flippant, I find that I must now ask whether Heidegger is dealing with real problems or pseudo-problems. Metaphysics (or ontology) ought to lead somewhere. That is, it ought to form the basis of a system (or at least a coherent body) of specialized and variegated philosophical theory. It seems somehow impoverished if it only leads back to an awareness of primal Being—

however deep such awareness might be. The metaphysical speculations of most philosophers lead fairly naturally into other sorts of
philosophical speculations, ethical (e.g., Kant), theological (e.g.,
Aquinas), political (e.g., Hobbes), cultural (e.g., Hegel), and so forth.
But where does Heidegger lead? Two answers are possible: Heidegger's metaphysics either leads nowhere at all or it leads into an
aesthetics. It certainly does not lead into an ethics—nor do I see how
it ever could, unless that ethics be a quietist, Taoist sort of mysticism
whose highest moral imperative is "Let Being be!" But isn't such a
motto just another way of saying that we should develop an aesthetic
awareness of pure Being, beyond any inclination we might have
toward an aesthetic awareness of "beings," always keeping in mind
that crucial difference between the truly ontological and the merely
ontic?

The result of the chess game? The contest is still in progress, and
will be for quite some time, but I would give the edge to Hegel. After
all, Hegel at least seems aware that the road between Being and
beings is a two-way street, i.e., mediation is a two-way process, and
the individual counts for just as much as the universal: Being mediates beings and beings mediate Being (witness the non-vicious circularity of the logic). By contrast, Heidegger whose ultimate concern
is for the disclosure of Being through the several basic meditative
(besinnlich) questions of fundamental ontology: Why is there something rather than nothing? How do beings stand with Being? What
is the sense of Being?—seems convinced that this road is (or ought
to be) a one-way street from beings to Being, because Being is con-
cealed or forgotten when we remain immersed in the immediate
ontic world of beings themselves, but disclosed when we move, by
means of such fundamental questions, from beings toward Being. In
Hegel's metaphysics, Being and beings seem to have equal and complementary importance; but for Heidegger, beings (die Seienden) are
always seen only as eventual means toward Being (Sein)—if not toward Being as such, then toward Being presencing itself in beings.
Indeed, even the authentic existence of Dasein is described in terms
of Dasein's being in tune with Being: "Die ontische Auszeichnung des
Daseins liegt darin, daßes ontologisch ist" (Sein und Zeit, § 4, emphasis
Heidegger's). "The ontic distinction of Dasein lies in the fact that
Dasein is ontological" (my translation). Here, as in most cases, Heidegger's use the term "ontic" is pejorative while his use of "ontological" is honorific.

In the last analysis, Heidegger's metaphysics must be seen as
"one-sided" in the Hegelian sense because of the low esteem in
which it holds particular beings relative to pure Being. Moreover,
Hegel's metaphysics must be said to recognize avant le lettre the

ontological difference and preserve it although, granted, in a style of preservation quite distinct from Heidegger's—in such passages as Paragraph 99 of the *Phenomenology*, where he writes:

> Dieser sinnlichen Gewißheit, indem sie an ihr selbst das Allgemeine als die Wahrheit ihres Gegenstandes erweist, bleibt also das *reine Sein* als ihr Wesen, aber nicht als Unmittelbares, sondern ein solches, dem die Negation und Vermittlung wesentlich ist, hiemit nicht als das, was wir unter dem *Sein meinen*, sondern das *Sein* mit der *Bestimmung*, daß es die Abstraktion oder das rein Allgemeine ist . . . (emphasis Hegel's).

> Since this sense-certainty has demonstrated within itself the universal as the truth of its object, *pure Being* thus remains as its essence— not as something immediate, however, but rather as something to which negation and mediation are essential, and consequently not as that which we *mean* by *"Being"* but *Being* which is *determinate* as abstraction or as the pure universal. (My translation.)

In sense-certainty, pure Being is disclosed or "unconcealed" as the universal in the empty demonstratives of *das Hier, das Dieser,* and *das Jetzt*—and, even though Hegel sees that the disclosure of Being at this stage is inadequate, he still sees it as an important result. Hegel is just as committed as Heidegger to the goal of revealing Being as Being; the main difference between them seems to be only that Hegel is able to see this goal in a balanced way in connection with other philosophical goals, whereas Heidegger is more like a fanatic, and interprets everything else just in terms of this goal.

NOTES

1. See our debate in *The Owl of Minerva*: Luft, 14, 1 (September 1982): 10; Williams, 14, 2 (December 1982): 9–10; and Luft, 14, 3 (March 1983): 7–8.

2. This paragraph does not mean to imply that your commentator holds a "strong" Hegelian view of history, namely, the view that historical transitions are necessary and logical. Rather, that question is bracketed, and all that is presented here is a "weak" interpretation of Hegel's *bon mot*: "Philosophy is its own time apprehended in thought." If I seem to be taking a Hegelian standpoint on the philosophy of history, it is not now for the purpose of advocating Hegel, but only for the purpose of criticizing Heidegger.

Chapter Eight

HEGEL, DERRIDA, AND BATAILLE'S LAUGHTER

Joseph C. Flay

In this paper I want to look at Derrida's treatment of Hegel in two sources: "Violence and Metaphysics: An Essay on the Thought of Emmanuel Levinas" and "From Restricted to General Economy: A Hegelianism Without Reserve."[1] I shall argue that there is something very insightful in Derrida's deconstruction of Hegel, but that, for reasons I will give, he misunderstood the actual power of his own deconstruction. I shall argue that the distinction between mastery and sovereignty on which the deconstruction turns is there for Hegel, as Derrida himself admits; but that sovereignty is taken up, in a way different from the way suggested by Bataille/Derrida, in order to get us to the domain of the discursive logic/metaphysics. Hegel, with this insight about sovereignty, has another path to the "place" to which Derrida wishes to lead us.

I

In the first of these two essays, Derrida begins with a critique of a criticism against Hegel given from the perspective of Emmanuel Levinas. Levinas' criticism centers on the insistence that the Other as an other person and as present to us through "*le visage*," cannot simply be brought under the otherness which lies within the domain of "the Same" or the "economy" that Hegel articulates on the basis of the relationship of lordship and bondage. This position and Derrida's version of its merits attention in itself but because it is used by him only to go beyond it, I shall pass over it for the present in order to examine what Derrida makes of it and how it brings him to his own critique, or rather deconstruction, of Hegel.

Derrida in effect criticizes the position of Levinas on very good Hegelian grounds. Using a discussion of Husserl's view of the Other,

163

Derrida introduces the notion of an "economy" which preserves both radical otherness and the otherness of same and other, and preserves them as necessary for the possibility of each other. According to Derrida, Husserl argues that the other self-consciousness can be recognized as other only because it is recognized as an ego, as an origin of the world. "If the other was not recognized as ego, its entire alterity would collapse . . ." There is here an irreducibility of the other to my ego, and thus it is not merely an entity in the economy of my ego, nor simply something transcendentally constituted in the domain of my ego. This means, according to Derrida, that for Husserl there is a symmetry as well as a dissymmetry, each being necessary for the other. That we are both egos lies at the basis of the possibility of a dissymmetry, lies as the foundation for recognition that the other as Other cannot simply be an element of my constituted world. The dissymmetry forms an "*economy* in a new sense, a sense which would probably be intolerable to Levinas . . .," and which can be designated as "the transcendental symmetry of two empirical asymmetries. The other, for me, is an ego which I know to be in relation to me as an other."[2] Then, as one is ready to leap on Derrida to point out that this is essentially just Hegel's view, he writes: "Where have these movements been better described than in *The Phenomenology of Spirit?*"[3] Derrida rightly argues, then, that for Hegel the radical otherness of the Other is an indispensable condition for the dialectic of independence and dependence, and thus that the Other is not simply reduced to an element of identity or of "the Same."

I have included the brief discussion of this criticism of Levinas' position so that we can be clear about what Derrida is *not* arguing; for it is important to see that he fully grants to Hegel the strongest form of negativity within "the economy of self-consciousness." But this, then, leads Derrida to argue that the dialectic of same and other, even including this radical form of otherness, has an "origin" which cannot be included in language; for, in general, the origin of language, meaning, and difference cannot lie in language, meaning, or difference itself. Derrida grants that language, meaning, and difference as we have spoken of them here form an economy within which all "transactions" between selves take place. But, he also argues, neither these transactions nor the logic/metaphysics consequent to the completion of the *Phenomenology* are self-grounding. There is no self-referential grounding: language does not determine the possibility of language; meaning does not determine the possibility of meaning; difference does not determine the possibility of difference. Here the issue is joined with Hegel; for on this problem Hegel maintains that, in the system of philosophical sciences, we have a discursive, self-grounding account of language, meaning, and difference, i.e., an account of what-is that grounds both other discourses and itself.

In "From Restricted to General Economy" Derrida takes up this issue of the self-grounding of metaphysics, and does so by using Bataille, whose project is to "laugh at philosophy." The actual deconstruction of Hegel is based on Bataille's "laughter," that is developed in terms of an opposition between "mastery" and "sovereignty." Derrida argues that the next "moment" in history, after Hegel's completion of metaphysics, is that of a laughter that signifies sovereignty and that reveals "the limit of discourse and the beyond of absolute knowledge."[4] In a very complex passage Derrida deconstructs Hegel by showing that what has been rejected by the latter as a possibility (namely, the total negativity which would result from the death of the master) is in fact the boundary within which is possible the rational discourse of lordship and bondage and the dialectic that follows from it. Let's look at this argument more closely.

Derrida begins by discussing the difference he means to make between sovereignty and mastery, the latter being a translation of "Herrschaft." He argues that in the case of mastery, it is the continued presence of life, through the surrender made by the slave, which makes mastery what it is, i.e., which makes it the giving of meaning to existence through the mediation of the slave. Without the surrender, there would be death, and not mastery; for the master would not surrender, but die, and thus cease to be master. But with the surrender, there arises mastery in the sense of the giving of meaning to our existence. "The putting at stake of life is a moment in the constitution of meaning, in the presentation of essence and truth." There are two conditions here: the preservation of life by the master and the emergence of the "truth" of the master or independent consciousness as "the consciousness of the bondsman." In the course of this development, "servility becomes lordship [and] keeps within it the trace of its repressed origin," viz., the surrender. The key to mastery is the presence of the slave. "It is this dissymmetry, this absolute privilege given to the slave, that Bataille did not cease to meditate. The truth of the master is in the slave; and the slave become a master remains a repressed slave."[5] Thus, if one did not have the reciprocity of mastery and bondage, there would not be the economy of the same, of meaning, language, and difference.[6]

This signifies for Derrida Hegel's violent rejection of what Derrida calls "sovereignty." For, with sovereignty, the mediating relationship would be given up, rejected, and would be replaced with, not a fight to the death, but laughter. What Derrida now argues I will quote in full; it is here that we find the crux of his argument for sovereignty and against Hegel's notion of mastery.

Burst of laughter from Bataille. Through a ruse of life, that is, of
reason, life has thus stayed alive. Another concept of life had been
surreptitiously put in its place, to remain there, never to be exceeded, any more than reason is ever exceeded . . . This life is not
natural life, the biological existence put at stake in lordship, but an
essential life that is welded to the first one, holding it back, making
it work for the constitution of self-consciousness, truth, and meaning. Such is the truth of life. Through this recourse to the *Aufhebung*,
. . . this economy of life restricts itself to conservation, to circulation
and self-production as the reproduction of meaning; henceforth,
everything covered by the name of lordship collapses into comedy.
The independence of self-consciousness becomes laughable at the
moment when it liberates itself by enslaving itself, when it starts to
work, that is, when it enters into dialectics. Laughter alone exceeds
dialectics and the dialectician; it bursts out only on the basis of an
absolute renunciation of meaning, an absolute risking of death, what
Hegel calls abstract negativity.[7]

Derrida's point is that the necessity for there to be meaning constituted in this way is taken to be a matter of "self-evidence." It is
"unthinkable" for Hegel that one could risk all through Bataille's
laughter. The blind submission to the hegemony of meaning is "the
essence and element of philosophy, of Hegelian ontologics."[8] The
"essence" of Bataille, on the other hand, is laughter at the notion of
Aufhebung itself, which latter

signifies the *busying* of a discourse losing its breath as it reappro-
priates all negativity for itself, as it works the 'putting at stake' into
an *investment*, as it *amortizes* absolute expenditure. . . . To be indifferent to the comedy of the *Aufhebung*, as was Hegel, is to blind oneself
to the experience of the sacred, to the needless sacrifice of presence
and meaning.[9]

Derrida now focuses on Hegel's "blindness" and his consequent
"displacement" and banishment of the otherness of sovereignty.

The blind spot of Hegelianism, around which can be organized the
representation of meaning, is the *point* at which destruction, suppression, death and sacrifice constitute so irreversible an expenditure, so radical a negativity—here we would have to say an expenditure and a negativity *without reserve*—that they can no longer be
determined as negativity in a process or a system.[10]

The criticism is that Hegel remained with the seriousness of the
negative, within the framework of a dialectic chained to the *Aufhebung*, rather than taking up the issue of sovereignty and its laughter
with the rejected "abstract negativity." In the process of completing
the *Phenomenology of Spirit* Hegel, according to Derrida, is caught up

in a simple economy of meaning, a restricted economy, which has as its purpose the prevention of rupture and the preservation of the "commercial values" of its own exchange of meanings.[11]

Here, doubtless, Derrida has an important insight. Hegel did, in fact, reject the radical laughter that Bataille represents.[12] He also uncovered, with the absolute negativity of death, what had to be refused, at this point, if there was to be a grounding of meaning. But was the sole outcome of this the continuation of a series of dialectical Aufhebungen which left Hegel blind to what he had uncovered? Is Derrida correct in arguing that the Aufhebung rules all? My answer is a resounding No.

II

What I now will argue should certainly not be construed as an argument that will end the discussion between Hegel and Derrida. My only claim is that, just as my earlier discussion of his critique of Levinas established one avenue that Derrida does not take toward Hegel, but could be construed to take, the present argument seeks only to establish that the criticism against Hegel on the grounds that the Aufhebung rules all and proscribes rupture of any sort will not hold.

I will discuss here two general reasons for this. First, there is no general character to the movement of Aufheben itself in the sense that it would involve an independent method or form that would in turn guarantee continuity. The way in which a particular, determinate negation is taken up and preserved, and yet changed into another form, must differ from particular to particular—and most importantly from one sort of particular to another sort of particular. The moment of an Aufhebung, like the moments of initial presentation and of original, dialectical negation, is governed by the nature of the content addressed, and not by an abstract form. Therefore, even if it were true that all such "third" moments were of the nature of Aufhebungen, this would not guarantee the absence of rupture; for it is conceivable that a particular "taking up" of a negation would rupture the previous economy.

But this is not the strongest sort of argument; for Derrida could counter that, even granting that the moment of an Aufhebung is governed by the content, the issue is not the economy of a particular phase of the Phenomenology, but rather the presupposition that meaning must be preserved and that only the appropriate Aufhebung can preserve it. Thus, he could turn this defense against itself and show that the very need to unite an Aufhebung to content in an appropriate way is generated and dictated by the prior need to maintain meaning without rupture of the restricted economy.

But there is a second, stronger reason. The *Aufhebung* simply does not govern, in an exclusive way, the overall movement of either the *Phenomenology* or the system proper. Since Derrida has concentrated his discussion on the former, I shall restrict myself to it as well. Before I address the issue directly, however, I should like to say something about the reason why Derrida overlooks the possibility of guarding against my defense here. The reason is that he works on Hegel, in the essay I am now discussing, through Bataille. By Derrida's own admission and the admission of Bataille as well, Bataille in turn works through the interpretation made by Kojève. I have heavily criticized elsewhere this influential interpretation, and must now concentrate on one of the many faults it harbors within it. For Kojève and those who will follow him, the master-slave dialectic governs all. This means that precisely what Derrida addresses here in his distinction between mastery and sovereignty is to be taken to hold for the *Phenomenology* as a whole. Thus, by the interpretation of Hegel via Bataille via Kojève, it is a *priori* the case that no break in the economy can be made. What Derrida cannot see—*his* blind spot—is the very possibility of something other than the structure of *Aufhebung* along the lines of the sort of preservation maintained in the rejection of death by the slave and thus, by default, by the master.

Now this is important because, however we interpret it, the very nature of master-slave relationship is shown by the *Phenomenology* to be insufficient as a way of approaching the possible ground of knowledge. It is shown to be insufficient, not because the master-slave structure is taken up into stoicism, skepticism, and unhappy consciousness—a movement which could be construed to continue along the lines of a series of *Aufhebungen* structured indeed by mastery—but because the whole possibility of self-consciousness as foundation must be given up at the end of the analysis of unhappy consciousness. And it is given up, and a move is made from self-consciousness to reason, not by means of an *Aufhebung* which would obey the dialectic of master-slave to which Derrida is committed, but with a radical break characterized as a "surrender" of self-consciousness (*ein Aufgeben*) to "a transcendent" (*ein Jenseits*) which characterizes this particular "*Aufgehobensein*" as something radical.[13]

I have carefully noted here that Hegel describes this surrender as having the character of *Aufgehobensein*. But there is nonetheless a rupture here; for at the very beginning of the discussion of reason which follows, Hegel writes that one element has been excised which was essential to the constitution of the structure of self-consciousness, viz. being-for-self: the unhappy consciousness "has successfully struggled to divest itself of its being-for-self and has turned [being-for-self] into mere being."[14] The verb Hegel uses here is a violent one, not fully reflected by its translation into "successful divestment [*es hat . . . sein Fursichsein aus sich hinausgerungen*]"; for it suggests something more final, such as an end to struggles because of death. Here we have an embracing of death by self-consciousness itself. We do not move to sovereignty as Derrida suggests we should, but to reason. However, the move to reason no less signifies a recognition of the insufficiency of mastery than does a move to the free play of laughter. It is because of this that I have suggested elsewhere that this movement is excellently represented by St. Augustine's surrender to the serendipitous command to take up and read, and the consequent salvation which had escaped him so long as he insisted on using his own will and desire to accomplish his unity with God.[15] The "economy" of mastery is here broken.

To be sure, this does not get us to Bataille's laughter, nor will any of the other radical moves that I discuss. But it does take us away from the paradigm of mastery that Derrida argues dominates Hegel's employment of the movement of *Aufhebung* in the *Phenomenology*. My argument is that if Hegel ends with the logic/metaphysics of the system, but does so *not* by means of a commitment to mastery, then his relation to Derrida/Bataille's sovereignty (granting it legitimacy for the moment) must be rethought and will in all probability turn out to be something quite different than Derrida has suggested.

There is a second significant break with the usual "smooth forms" of *Aufheben*. At the end of Hegel's discussion of reason as simple observation, the last moment of which is the notorious phrenology discussion, the move that is made is characterized as a "reversal" (*eine Umkehrung*). The reversal of reason becomes necessary precisely because the project of finding reason as ground in the simple observation of what-is has been shipwrecked in the very attempt. The project literally comes to a point of laughter, where the old-wives' sayings about hanging the wash causing rain, and observations about the unity of the organ of generation and the organ of urination, become the focus of our attention.

Again, it is true that the reversal is made in order to preserve meaning. It is even true here that the threat to meaning may be taking the form of something close to that "domain" of free laughter where nonmeaning confronts meaning. Here we actually do retreat in the face of the absolutely ridiculous. But it is also true that this retreat toward meaning is not on the grounds of mastery as in the master-slave relation; the search for reason here is not the search for a ground in self-consciousness, but rather for a ground in the transcendent. Nor is this reversal a surrender. In fact there is a very nice irony here. On the one hand, the transcendent ground of reason to which we have surrendered has brought us back to our own skulls, genitals, and simple household tasks such as washing and cooking; on the other hand, the outcome of the reversal is that at this very point we turn away from the transcendent and toward ourselves as actors and shapers of the world.

Could this irony support a Derridean point, namely that in turning to the actualization of self-consciousness we have returned to master-slave? I think not; for we are still under the presupposition that reason, not self-consciousness, is the possible ground of certainty; and thus we still *reject* the reciprocity of the independence and dependence of self-consciousness as the possible ground of certainty. Is this nevertheless only a thinly disguised version of master-slave, or a refinement of sorts? Again, I think not; for what this actually leads us to is spirit, *Geist*, which has lost all the abstraction of self-consciousness, mastery, and slavery, and gives us actual forms of world-history in which individuals with their self-consciousness are neither masters nor in bondage, but rather co-originators with a transcendent that at the same time governs them. Here we have, then, neither mastery nor laughter, but a living, embodied self-constitution through history, a unity of diachrony and synchrony which involves neither surrender to pure meaning nor the noble defiance of Bataille's laughter.

There are at least two more forms of renegade transition. The first is the reconciliation of opposing conscientious actors, which gets us beyond objective spirit and into the transcendent orientation of religion—a move that takes us to *a form of self-awareness radically opposed to self-consciousness as mastery*. The second is the culminating move to absolute knowing, which is made on the ground of a collapse of representational knowledge, and which in turn brings us to the unconcealment of that which has been hidden, something Hegel characterizes as an unconcealment of disclosure as disclosure. I have not the time to discuss this last movement in detail, but I wish to point out what is relevant here for our present discussion of Derrida.[16]

Hegel resorts, at the moment of entry into the domain of the system of philosophical sciences, to an *Hinausgehen* which is undertaken under *compulsion* [*ein Drängen*].[17] There is given up here all semblance of a movement which could be characterized as an *Aufheben*; for the movement of an *Hinausgehen*, taken up not rationally but under compulsion, leaves us with a confrontation with a ground which Hegel will characterize in the *Science of Logic* as one which can emerge only when the interests that move individuals and nations are hushed. That is to say, the point at which we arrive at the end of the *Phenomenology* is indeed one of a grounding of meaning on the basis of a commitment to meaning; but it is *not* one in which that meaning can be characterized as Derrida characterizes it, namely as built on a commitment to mastery and a denial of sovereignty. The economic, political, and military metaphors are here out of place. Rather, what we have are figures of shelter, of being-at-home. Hegel's view of the domain of the logic/metaphysics is one which is closer to Heidegger's view of language as the temple of being, as dwelling (e.g., as discussed in "Building, Dwelling, and Thinking"), than to Kojève's view of a battlefield in history, a monarchy of categories. And this is so because the route taken in the course of the *Phenomenology* has been governed at crucial junctures by breaks: a *surrender* of self-consciousness to a spectatorial reason, leading to the need for a *reversal* to active participation of the individual in the rational, leading to the need for a *mutual recognition* of others united in a religious community (the first homecoming), and finally leading to a *leaving-behind* of the transcendent caused not by reason or desire, but by a *compulsion* to dwell in the unity of being and time.

The mastery-theme upon which Derrida focuses has therefore been transcended. To be sure, there is not a sudden, meaning-shattering move to laughter; rather there is a patient, continued search for a ground, an origin of meaning in a unified logic/metaphysics. Does the fact that we end up nevertheless in a discursive self-grounding signify that Bataille and Derrida indeed have the last laugh? I think not; for although there may be a play "beneath" the serious business of this logic/metaphysics, a play which Hegel does not attend to in itself, it is not one necessarily imprisoned in the mad laughter of Bataille and Artaud and in the anarchy of interpretation which is at least suggested by Derrida. As I have argued in *Hegel's Quest for Certainty* and elsewhere, there *is* a relativity of intelligibility frameworks that is not grounded in any ultimate framework of meaning and this relativity *could* be understood as a manifestation of the play of play. But the route to the discovery of this "domain" of play is through a constructive dialogue with Hegel, not through a deconstruction based upon the assumption that Hegel cannot see beyond mastery. His moves away from self-consciousness as the foundation for meaning are evidence of his vision of something beyond mastery. And the breaks marked by surrender, reversal, reconciliation, and the iconoclastic rejection of the comfort of religion and the Holy Spirit are indications of the risk-taking involved in turning one's back on mastery.

So Hegel *can perhaps* be criticized for not considering the play of play itself which is pointed to by Derrida, but he *cannot* be criticized for denying the presence of the domain or for remaining with the seriousness of mastery. The reason, in my view, that Hegel did not address play itself was that he was completing the task of that tradition which sought the ground of meaning as a fundamental or foundational meaning (metaphysics). But, standing at the birth of a new time, he also made possible the view of what might be beyond such a unitary foundational meaning, as Bataille's and Derrida's reflections show. Hegel's arrival at the home constituting his system, breaking with the subject-object division of modernity, opens up the question of the real ground, the real foundation, on which this home is built. In coming to know God, one comes to know God's domain, to be familiar. Once one feels at home, one begins to explore the domain and finds, perhaps, that there is yet another horizon which makes possible the meaning-structure of our existence. However, familiarity here breeds not contempt, but a daring curiosity.

NOTES

1. Both essays are found reprinted in Derrida, *L'écriture et la différence* (Paris: Éditions du Seuil, 1967), hereafter cited as *ED*. The English translation used in the present essay is to be found in Derrida, *Writing and Difference*, trans. by Alan Bass (Chicago: The University of Chicago Press, 1978), hereafter cited as *WD*. I don't pretend here to be able to take account of anything else that Derrida may have said about Hegel in other places. I am interested in this particular "critique" or deconstruction of Hegel because it represents a subtle and profound version of one of the traditional critiques, namely that Hegel submerged all particularity or existing individuality in a logic/metaphysics.

2. *ED*, pp. 84–85; *WD*, pp. 125–26. The passage in full is the following. Husserl "seeks to recognize the other as Other only in its form as ego, in its form of alterity, which cannot be that of things in the world. If the other were not recognized as a transcendental alter *ego*, it would be entirely in the world and not, as ego, the origin of the world. . . . If the other was not recognized as ego, its entire alterity would collapse. . . . The other as alter ego signifies the other as other, irreducible to *my* ego, precisely because it is an ego, because it has the form of the ego. The egoity of the other permits him to say 'ego' as I do; and this is why he is Other, and not a stone, or a being without speech *in my real economy*. . . . Dissymmetry itself would be impossible without this symmetry, which is not of the world, and which, having no real aspect, imposes no limit upon alterity and dissymmetry— makes them possible, on the contrary. This dissymmetry is an *economy* in a new sense; a sense which would probably be intolerable to Levinas."

3. *ED*, p. 185; *WD*, p. 126.

4. *ED*, p. 383; *WD*, p. 261.

5. *ED*, p. 374–75; *WD*, p. 254–55. The passage is the following. "It cannot even be said that this difference [between sovereignty and mastery] has a sense: it is the *difference of sense*, the *unique* interval which separates meaning from a certain non-meaning. Lordship has a meaning. The putting at stake

of life is a moment in the constitution of meaning, in the presentation of essence and truth. It is an obligatory stage in the history of self-consciousness and phenomenality, that is to say, in the presentation of meaning. For history—that is, meaning—to form a continuous chain, to be woven, the master must *experience his truth*. This is possible only under two conditions which cannot be separated: the master must stay alive in order to enjoy what he has won by risking his life; and, at the end of this progression . . ., the 'truth of the independent consciousness [must become] the consciousness of the bondsman' . . . [W]hen servility becomes lordship, it keeps within it the trace of its repressed origin, 'being a consciousness within itself, it will enter into itself, and change round into real and true independence'. It is this dissymmetry, this absolute privilege given to the slave, that Bataille did not cease to meditate. The truth of the master is in the slave; and the slave become a master remains a 'repressed' slave."

6. Even allowing for differences in interpretation—and I cannot accept the Kojèvean interpretation on which Derrida relies here—this is a point well-made.

7. *ED*, p. 376; *WD*, pp. 255–56.

8. *ED*, pp. 377–78; *WD*, pp. 256–57.

9. *ED*, p. 378; *WD*, p. 257

10. *ED*, p. 380; *WD*, p. 259.

11. *ED*, p. 399; *WD*, p. 271. "Since it relates the successive figures of phenomenality to a knowledge of meaning that always already has been anticipated, the phenomenology of the mind (and phenomenology in general) corresponds to a restricted economy: restricted to commercial values, one might say, picking up on the terms of the definition, a 'science dealing with the utilization of wealth,' limited to the meaning and the established value of objects, and to their *circulation*."

12. Not only here, but elsewhere, throughout the system. See for example his remark in *Reason in History*. "To him who looks at the world rationally the world looks rationally back." (*Werke*, 12 [*Vorlesungen über die Philosophie der Geschichte*] (Frankfurt am Main: Suhrkamp Verlag, 1970), p. 23; *Reason in History*, trans. Robert S. Hartman (Indianapolis, New York: Bobbs-Merrill Company, 1953), p. 13.) The remark is to be found near the beginning of the section titled "Reason as the Basis of History."

13. Hegel, *Phänomenologie des Geistes* (Hamburg: Felix Meiner Verlag, 1952), pp. 170–71. Translated as *Hegel's Phenomenology of Spirit*, by A.V. Miller (London: George Allen & Unwin, Ltd., and New York: Humanities Press, 1969), p. 138. The German and English will be referred to hereafter, respectively, as *PhG* and *PhS*.

14. *PhG*, p. 175; *PhS*, p. 139.

15. See my *Hegel's Quest for Certainty* (Albany: State University of New York Press, 1984), p. 111.

16. See *Ibid.*, p. 242–48 and appended notes.

17. *PhG*, p. 535; *PhS*, p. 466.

Commentary on Joseph Flay's
"Hegel, Derrida, and Bataille's Laughter"
Judith Butler

Professor Flay's paper elucidates the alleged difference between Hegel's notion of *Aufhebung* and Bataille's laughter, a difference that both Derrida and Bataille understand to be quite fundamental, indeed, a difference that one might in Hegelian terms understand as purely external, resistant to any kind of synthetic appropriation. Indeed, the difference that is outlined is one between a philosophical procedure, that of the *Aufhebung*, which is said to be purely appropriative, and that of *laughter* which is described as "an expenditure without reserve." The restricted economy is clearly Hegel's, for as Derrida says, it "restricts itself to conservation, to circulation and self-production as the reproduction of meaning"; it is also the economy of the "same" whereby all ostensibly external relations are recapitulated as internal relations, assimilated or appropriated into a single totality. In opposition to this single totality is a philosophical or, perhaps, anti-philosophical procedure designated by "laughter" and which signifies that aspect of life that resists or exceeds any effort at totalization; it is excess itself, that which cannot be conceptually captured or contained.

Professor Flay's paper strikes me as offering an extremely significant response to some of Hegel's contemporary French critics. Flay outlines the kinds of transitions operative in the *Phenomenology* that are not adequately understood in terms of *Aufhebung*, and I think he is right that there are breaks and ruptures and different kinds of reversals in the *Phenomenology* that cannot be rightly accounted for as forms of *Aufhebung*. If Professor Flay is right, then Hegel may well be promoting a restricted and appropriative philosophical procedure when employing the *Aufhebung*, but he is doing something else—in fact something closer to Derrida and Bataille—when his text admits of ruptures and reversals of another order indeed. Indeed, to extend the point made in Professor Flay's *Hegel's Quest for Certainty*, it appears that inasmuch as Hegel entertains a number of different frameworks of intelligibility, he offers a play of textual strategies that look very much like Derrida's own notion of a play of play, a fluid interchangeability of frameworks which resist reduction to a single model of philosophical truth. And though Professor Flay may well be right to point out these various textual strategies that differ from the more serious *Aufhebung*, I wonder whether *Aufhebung* itself is as self-serious, totalizing, and appropriative as Bataille, Derrida and, indeed, Flay suggest. Indeed, I would suggest that *Aufhebung* is actually more comic than its critics tend to realize, and that its sense of humour is generally underrated. Moreover, I would like to suggest further that once one has understood this peculiarly Hegelian sense of humour, one can see that *Aufhebung* is not a purely appropriative structure and, moreover, cannot be easily equated with a project of totalization.

Consider that those transitions in the *Phenomenology* that are effected by an *Aufhebung* exemplify an ironic reversal of sorts. Like Cervantes' *Don Quixote*, Hegel's journeying subject, whether as consciousness, self-consciousness, spirit, or even reason, at every stage of its experience takes some configuration of reality to be absolute only to discover that what that defining configuration excludes returns to haunt and undermine that subject in its self-definition and in the basic metaphysical presumption into which that self-definition is integrated. At the end of each stage, there is a false arrival of the absolute, a resolution of the latest contradiction which postures as a false though convincing synthesis. As readers of his text, we undergo the drama of accepting false certainties and then being rudely and, indeed, comically confronted by that which they unwittingly exclude. It is this domain of inadvertent and undermining consequences that is the insistent source of comedy in the *Phenomenology*. Indeed, the narrative journey of Hegel's emerging subject in the *Phenomenology* is marked by a repeated and insistently premature proclamation that the absolute has been achieved. Like Cervantes' *Don Quixote*, a text that Hegel clearly admired, reversal propels the narrative, and though Cervantes' text plunges ever deeper into irreversible fantasies of the absolute, Hegel's text, driven by a similar comic blindness, portrays an infinitely resilient subject who not only recovers from every deception and reversal, but proves more capable and accommodating as a result. According to Derrida, this everexpansive and ever-accommodating activity is also *fantastic*, a trope of appropriation that not only lacks plausibility but seeks to possess and control conceptually that which ought simply to be affirmed as exterior and let go.

Let us consider more closely the meaning of expansion and accommodation as it is dramatized by the Hegelian *Aufhebung*. In particular, what kind of expansion does ironic reversal effect? Insofar as *Aufhebung* clearly implies the preservation of what is negated, it is appropriative as Derrida describes. But *Aufhebung* is not an independent agency, the personification of a logical and ontological term, as Derrida suggests, but a relation that mediates between substance and subject. Indeed, concretely, the subject, regardless of which stage in its development, revises its conception of the absolute to appropriate or render internal what has initially appeared as an external relation. In this process, however, the subject is forced to relinquish itself in a significant sense. It forfeits its prior self-definition and the boundaries that it falsely considered to be all-inclusive.

In an article on the ecstatic origins of Hegel's concept of alienation, Nathan Rotenstreich emphasized the structure of Hegelian self-consciousness as that which is insistently impelled outside itself.[1] He suggests that self-consciousness is continuously forfeiting itself and discovering its own fundamental exteriority, the necessity that it be other to itself. And although the self-consciousness that is forfeited and exteriorized is also "recovered," it is important to note that this recovery is not the same as what Derrida terms "appropriation." According to Derrida, what is external is assimilated back into a self-identical subject, but for Hegel, the act of assimilation is simultaneous with a radical revision of the subject itself. Indeed, the former self-definition must be forfeited to accommodate this externality, so that, strictly speaking, *Aufhebung* designates both appropriation and expenditure at once.

The Derridean response, of course, is to argue that expenditure is always subordinate to appropriation and therefore exemplary of an economy of the Same. But what Derrida fails to realize or, perhaps, refuses to acknowledge is that the totality that Hegel describes at the close of the *Phenomenology* is not a static totality; indeed, the final word of the *Phenomenology* is "infinity" and not totality. Interestingly, Derrida brings in Levinas to counterpose a notion of infinity to Hegel's notion of totality, although Derrida nowhere considers Hegel's own procedure for reconciling those terms. And though the question of their relation cannot be adequately answered in this context, it is ironic that Derrida's teacher, Hyppolite, was the one who most strongly argued that the Concept was the thought of the infinite.[2] Almost as if Hyppolite had never made his argument, Derrida promotes a view of Hegel, now prevalent in France, that his system represents a static, closed, and "conservative" economy—"conservative" in many senses, but most prominently in the sense of "all-consuming."

Although Hyppolite also cautioned against a reading of Hegel that centered exclusively on the *Phenomenology*, Derrida appears to ignore that warning and to center on a given reading of the master-slave section as indicative of Hegel's entire metaphysics. Since Derrida knows there is another Hegel, as it were, why does he focus on the notion of mastery which becomes quite pivotal in Derrida's distinction between mastery, designating an economy of ever-circulating resources, and sovereignty, designating a metaphysics of unlimited funds. My suggestion is that this is a tactical misreading on his part which facilitates the comparison of the Nietzschean notion of mastery, embodied in the will to power, with Hegel's master. Implicitly, Derrida seems to be suggesting that what Nietzsche offers as the opposite of slave morality is superior in some sense to what Hegel offers as the opposite of the slave of the *Phenomenology*. Of course, in Hegel, it is the slave whose triumphs over and assimilates the master, but Derrida wilfully resists Hegel's text in this regard in order to justify his own point, namely, that the dissociated, abstract, and repressive figure of the master is characteristic of the entire project of Hegel's economy, and that *Aufhebung* generally is a mode of domination and appropriation. In particular, it seems, the *negation* included in *Aufhebung* is interpreted by Derrida as a prohibition or a repression of that which threatens to exceed dialectics and to reveal its status as less than absolute. Indeed, *Aufhebung* itself is a strategy of concealment and repression that silences an entire domain of life through an appropriative strategy.

This repressed domain of life is characterized by non-dialectical differences which, in Nietzschean fashion, ought to be simply affirmed and set free, as it were, from their dialectical trappings. In his book *Nietzsche and Philosophy*, Gilles Deleuze maintains that dialectics is always symptomatic of slave morality because it refuses that excess of will that designates the truly creative capacity of human beings. Although this is not exactly Derrida's view, he nevertheless promotes a kind of expenditure that he understands to be inimical to dialectics itself. For Bataille, this expenditure represents the unleashing of the negative from dialectics, a loss that cannot be recuperated, a sacrifice that disperses itself into an unrecoverable multiplicity. This is the dissipation of *laughter*, but it seems we must ask what happens after this laughter is over, or is it the case that this laughter is eternal, the sound of the play of the signifier as it chortles its way through all signification *ad infinitum*? Is it the arbitrary ground of signification that periodically sends its laugh up through the rupture of the signifier and signified and reminds us of the necessary limits of signification?

Derrida tells us this laughter is totally Other to dialectics; it is its "outside" and, hence, distinguished from dialectics, which assumes the self-grounding of all signification. But is there perhaps a different sort of relation between the groundless and the self-grounding that has not been explored? If dialectics suppresses laughter, could it be that laughter catches its breath, as it were, in a moment of necessary self-conservation? What kind of exhalation, indeed, *psyche*, is this that frees itself of temporal determinacy? I wonder whether the self-consciousness that seeks to risk its life at the outset of the master-slave dialectic does not represent the project of total and unrecoverable expenditure that Bataille seeks, and whether a phenomenological narrative would not reveal that self-sacrificial laughter as one subject to its own ironic reversal. Surely Bataille would want to retain the determinate life of his own body as that which grounds his laughter or even the determinate life of that fashioned text of his which communicates that laugh to his readership. And when that laugh becomes determinate, and *his* laugh, the laughing *text* that he provides, doesn't that ostensibly groundless laugh meet its own inevitable ground. He may laugh and laugh, but if he were engaging in a self-sacrifice that included the sacrifice of that determinate body and text, perhaps then the laugh would come to an abrupt end; indeed, perhaps he can only laugh while risking his life in a total expenditure because he has not yet learned the key Hegelian lesson about life, namely, that it requires continued and determinate form. Indeed, when Bataille's laughter is spent, and he finds that he himself remains, perhaps then it will be Hegel who, in a characteristic moment of ironic reversal, has the last laugh.[3]

NOTES

1. Nathan Rotenstreich, "On the Ecstatic Sources of the Concept of Alienation," *Review of Metaphysics*, March 1963.

2. Jean Hyppolite, *Genesis and Structure of Hegel's Phenomenology of Spirit*, trans. Samuel Cherniak and John Heckman (Evanston: Northwestern University Press, 1974), pp. 147, 166–67.

3. For a further consideration of Hegel's "Comic" procedure in the *Phenomenology*, see the introduction to Jacob Loewenberg, *Hegel: Selections* (New York: Charles Scribner's Sons, 1957).

Chapter Nine

AN HEGELIAN CRITIQUE OF REFLECTION

David S. Stern

Although it has gone largely unnoticed in philosophical circles in this country, one of the most remarkable developments in contemporary German philosophy has been the effort to effect a rapprochement with that mode of philosophizing known as "analytic," which has enjoyed ascendancy in the English speaking world since Russell and Moore drove the baneful influence of German Idealism underground. In Germany, Hegel and the other post-Kantians have found a more hospitable reception, though even there Hegel was considered a "dead dog" from the middle of the 19th century until Dilthey's studies rehabilitated him in the early years of this century. Now, however, one of the most influential German exponents of analytic methodology, Ernst Tugendhat, has enlisted the aid of analytic philosophy in an effort to displace Hegel from the place of honor to which, in Germany at least, he has laid claim.[1]

Sketched in broad strokes, Tugendhat's indictment of Hegel seems to amount to nothing more than a recrudescence of the charges, first leveled by Rudolf Haym in his book *Hegel und seine Zeit* of 1857, that contributed not a little to making Hegel seem a "dead dog." Tugendhat explicitly calls the closing chapters of *Selbstbewusstsein und Selbstbestimmung* a "last dance with Hegel," and admits that his polemic is motivated by moral outrage due to the "perversion" represented by Hegel's "denigration of the idea of responsibility" and his negation of the notion of practical truth.[2]

Because such charges have elicited from both critics and defenders of Hegel subtle interpretations of the ethical and socio-political issues involved, I do not wish to discuss these topics in the present essay. Moreover, to engage Tugendhat at this level would be to fail to appreciate the true force of his criticism of Hegel. What must ultimately command the attention of anyone seriously interested in testing the strength of Hegel's philosophy are not the socio-political theses, but rather the theoretical principles that underlie them. The significance of Tugendhat's challenge shows itself in just this light.

What is novel in Tugendhat's critique is the attention he focuses on Hegel's conception of self-consciousness. He contends that Hegel's quietist affirmation of the moral and political *status quo*, and the concomitant conversion of freedom into abject subjection to existing authority, are rooted in his theory of self-consciousness. Thus, unlike most who levy these sorts of charges, Tugendhat acknowledges Hegel's constant insistence that the ground of his political theory must be sought at a different level, and undertakes to criticize the theoretical structures he (rightly, I believe) holds to be the underpinning of Hegel's practical philosophy. It is for this reason that, despite its polemical excesses, Tugendhat's critique deserves to be taken seriously.

According to Tugendhat, Hegel uncritically assumes the subject-object model of self-consciousness in the form that Fichte had given it, and then proceeds to define both truth and freedom in terms of identity of subject and object. In what follows, I do not propose to undertake a point by point discussion and evaluation of Tugendhat's interpretation of Hegel, let alone of the alternative conception of self-consciousness that he draws from Wittgenstein, G.H. Mead, and Heidegger. Instead, I shall pursue the issues only indirectly, via an interpretation of Hegel's theory of self-consciousness, which should demonstrate that (1) Hegel provides arguments against the uncritical assumption that self-consciousness should be interpreted on the model of consciousness, a procedure Tugendhat himself adopts. Since Hegel thinks consciousness exemplifies the subject-object relation, it follows that (2) he should be explicitly concerned to reject this model as appropriate to self-consciousness. If these two points can be established, then the basis for Tugendhat's global critique will have been destroyed; more importantly, the way will be opened for an understanding of Hegel's own theory.[3]

Hegel announces at the beginning of the second section of the *Phenomenology of Spirit*[4] that with self-consciousness we "enter the native realm of truth" (9:103,28–29/104) in which "certainty is identical with its truth" (9:103,13/104). The conception of self-consciousness as an introspective, inner perception that affords an immediate certainty of oneself in thought is, of course, the fundamental principle of Descartes, and by extension, of much of modern (post-Cartesian) philosophy, and there are many who have read Hegel himself as little more than a bearer of the Cartesian inheritance. Although it is undeniable that Hegel stands in the tradition of theories of subjectivity

inaugurated by Descartes, attention to the notion of truth as it functions in the *PhG* reveals that Hegel not only is not concerned with
the indubitability of my thought of myself, but that he denigrates the
direct and immediate self-awareness as empty and sterile.

The preceding section on "consciousness" demonstrates that a
non-reflexive epistemological stance that treats its object as a given
to which knowledge must conform, and that holds the subject's
contribution to be inessential, a mere reception of what is given,
cannot be consistently maintained. The efforts to uphold such a non-
reflexive, objectivistic orientation described in the opening chapters
of the *PhG* all exhibit one fatal difficulty: they are unable to defend
the truth of the knowledge they claim without recurring to explanatory principles that ought to be unavailable if strict consistency is to
be maintained.[5] For example, the initial, most immediate form of
consciousness, sense-certainty, believes that it has a direct and immediate grasp of its object, which it takes to be a sensed-particular,
or a "this." But in its effort to say what it knows, and thereby to
establish the truth of its knowledge, sense-certainty discovers that it
subverts the very objects it claims to know: to know a "this" *as* a
"this" requires that the particular be known as a general type, as a
universal or a "this-such." More specifically, it is a thing with properties. But this is no longer the object that sense-certainty initially
claimed to know, nor is the mode of knowledge appropriate to that
new object an immediate sensory awareness. Rather, the new mode
of knowledge, or "shape of consciousness," is perception.

As a mode of intentional consciousness *in sensu stricto*, perception
also takes the objective thing to be an independent and self-subsistent entity, distinct from the ways in which it is perceived. But, as
Descartes endeavors to point out in his famous discussion of the
lump of wax in the *Meditations*, at the level of perception itself there
is a "contradiction" between what the object is supposed to be—a
particular perduring thing—and the many properties we perceive,
but which, as Descartes' example shows, cannot themselves account
for the required unity.[6] Thus, in order to know its object as what it is
said to be, perceptual consciousness must also transcend itself; the
superior resources of conceptual understanding must be called into
play in order to account for the sort of unity that the standard of
perception requires.

This process is what Hegel calls the experience of consciousness.
At each stage it learns, first, that the object it originally took to be
independent of knowledge is in fact only for consciousness insofar
as it is known, and secondly, that what it knows in knowing its
standard is a different kind of object than that which the standard
defines as the truth of a given mode of knowledge. Thus when

sense-certainty knows its standard, what is known is not a sensed-particular but a universal. This means, with regard to experience in general, that the justification at any stage in the dialectic of the necessity of the move to a higher stage rests on what consciousness itself experiences, namely, that it cannot account for what it knows. It is driven by internal necessity to recur to a higher level just in order to avoid a *reductio*. What drives it on is the discrepancy between knowledge and truth or subjective certainty and objective standards of truth. So long as these remain separated, consciousness will be unable to explain how what it knows can be known to be true. For knowing something *as* true under these conditions always subverts the first-order knowledge claim.

The first main stage of the process culminates in the section on the "inverted world." Here consciousness itself discovers that it is compelled to recur to increasingly higher order principles just in order to be able to account for what it claims to know at a lower level. Yet this process does not continue *ad infinitum*: the very defining principle of the irreflexive natural consciousness—its assumption that its object is in a strict sense independent, so that knowledge consists in conforming to that object—must be sacrificed. This is clearly a self-sacrifice, for the paradigm that consciousness seeks to establish, and which defines the ordinary self-understanding of the natural attitude, cannot be upheld. Consciousness thus begins to comprehend the error of its misplaced objectivism and in so doing begins the process of understanding itself, of becoming self-conscious.

What emerges is thus not yet another independent object that serves as the standard of knowledge, for the dialectic of consciousness discloses that the domain of truth is not the "objective" world opposed to consciousness. This too has superficial similarities with the Cartesian thesis that the whole realm of external reality and our purported knowledge of it are subject to doubt, but the lesson of the dialectic is in fact quite different: the discovery that truth does not lie in the objective world, has nothing to do with the dubitability of the existence of that world, but rather concerns that basic insight that the truth of the knowledge of the objective world cannot be known by appeal to that world. It is for this reason that Hegel calls self-consciousness the "truth" of consciousness: the truth of the claims made by object-level consciousness can only be defended, so Hegel thinks he has shown, by appeal to self-consciousness, or in terms of the subject's contribution to knowledge.

The thesis that self-consciousness is the truth of consciousness is not to be found in Descartes, but instead is Hegel's way of describing the advance Kant made on the Cartesian position. For Descartes the immediate self-certainty of the *cogito* remains wholly subjective despite its indubitability; even though he asserts that the procedure of methodological doubt allows him to discover a ground and basis for knowledge, Descartes must introduce God as a sort of epistemological guarantor in order to assure the possibility of knowledge of the external world. Thus he is unable to demonstrate that the self-certainty revealed in the *cogito* is a basis for further knowledge. It was Kant who saw that the need for God in this context can be eliminated by radicalizing the subjective turn inaugurated by Descartes: for Kant, objectivity itself is constituted by subjective a priori principles, the pure concepts of the understanding, which thus are ontological principles. In effect, Kant takes Descartes' fundamental insight that every thought is a thought of myself (*cogito me cogitare*) to its logical conclusion by arguing that the rules of thought are at the same time the principles of objectivity, so that Descartes' skeptical restriction of his insight, according to which I think only myself, is overcome.[7] The lesson of the dialectic of consciousness, that consciousness must become self-conscious, is not the discovery of an absolute certainty of self, but rather the revelation of the necessity of the transcendental turn. Thus the opening section of Hegel's *PhG* is intended as an alternative to Kant's effort to "deduce" the necessity of the move to self-consciousness. The key to Hegel's phenomenological approach—designed to obviate the need for a further justification of the transcendental turn at a higher level, and thus to avoid the regress to which Kantian transcendental theory is subject—is the experience that consciousness has of itself, by which it discovers that it must become self-conscious if it is to be able to explain what it claims to know. Intentional consciousness cannot itself account for or explain intentionality so that the ground of intentionality must be sought not in intentionality itself, but in self-consciousness. Yet this only serves to emphasize the significance of our question: how is self-consciousness to be understood?

* * *

Kant first pointed to a problem confronting the theory of self-consciousness, namely that it is burdened with a circularity it apparently cannot overcome, and he stated in concise fashion the nature of the difficulty: "Now it is indeed very evident that I cannot know as an object that which I must presuppose in order to know any object,"[8] so that we "can only revolve in a perpetual circle, since any judgment about [the subject] must have always already made use of the representation of it."[9] Although Kant recognized this as an "inconvenience" and as a limit on our knowledge, he thought it a virtue of his theory to be able to explain the reason for the unavoidability of the circle. His account involves the thesis that the self-identical ego is the subject of knowledge insofar as it is the ground of the use of the categories; since all knowledge must invoke the categories, it is impossible for the transcendental subject to be known. The result is that Kant holds that self-consciousness, which the transcendental inquiry reveals to be necessary, can only be presupposed, so that the transcendental subject=X.

This position is sharply criticized by Hegel in a way that anticipates one of the leading themes of modern phenomenology. At issue is the tendency to construe the subject in terms of the ontology of things. It might seem odd to suggest that Kant is guilty of this "category mistake," given that his arguments against rational psychology in the Paralogisms are designed to undercut the very objectification of the subject which yields the illegitimate notion of a soul-substance. Nonetheless Hegel rejects Kant's reasoning in this matter, on the grounds that the contention that the subject is unknowable because there is no category with which to think the subject as subject rests on the unfounded assumption that there are only categories of objects.[10] In the vivid language that Hegel employs in the section on observing reason, "the intention is not to state that Spirit . . . is a thing; no materialism, as it is called, is intended. . . . But that Spirit *is* means nothing other than that it is a thing. When *being* as such or thinghood is predicated of Spirit, the true expression of this is that Spirit is the same sort . . ." of being as a thing (9:190, 18–24 / 208). With this Hegel seeks to indicate the ultimate consequence of a theoretical position that confines itself to the categories of objectivity, so that either no place is left for subjectivity, or the subject is reduced to one object among others.

In this regard Hegel's criticism is very much like that of Heidegger, who also rejects Kant's effort to explain "that and why . . . the mode of being of the I cannot be explicated."[11] For "the impossibility of an ontological interpretation of the I does not follow from the inappropriateness of the categories of nature. It follows only under the assumption that for the knowledge of the I, the only possible mode of knowledge is that which is valid for the knowledge of nature."[12] However, the ultimate force of these objections depends on Hegel's (or Heidegger's) ability to provide the alternate, non-objectifying categorical account of the subject which is demanded, and it is to this that Hegel devotes considerable effort. Most significant is his argument in the *Science of Logic* that what Hegel calls the "objective logic," which he explicitly associates with Kant's transcendental logic, and thus with the categorical ontology of *ens* or objects,[13] must be supplemented by a "subjective logic" in which the required categorical account of the subject is provided. But this is an exceedingly complex matter, and cannot be taken up in the context of this brief essay.

* * *

This would seem to leave us in the lurch: either Hegel's alternative must be both understood and assessed, or his objections, important though they may be, lose their apparent force. Fortunately, closer attention to Hegel's position provides a way to avoid this dilemma. The real target of his criticism is not so much the ontology of things as the prior mistake that leads Descartes, Kant and others to construe self-consciousness in such a way that the categorical and ontological problem arises: the adoption of the model of reflection.

Thus far the issue of self-consciousness has been described wholly within the context of Hegel's relation to Kant. This historical approach could of course be further elaborated, and the contributions of Reinhold, Schelling and especially Fichte could be usefully analyzed and assessed. But this might suggest that the problematic is historically specific. In order to counter this impression it is important to recognize that the aporia to which Kant drew attention is not confined to the Kantian systematic, despite the fact that he situates the problem of self-consciousness within the elaborate argumentation of his theory of apperception.

Even in Kant's appeal to his theory of apperception as the ground of the categories, we can see that self-consciousness is conceived of as reflection. That is to say, it is construed as the turning away from the objects of consciousness so as to make itself its own object. As Dieter Henrich and others have recently shown, the circularity to which Kant first pointed is a direct consequence of the adoption of the model of reflection, regardless of the larger philosophical context in which this model is employed.[14] The objective of the theory of reflection is to explain self-consciousness, and its most fundamental thesis is that self-consciousness arises as a result of reflection (or, as it is frequently put, of a reflective act). Only when the identity of subject and object, of knower and known, is established is there self-consciousness, and such can only be established insofar as I turn away from objects of thought which are other than I am, and make myself the object of my thought.

As Descartes had already recognized, there are considerable difficulties involved in specifying what it is I know when I know myself, but for the moment these need not concern us. For now we are only interested in the claim that the theory of reflection, and not the phenomenon itself, is circular, and as such cannot provide an account of the phenomenon—self-consciousness—it is designed to explain.

The apparent explanatory power of the theory of reflection depends on a fundamental ambiguity with regard to the subject. It is unclear whether the subject, which is supposed to come to self-consciousness via reflection, has knowledge of itself prior to reflection. If so, then the theory clearly presupposes what it is supposed to explain; if not, then reflection cannot explain how the ego knows that it is identical with its object; the self-objectification that the act of reflection brings about must presuppose that the subject already has knowledge of itself such that the identity, I=I, is recognized.[15]

In the first part of his book, Tugendhat draws out the consequences of these analyses of the theory of reflection. The virtue of Tugendhat's presentation of the theory of reflection is his demonstration that the aporia of reflection is a result of the employment of the subject-object model. The paradoxical circularity of the theory of reflection amounts to a *reductio ad absurdum* of the traditional theory, and forces us to examine the very presupposition that underlies the theory of reflection: the subject-object model.

Tugendhat has little difficulty in establishing that this is indeed the presupposition of the theory. As we have seen, reflection is postulated as the explanation of self-consciousness, and this latter is understood to be the unique situation—distinguished from ordinary, intentional consciousness—in which consciousness has itself as its object, such that the knower and the known, *noesis* and *noema*, or, in general, subject and object, are identical,[16] and which thus finds expression in the equation I=I.[17]

It is significant for our further analysis of self-consciousness in Hegel that Tugendhat proceeds in exactly the same fashion as those who employ the subject-object model. He argues that we must eliminate the subject-model even in its original function as the model of the intentionality of consciousness, substituting instead the notion of a propositional attitude. However this may be evaluated, Tugendhat proceeds to argue that self-consciousness, as "consciousness of itself,"[18] must be assumed to have the same structure. That is, Tugendhat interprets self-consciousness on the model of consciousness, and concludes that it must take the form "I know that I am (in a certain state) p." This move has important consequences, but these cannot be treated here. We must confine ourselves to the two most important aspects of Tugendhat's approach: (1) he demonstrates that self-consciousness must not be construed on the model of subject-object; (2) he interprets self-consciousness on the model of consciousness, which now is taken to be essentially propositional. The importance of these two strategies should become apparent below.

We have already noted why Hegel describes the transcendental turn as the "inverted world." Simply put, the point is that to account for the truth of our knowledge always "inverts" what it is that we claim to know. To take an example closely related to the Kantian project, even if true knowledge has as its object an empirical or objective world existing independently of our knowledge of it, the truth of such knowledge cannot be known or established empirically. For Hegel self-consciousness is the truth of consciousness, and given what we know about the nature of such transitions from the level of the *explanandum* to that of the *explanans*, we can anticipate that Hegel must think it gravely mistaken to interpret self-consciousness in terms of consciousness. Moreover, we have also seen that the lesson of the dialectic of consciousness has been that the characteristic structure of consciousness assumed from the outset has been disqualified: the utter independence of the object of consciousness is seen to be untenable, so that consciousness can no longer stand on its own terms. Thus to suppose that self-consciousness ought to be interpreted in terms of consciousness is wholly to miss the lesson of the opening chapter.

In addition to these somewhat formal points, Hegel also provides an immanent analysis of the subject-object-reflection model of self-consciousness. When self-consciousness is interpreted as consciousness of self, then by contrast to consciousness and its relation to an other, in self-consciousness this other has disappeared (9:103,30–32 / 104–105). Insofar as self-consciousness is a mode of consciousness in which subject and object are identical, so that it "distinguishes only itself as itself from itself, the difference as an otherness is immediately cancelled. The difference is not, and [the purported self-consciousness] is only the motionless tautology of I=I" (9:104,10–13 / 105). Thus we see that if self-consciousness is modeled on consciousness, so that it has an object only by objectifying itself in reflection, then the defining characteristic of the model is lost, for the difference between consciousness and its object has collapsed into the mere identity I=I. This Hegel explicitly notes in § 424 of the *Encyclopedia*: "for self-consciousness, which is the object of itself, is not an object, since there is no difference between it and its object."[19] And in a lecture manuscript from 1825 we read that "what is lacking here is what there was too much of in consciousness, in which there was a preponderance of difference."[20] Thus Hegel says in § 424 that self-consciousness so conceived is "without reality," and says in the *PhG* even more forcefully, that "insofar as the difference does not have the form of being" the "motionless tautology I=I . . . is not self-consciousness" (9:104,13–14/105).

This is, I think, Hegel's most powerful argument against the ordinary conception of self-consciousness, for it shows that the Cartesian notion of a direct, inner perception on the one hand, and the Kantian thesis about the impossibility of self-knowledge on the other, are both the result of the transposition of the subject-object-reflection model from its proper place in intentional consciousness to the phenomenon of self-consciousness. Almost incomprehensibly, Tugendhat reads the passages we have elucidated as urging the very conception Hegel is at such pains to devalue. Moreover, Hegel's subtle analysis of this issue succeeds in showing what Tugendhat has altogether failed to appreciate: that the error to be avoided is not merely the employment of the subject-object model, but also the interpretation of self-consciousness as if it were a mode of consciousness (of self). Such an interpretation is self-defeating, for it eliminates the very structure of consciousness that is supposed to provide the model of self-consciousness.

The lesson to be drawn from this failure is also the definition of the task at hand: the development of a conception of self-consciousness able to reconstruct the very moment of consciousness which the theory of reflection eliminates, namely that of difference or objectivity.[21] Such a reconstruction of difference in self-consciousness is only possible so long as the model of consciousness, and with it the pure self-relation of I=I or consciousness of self, is rejected. Hegel's analysis permits us to formulate concisely the *desideratum* for any adequate theory of self-consciousness: the articulation of an alternative mode of self-relation able to integrate into itself the relation to otherness characteristic of consciousness. That such is one of the foci of Hegel's philosophical efforts is surely one of the most significant merits of his thought.

NOTES

1. Ernst Tugendhat, *Selbstbewusstsein und Selbstbestimmung* (Frankfurt am Main: Suhrkamp Verlag, 1979). Now available in English: *Self-Consciousness and Self-Determination*, trans. Paul Stern (Cambridge: MIT Press, 1986).

2. *Ibid.*, pp. 349; 351.

3. This does not mean, however, that all of his interpretation is thereby rendered invalid. For a discussion of some of the issues that cannot be treated here, see Ludwig Siep, "Kehraus mit Hegel? Zu Ernst Tugendhats Hegelkritik," *Zeitschrift für philosophische Forschung*, XXXV, Nos. 3/4 (1981), pp. 518–531.

4. Hereafter I shall use the abbreviation "*PhG*" to refer to Hegel's *Phenomenology of Spirit*. References to this work, provided in the text, will be given as follows. The first reference will be to the volume, page, and line number of Hegel, *Gesammelte Werke*, edited by the Rheinisch-Westfaelische Akademie der Wissenschaften (Hamburg: Meiner Verlag, 1968-). The second reference,

separated by a slash from the former, will be to *Hegel's Phenomenology of Spirit*, trans. by A.V. Miller (Oxford: Clarendon Press, 1977). All translations are, however, my own.

5. For a good, recent account of the opening chapters of the *PhG* in terms of the objectivistic intentionality of the "natural attitude," see Joseph C. Flay, *Hegel's Quest for Certainty* (Albany: State University of New York Press, 1984), Chapter III.

6. See Descartes, *The Philosophical Works of Descartes*, Vol. I, trans. by E.S. Haldane and G.R.T. Ross (Cambridge: Cambridge University Press, 1979), pp. 154–155.

7. One revealing way of articulating the differences between Kant and Hegel shows itself here. For Hegel, the skepticism implicit in realist epistemology is correctly diagnosed by Kant, and the transcendental turn, with its effort at a immanent justification of the objectivity of thought, is the appropriate way of meeting the challenge. But Hegel seeks to show that there is a remnant of the skepticism born of realist assumptions in Kant, as his retention of the notion of a thing in itself independent of our modes of conceiving it makes clear.

8. I. Kant, *Kritik der Reinen Vernunft*, ed. Raymund Schmidt (Hamburg: Felix Meiner Verlag, 1976), A402.

9. *Ibid.*, A346/B404. See also B422; A366.

10. Cf. B422, and the discussion of this passage in H.E. Allison, *Kant's Transcendental Idealism* (New Haven: Yale University Press, 1983), p. 292.

11. Cf. Martin Heidegger, *Grundprobleme der Phänomenologie*, in *Gesamtausgabe*, ed. by Friedrich-Wilhelm von Hermann, Vol. 24 (Frankfurt am Main: Vittorio Klostermann, 1975), p. 202.

12. *Ibid.*, p. 207.

13. Cf. *Wissenschaft der Logik*, I, ed. Georg Lasson (Hamburg: Felix Meiner Verlag, 1932), pp. 44–46.

14. Dieter Henrich, "Fichtes ursprüngliche Einsicht," in *Subjektivität und Metaphysik. Festschrift für Wolfgang Cramer*, ed. Dieter Henrich and Hans Wagner (Frankfurt am Main: Vittorio Klostermann, 1966), pp. 188–232.

15. Cf. D. Henrich, "Selbstbewusstsein," in *Hermeneutik und Dialektik I*, ed. by Rüdiger Bubner, *et al.* (Tübingen: J.C.B. Mohr, 1970), pp. 257–284. In this essay Henrich argues that the difficulty applies equally to a non-egological theory. Developing this point, Konrad Cramer has demonstrated that even Husserl's non-egological theory of consciousness in the *Logical Investigations*, which rejects the necessity of a relation to a subject in order to explain the intentionality of mental phenomena, nonetheless falls victim to this circle insofar as it describes self-consciousness as inner perception, and thereby imports the relational model which yields the aporia. Cf. Konrad Cramer, "Erlebnis," *Hegel-Studien, Beiheft* 11 (1974), pp. 569ff.

16. Tugendhat, *Selbstbewusstsein und Selbstbestimmung*, p. 54.

17. Tugendhat also argues that an important peculiarity of this model of self-consciousness is the supposition that the identity which is said to obtain

between subject and object is also a relation of knowledge. This is nonsensical for Tugendhat, for he assumes from the outset that all knowledge is propositional; a sentence of the sort "I know me" is either nonsensical or elliptical because it is not propositional. Indeed, Tugendhat proposes that we eliminate the subject-object model even in its original function as the model of the intentionality of consciousness. This too should be understood as a propositional attitude. The consequence is that "by 'intentional consciousness' is meant relations which are distinguished from other relations in that they are relations of a spatio-temporal entity—a person—to a proposition or imply such a relation" (p. 20). Though it is usually Tugendhat's intention to furnish commonsense with arguments against the extravagances of philosophers, I fail to see how this suggestion about the structure of consciousness and intentionality preserves the original *explanandum*, the fact that our thoughts, dreams, desires, and so forth are thoughts, dreams, desires of something. Recognizing this, some contemporary theorists have distinguished between propositional attitudes on the one hand and intentionality on the other. The former remains a relation between a person and a proposition, while intentionality as such is distinct from attitudinal consciousness. In phenomenological terms this way of drawing the distinction would make the consciousness "that p" noetic, and thus not adequate to the explanation of the noematic content of an intention. Though this might serve to obviate the difficulty Tugendhat incurs, it cuts in a direction opposed to the one he urges on us, and would seem to reintroduce the relation of subject and object.

18. *Ibid.*, p. 21.

19. See the discerning analysis of § 424 by Konrad Cramer, "Bewusstsein und Selbstbewusstsein," *Hegel-Studien, Beiheft* 19 (1979), pp. 215–225. Cramer's thesis is that the reflection theory is self-defeating, for it "cannot preserve in self-consciousness the structure of consciousness" (p. 222).

20. Cf. *The Berlin Phenomenology*, ed. M.J. Petry (Boston: D. Riedel Publishing Co., 1981), p. 57.

21. Cf. Cramer, "Bewusstsein und Selbstbewusstsein," p. 223.

Chapter Ten

IS HEGEL'S *LOGIC* A LOGIC? ANALYTICAL CRITICISM OF HEGEL'S *LOGIC* IN RECENT GERMAN PHILOSOPHY

Walter Zimmerli

Whether Hegel's *Wissenschaft der Logik* of 1812/16 actually is a logic is a question that has preoccupied readers/critics ever since this mysterious book appeared. A number of critical arguments suggesting a negative answer to this exist since Trendelenburg's *Logische Untersuchungen* of 1840. We seem, however, to have lost sight of the fact that this question itself is not very clear indeed. When we speak of "Hegel's Logic," we could mean both his book (*Die Wissenschaft der Logik*), as well as its formal structure, or rather the formal structure of all his encyclopedic writings, and we must furthermore also determine what is meant by the second reference to "logic."

In professional philosophical language we define "logic" as either being the stock of syntactic connection-rules which standardizes what we call "correct inference," or the theoretical discussion of these rules. The respective semantics of the collection of syntactic rules no longer constitute a characteristic object of logic, at least if we do not refer to the syntax of the connection-rules themselves. The pragmatics of logical arguments do not (or perhaps we should express it historically: no longer) fall under the domain of logic. But at this point the timeless/timely scandalon of logic arises, namely, that it appears neither to require justification nor be able to be justified, for it thematizes all of the logical connection-rules which are presupposed for itself. In other words, the very core of formal philosophy, i.e., the canon of argumentation-rules, is stated, but seemingly without presupposing anything at all.

My thesis, which I wish to exemplify by drawing on some of the more recent views and their shortcomings expressed in current German Hegel criticism, is:

We can, by means of a pragmatic interpretation of Hegel's *Wissenschaft der Logik*, understand this work as a formal logic which, by dealing with the semantics of metaphysics justifies itself, and as a metaphysics which legitimizes itself as a result of the self-justification of formal logic itself.

I intend to expound this thesis as follows: first of all I shall analyze Dieter Henrich's views, which he has expressed in various articles in the seventies; secondly, I shall examine Michael Theunissen's theses, which have generated much discussion at the beginning of the eighties. The third part of this paper will contain an explication of my own views, which expound the dilemma of logical self-justification as seen from but independent of Hegel's logic problem.

I

Since 1973 Dieter Henrich has made several attempts to acquire an understanding of Hegel's most essential and basic logical operation, "Hegels Grundoperation" (Henrich, 1976), by means of an analytic reconstruction of language, and in particular of "Formen der Negation in Hegels Logik" (Henrich, 1975). He is obviously not simply concerned with reconstructing *Wissenschaft der Logik*, but rather with "Hegel's logic" in the sense of the structure of his argumentations.

In view of this Henrich's thesis reads as follows:

> In "Wissenschaft der Logik" Hegel does more than merely recapitulate and comment on a primary sequence of concepts, of which it can only maintain that it establishes itself intuitively and automatically. It deals even less with the basic concepts of cognition logically and arbitrarily or only according to the aesthetic principles of order. It contains a constructive basic idea which we are able to follow. The methodic key-formulae and the basic terms which this logic uses are derived from it. By virtue of this idea, it possesses a checkable, methodic arsenal. Both can be developed, even before the systematic analysis of basic concepts has begun . . . Hegel's basic operation emerges from his approach in dealing with negation (Henrich, 1976, 213).

On the other hand, Henrich, corresponding to the ontological status of Hegel's *Wissenschaft der Logik*, uses "negation" also as the expression for the thematized content:

> Hegel's real idea therefore also rests on a quite different consideration, in which the form of the negative statement is not disregarded: if it is the case that all Dasein can only be understood as the unity of reality and negation, and if we cannot extract the concept of this unity by considering the being from the very beginning as a theme

of a statement, that is of cognition, then we must grant it, i.e., the being in itself, as a principle of its constitution, the quality of *being* negation (Henrich, 1975, 247).

Henrich could have meant at least two different things by the combination of these two assertions (which can be found in two different essays, although Henrich himself explicitly says that they "belong together," Henrich, 1976, 230):

(1) In some sort of a quasi-transcendental argument the inference from the *operation* of thinking to a structure within the realm of the *contents* of thinking could be meant which renders the operation of thinking itself possible:

(a) Either in the applicative (Kantian) sense: If the basic operation of negation can be applied to all Dasein, then it must have, provided that all Dasein is determined by thinking, the structure of negation.

(b) Or in the genetic (Schellingian) sense: If the basic operation of negation can be applied to all Dasein, then it must, provided that forms of thinking are products of Dasein, itself be thought of as negation.

(2) However, when we regard the ontological meaning of Hegel's *Wissenschaft der Logik* already asserted, he could also mean: since Hegel's *Wissenschaft der Logik* deals with a theory which successively thematizes all conceptual determinations and thus has as its object one "ontological core" (Henrich, 1978) after the other, it must at some time or other thematize its own basic operations. In order to do this, however, it must be both the logical basic operation and Dasein.

It is not until we reconstruct Henrich's analysis of negation (which we shall now undertake), that we realize that he has in mind the second of the two meanings.

In the following five steps Henrich (Henrich, 1976, 214 ff.) reconstructs what he holds to be Hegel's basic operation:

1. Negation must, if it is to be Hegel's one independent operation, be freed from all relations in which it otherwise stands within the logic of propositions. Therefore, Henrich also speaks of "autonomized negation," in order to express that, if negation is thought like this, it will not be viewed as a negated proposition, that is not as the negation of something presupposed. But in order to still make sense in speaking of "negation," the rules according to which it is to be applied, must correspond to those of the logic of propositions: "(1) Negation negates something. (2) Negation can be applied to itself. (3) The self-referential usage of negation has a result" (*ibid.*, 214).

2. If negation is actually to be negation, then it must have a negating relation to something in accordance with the rules of negation stated. Since, however, nothing can be presupposed if negation is really to be autonomous, then negation must relate to nothing else but itself. This means that we must conceive negation as a double negation right from the very beginning. The stage of absolute negation reached by doing this is indeed different from the classical double negation. Whereas the classical double negation proves to be the application of a negation of the second stage, Hegel thinks of the double negation in a strictly self-referential way: "However, it follows from this that we cannot differentiate between both forms of negation by saying that they belong to two different stages. In fact we must say that we cannot differentiate between them at all. Negation, which is negated by negation, negates *itself*" (*ibid.*, 216).

3. But since the negation of negation has a result corresponding to the rules stated, and yet defines a negation as internal structure, and since that which it negates is negation, the state at which we arrive can only be described as the self-nullification of negation, as "no negation at all." Whereas the double negation in classical logic brings about the initial state again, which is negated by classical negation and is re-established by the doubling of it, a state arises in Hegel's operation of negation which is determined by the non-existence of every negative relation. Hegel calls this new state "pure immediacy," "an immediacy which involves neither negation nor mediation" (*ibid.*, 217).

4. Since a stage is now reached about which nothing more can be said, the basic operation appears to be completed. But this consideration is only feasible for an external approach, for we immediately see in an internal approach that, owing to the fact that it constitutes the counterpart of autonomous negation, functionally this state still has the meaning of being a result actually different from it. The state which emerges in this way, which shifts autonomous negation back into a relation, does so necessarily in only one direction: "Autonomous negation is only conceivable in relation to an opposite, but to an opposite that only follows and does not also precede it" (*ibid.*, 218). If it were also to precede it, we would then have to deal not with autonomous negation, but with negation within the logic of propositions.

5. The danger we are now faced with is that the opposite of autonomous negation reached in this way appears like something added externally which endangers the autonomy of negation. For it was this very supposition of self-reference that made it necessary to suppose an opposite of autonomous negation. The only possible way

Hegel sees to avoid the collapse of the idea of autonomous negation is, according to Henrich, to use the idea of self-reference self-referentially. That means, however, that the opposite of autonomous negation must at the same time be identical with it: "The opposite of the autonomous double negation must itself also be a double negation. The double negation can only be conceived as a self-reference if it is thought of twice" (*ibid.*, 219).

When Henrich adds here that everyone understands the speculative weight of this idea, he means both the vertical as well as the horizontal symmetry which this model contains. We could now believe that herewith a formally harmonious operator has been attained, which in Hegel's sense is "concrete," and has the function of a "key" that, when put in the keyhole correctly, reveals the secrets of Hegel's *Wissenschaft der Logik*. Henrich, however, explicitly opposes this: in his opinion *Wissenschaft der Logik* is not some form of code, referring to something different behind it. The logic has "no secrets which necessitate that the meaning of the printed text be deciphered in search of a hidden underlying meaning." It is therefore true that:

> Negated negation cannot be the key to the reconstruction of the entire logic. It does indeed rest on a formal operation and permits a purely formal development in several stages. At the same time, however, it leads to consequences which cannot be mastered by the concept of self-referential negation only. For this we require new unified concepts of negativity, which cannot be deduced deductively, even though the deductive development of the thought of negativity gives a direction as to what form they should take (Henrich, 1978, 319).

We then see, as we have presumed, that negation as Hegel's basic operation must belong to the thematizing structure, i.e., to the logic of *Wissenschaft der Logik*, but at the same time must be an element of the thematized structure, i.e., of *Wissenschaft der Logik*, as assumed in variant (2) above. On the other hand we see here that in Henrich's opinion, as a basic operation, negation is not the same basic operation that determines the course of the entire *Wissenschaft der Logik*. Additionally, as Henrich explains in his essay on "Hegel's Logik der Reflexion" (Henrich, 1978, 309 ff.), the consequences which are typical for Hegel's dialectics (*ibid.*, 312) are to be interpreted as meaning-variances of concepts, i.e., as "successor-concepts" as defined by Sellars and Feigl (*ibid.*, 312). According to Henrich, the claim of Hegelian logic therefore fails to develop from an autonomous basic operation by, as it were, questioning itself from a distance that is to be understood as the capability to master this theory autonomously.

II

Theunissen explicitly refers to Henrich's thesis when he states:

> We have no doubt that the logic of reflexion, in particular as the logic of the definitions of reflexion, contains a criticism of understanding. In accordance with more modern research it pursues predominantly the methodic goal of explicating the means already made use of by the logic of being (Henrich, 1963). It thematizes . . . the operative concepts of the logic of being (Theunissen, 1980, 27).

Nevertheless Theunissen's critical intention is not identical with that of Henrich, for the former is not concerned with the identification and criticism of Hegel's one basic operation:

> Even the question which has been discussed for a long time, namely whether and to what extent Hegel's retrospective generalizing reflection on methods really does justice to that which he has previously practised, must be left out of our deliberations (*ibid.*, 150).

Owing to the fact that on many occasions Theunissen asserts that he agrees with Henrich, we tend almost to overlook the decisive difference between them: Theunissen sticks to his previous thesis (Theunissen, 1970) that at least Hegel's doctrine of the absolute spirit must be read as a political theology. It is true, as Fulda and Horstmann rightly stress "that both books coincide as far as their orientation is concerned" (Fulda/Horstmann, 1980, 11). We then realize why Theunissen objects to Henrich:

> The point that Henrich (Henrich, 1976, 228) is disputing, that Hegel's theory of "autonomous negation" is the logical center of his system, emanates "from an absolute" which is associated with God's metaphysical doctrine. Ultimately we must even say, that this theory stands and falls with the metaphysical doctrine of God (Theunissen, 1980, 177).

But this is only one of the matters which Theunissen endeavors to weld together as it were in his book on Hegel's *Wissenschaft der Logik*. Another aim of his study is at least equally important for him, but which we might regard as even more important, is to show that Hegel's *Logic* is concerned with a theory of communication; to put it more mildly, that the means of "communicative freedom" can be usefully and productively inserted into the Hegel-interpretation. When this is taken into account together with the political theology-thesis of interpretation above mentioned, the following emerges:

> The logic of concepts is relevant in terms of a theory of communication only in as far as it meets in the *proposition* relations, in the movement of which we can see the sublation of estranged dominat-

ing relations in communicative freedom in the code of the Logical. It is, as far as it does not restore metaphysical theology, *immediately* theory of the dialectic movement of the proposition and only *as such* indirectly a universal communication theory also (*ibid.*, 60).

It is therefore not the logic of reflexion or objective logic as such that becomes the center of Theunissen's interpretation, but the logic of concepts, the "logical analogue for sublating estranged domination."

What I find fascinating about Theunissen's interpretation and criticism of Hegel's logic is that he shows that although the theological thesis, the logical thesis, and the theory of communication thesis appear to be almost inextricably tied up with one another, each one of the three can be true without the other two also being true. In other words, the theses of interpretation are for their part logically independent of one another. This may be due not least to the fact that Theunissen introduces a fourth interpretation. This fourth thesis links up the other three, but does not have logical status in the narrow sense but a historical status. Not only does Hegel intend presentation, but also criticism, and that apparently in a threefold way: as a criticism of traditional metaphysics and its determinations, as a criticism of the relations of communication and as a criticism of traditional logic. In Theunissen's opinion the latter does not live up to its claim of revealing truth, but diminishes considerably in the form of a drastic loss of standard.

The uncoupling of Theunissen's various intentions of interpretation has also the effect that by potentializing the intentions of proof, which would otherwise become unavoidable, an exhaustive overtaxation can be avoided. That which Theunissen, together with Hegel, calls "the Logical," is now of interest to us. Theunissen expresses this with explicit reference to Kant and the paradigmatic function of dethroning which his philosophy had for Hegel, in the following way:

> The speculative and logical program of a sublation of transcendental philosophy implies the conviction that the goal Kant is striving for by means of the self-reflection of the subject can only be attained by reflective self-assurance of language. The concept of the Logical is the very element in which we have always moved as soon as we speak and by speaking utter determinations of thinking (*ibid.*, 53).

Theunissen would now determine the Logical as that which "we must have always understood, in order to be able to understand something like the proposition itself" (*ibid.*, 54). In other words, in the framework of subjective logic the thematization of the proposition in the doctrine of judgment receives first and foremost the central position. Mere negation as an operation counts for nothing as long as it is not contained in judgments. That this distinction awarded to the doctrine of judgment in subjective logic is strangely contrasted with the negative assessment of subjective logic as far as its originality is concerned, can again be attributed to the interaction of Theunissen's various purposes of interpretation and therefore should not trouble us for the time being.

The position of precedence accorded to the doctrine of judgment in subjective logic over that of the conceptual determinations of objective logic is not justified by the fact that the chapter on judgment in Hegel's logic occupies the "rank of a main text." To assume this position would be "absurd," to use Theunissen's words. The "key-position" of the doctrine of judgment implies more. Corresponding to the difference between thematized and thematizing thinking which Theunissen has already introduced, it is simply the fact that the chapter on judgment adopts "a meta-theoretical position towards the entire logical theory in as far as it exposes in the analysis of its object the one truth in the truth of all determined concepts" (*ibid.*, 422). Hegel's *Wissenschaft der Logik* would be in this respect a logic, insofar as it is a theory of judgment, and theories of judgment constitute an inherent object of logic.

Theunissen quite obviously outdoes Henrich's basic assumption by going one step further as far as reflection is concerned: like Hegel he argues explicitly that the doctrine of judgment in subjective logic represents the reflection of the logic of reflection, the "setting of the determined concepts by the concept itself" (cf. Taylor, 1975, 308 ff.). On the other hand, Theunissen distances himself from the obvious view held by both Kant and Hegel that the truth of the judgment is the conclusion and as a result the logical operation at stake which expresses the truth of concept determinations, is not the judgment, but rather the conclusion:

> The judgment does not succeed reflection in the same way as the conclusion. The conclusion sets reflection once again, but, of course, under the changed circumstances of the logic of concepts, whereas the judgment replaces reflection. The conclusion reproduces reflexion's own structure, as well as that of affirmative infinity by renewing the circular movement of its termini in the changed form of a permutation. However, judgment accomplishes what reflection was supposed to accomplish—a structurally different formation (*ibid.*, 424).

At this stage it seems to me that, on the one hand, Theunissen does not satisfy his own purposes of interpretation and, as a result, does not go far enough. But on the other hand, this opens up the possibility for us to identify the decisive weakness in his argument (and, moreover, that of Henrich also). Both of them conceive the argumentation structure of logic as linear, and indeed as merely having one meaning in one direction. What I am getting at is that they neglect the *aim of justifying logic* which, in accordance with the scandalon of logic mentioned at the beginning, must be the main purpose of every dialectical logic. If we do not do this, it is no longer a question of which basic logical operation is actually Hegel's or at which point this logical basic operation itself actually becomes thematic, but rather the reverse: how we could justify the validity that has always been assigned to the structure of argumentation. Theunissen earns credit for drawing our attention to the communication-theoretical undertaking. However, he projects what he means by this not onto the argumentation structure itself, but only onto the meaning structure. When doing this, one would have to take the pragmatics of the argumentation in the communicative context into account. And this means that neither the concept nor the judgment maintained, but only the justification, i.e., the conclusion, should be made the subject of reflection.

I shall now deal with this in the third part of my paper.

III

In my own contributions to the debate on the formation and structure of Hegel's logic (Zimmerli, 1981, 1982, 1986) I endeavored to advance the comprehensive interpretation of *Wissenschaft der Logik* as well as Hegel's argumentation-structure ("logic" as in the second meaning). The result of this was that we see in the historical development of Hegel's various conceptions of logic that he successively "contradicts" the logic oriented towards Kant and restocks it with his own content, before writing up *Wissenschaft der Logik* as the end result of this development. We are to understand objective logic here as a criticism of existing metaphysics, as formulated and criticized above all by Kant, and which consequently has simultaneously a "presentation" function and beyond that the pragmatic function of preparing ground for the use of logical operations.

From a more systematic perspective rather than from that of historical development we can basically argue as follows:

If it is at all true that we can differentiate between true and false propositions by proceeding—transcendentally—from the *fact* that propositions are true or false, as we have done throughout Western philosophy since Plato and Aristotle, and throughout the whole history of metaphysics, then the question as to a justification for this is a basic question of transcendental philosophy. We can indeed find diverse forms of criteria in accordance with which we can decide when a proposition should be called "true" and when "false," and many different types of truth theory are tied up with this. Nevertheless we must presume when considering these approaches that there is a point in talking of the truth of propositions. The task of a logic justifying logic should be to discuss the *quaestio juris* of this prerequisite. Hegel himself also realizes this:

> If we were only supposed to see the formal functions of thinking in logical forms, then they would be worthy of examination, if only for the purpose of ascertaining to what extent they for themselves correspond to *truth*. A logic which does not achieve this can at most claim the value of a natural-historical description of the manifestations of thinking as they are to be found (*Logik* II, 234).

But neither in view of the correspondence theory nor of the theory of consensus nor of any other kind of theory of truth is it possible to explain the truth of propositions as located in the reality described by them. The question then is: what is supposed to be "true" when something is thus and not otherwise or behaves in such and such a manner and not otherwise? On the other hand, it is just as obvious that the reason for the truth or falsity of propositions cannot also be substantiated in the form of the proposition as such. For then it would not be clear why of all other forms of proposition this very one should permit truth. Finally, however, the reason of truth cannot only rest with the users of propositions and their historical and social background; it is indeed true that as a rule all reasonable people endorse true propositions and reject false ones; but on the other hand, it is by no means always like this, and even if it were, it is a matter not of a justification, but merely of a description.

The reason for the truth of propositions (whether so-called "formal" or "empirical" propositions is irrelevant) therefore is located in some form of relation of signs, designated reality, and pragmatics of signs. And this relation cannot be seen either in the signs, or in the designated reality or in the pragmatics of signs. Whatever this relation may be and however we may for its part theoretize it, it is at any rate *necessary* to presuppose it. We could, of course, object to this by saying that it is surely possible to negate what I have called the "fact of truth" and that it is not absolutely necessary to presuppose the truth-establishing relation of signs, designated reality and pragmatics of signs. We can, however, only deny the fact of truth under the condition of its existence, as is shown in the manifold variants of the refutation of skepticism. And even the affirmative indication of the possibility of another "higher" truth, which has nothing at all to do with logical truth, does not get us any further, since those who go into the function of justifying the logic of logic have already gone into "the Logical." In other words we must differentiate between the assertion, "Since truth does not exist, it is wrong to maintain that it is necessary to suppose a truth-establishing relation between signs, designated reality and the pragmatics of signs," and the proposition, "I do not know whether truth exists." Neither of them, however, constitutes a counter argument: the assertion because it is contradictory, and the proposition because it is not an argument at all.

The examination of logical forms as the "formal functions of thinking in order to find out to what extent they correspond to *truth*," as Hegel expresses the quasi-transcendental task of logic derived from this (*Logik* II, 234), is now doubly reflexive: If we work from the basis of the correspondence concept of truth, this task consists in examining the analogy between logical forms and truth, i.e., the analogy of logical forms on the one hand and the analogy of concept and reality on the other. The function of truth in logic is both that of an *element* and that of a *relation* to be examined. We are now not very far away from a truth-functional approach, which reinforces Theunissen's (Theunissen, 1980, 66) meta-criticism of Tugendhat's criticism of Hegel *and* at the same time renders it superfluous. As a result of this, however, as we have already mentioned, it is not ultimately Hegel's theory of propositions that is placed in the centre of the critical reconstruction, but his doctrine of conclusive inference. The question of justifying logic raised in the *Wissenschaft der Logik* is not how we can assert truth, but how we can represent the truth of our assertions to an opponent who doubts them.

It should not surprise us that, under these circumstances, nothing more emerges from Hegel's reconstruction of valid logic in the subjective logic than the traditional conception of syllogism. The truth-functional reconstruction of the logic used here does indeed show that the identity that Hegel maintained to exist between the structure of *Wissenschaft der Logik*, the logic substantiated in it, and the logic that substantiates it, *in fact does not exist at all*. The function of legitimizing logic from the history of metaphysics ought also to apply to classical logic. The argumentation-structure itself, however, transcends classical logic and, presumably, has to do so necessarily. Hegel's thesis that the logical structure thereby becomes completely transparent proves, luckily, to be inappropriate.

LITERATURE

J. Burbidge, *On Hegel's Logic* (Atlantic City: Humanities Press, 1981).

H.F. Fulda/R.P. Horstmann/M. Theunissen, *Kritische Darstellung der Metaphysik* (Frankfurt a.M.: Suhrkamp, 1980).

G.W.F. Hegel, *Wissenschaft der Logik*, 2 vols. (Hamburg: Meiner, 1963).

D. Henrich, 1963, "Anfang und Methode der Logik." Reprinted in D. Henrich, *Hegel im Kontext* (Frankfurt a.M.: Suhrkamp, 1971), pp. 73–94.

"Formen der Negation in Hegels Logik," in *Hegel-Jahrbuch—1974* (Cologne: Pahl-Rugenstein, 1975), pp. 245–256.

"Hegels Grundoperation," in *Der Idealismus und seine Gegenwart*, Festschrift für W. Marx (Hamburg: Meiner, 1976), pp. 208–230.

"Hegels Logik der Reflexion. Neue Fassung," in *Hegel-Studien, Beiheft* 18, 1978, pp. 203–324.

C. Taylor, *Hegel* (Cambridge: Cambridge University Press, 1975).

M. Theunissen, *Hegels Lehre vom absoluten Geist als theologisch-politischer Traktat* (Berlin: De Gruyter, 1970).

Sein und Schein. Die kritische Funktion der Hegelschen Logik (Frankfurt a.M.: Suhrkamp 1980).

A. Trendelenburg, *Logische Untersuchungen* (Berlin: G. Bethge, 1840).

W.C. Zimmerli, *Die Frage nach der Philosophie* (Bonn: Bouvier, 2nd enlarged ed., 1986)

"Inweifern wirkt Kritik systemkonstituierend?" in, *Hegel-Studien, Beiheft* 15, 1980, pp. 119–138.

"Aus der Logik lernen?" in W.R. Beyer (ed.), *Die Logik des Wissens und das Problem der Erziehung* (Humburg: Meiner, 1981), pp. 66–79.

"Die Wahrheit des impliziten Denkers," in *Studia Philosophica*, 41, 1982 pp. 139–160.

"Potenzenlehre versus Logik der Naturphilosophie," in R.P. Horstmann/ M.J. Petry (eds.), *Hegels Philosophie der Natur* (Stuttgart: Klett-Cotta, 1986), pp. 309–327.

Chapter Eleven

HUSSERL'S CRITIQUE OF HEGEL

Tom Rockmore

The most interesting criticisms of a position do not necessarily appear in the scholar's reception of a great philosopher. They often occur in the comments of one major thinker on the work of another. A possible instance is provided by one of Husserl's rare remarks on Hegel.

It is obvious that important philosophers do not always provide deep insight into their predecessors' views, in part because they do not invariably possess the necessary historical knowledge. Now there is reason to believe that Husserl lacked precise knowledge of the history of philosophy in general.[1] There is further reason to believe that he lacked detailed acquaintance with Hegel's position. Following his teacher Brentano, who apparently regarded Hegel as a case of the extreme degradation of human thought (!), Husserl seems not to have studied Hegel more than casually.[2]

A casual acquaintance is certainly insufficient to understand one of the most difficult positions in the philosophical tradition. But it does not necessarily follow that Husserl's criticism of Hegel is incorrect. Husserl's lack of precise knowledge did not prevent him from offering a severe verdict on Hegel's thought. In the introductory section to his programmatic article, "Philosophy as a Rigorous Science," he writes:[3]

> A change began with the Romantic School. Although Hegel insists on the absolute validity of his method and doctrine, his system lacks the philosophical scientificity [*Wissenschaftlichkeit*] deriving from the most fundamental critique of reason [*allererst ermöglichende Vernunft-kritik*]. In relation to it, philosophy, like romantic philosophy in general in the following period, brought about a weakening [*Schwächung*]

or a falsification [*Verfälschung*] of the drive to the constitution of
rigorous philosophical science.

This passage provides a multi-pronged, fundamental criticism of
Hegel's view. What that criticism is can only be understood in the
context of the passage in Husserl's article. From the title, we know
that the article concerns an as yet never realized concept of philosophy. As Husserl reads the history of the tradition, it is composed of
unavailing attempts to realize this concept, offered in replacement of
earlier efforts, which have been criticized and rejected. As such decisive moments, Husserl names the Socratic-Platonic view, the rejection of Scholasticism, and the impulse towards conceptual rigor—
identified with the views of Descartes, Kant, and Fichte—which ter-
minates with the rise of romanticism.

This general characterization of Husserl's criticism calls for three
comments. First, Husserl's reading of the tradition is interesting in
that he understands that the impulse towards rigorous, scientific
theory is not confined to the modern moment. He thus avoids a
frequent simplification, even if it would be an error to compare the
depth of his knowledge of the tradition to Hegel's. Second, we can
note a change in perspective from Hegel to Husserl. Unlike his great
predecessor, Husserl is explicitly unconcerned to build upon previous views in the history of philosophy. To put this point bluntly,
although I believe accurately, he holds that while much has been
attempted, nothing has been accomplished. Since a true beginning
for scientific philosophy has yet to be made, it is necessary to start
over. The entire positive legacy of the past tradition, as Husserl read
it, resides in the idea of philosophy as distinguished from its
realization.[4]

Third, we can note that Husserl's criticism is formulated in a
general manner which refers neither to a particular passage, nor even
to a particular text. This generality is to be expected, if, as I believe,
Husserl did not possess more than a passing acquaintance with
Hegel, perhaps similar to Kant's knowledge of Hume. In virtue of
its generality, Husserl's remark resembles the comments on many
important thinkers on their predecessors or contemporaries. A good
example is provided by Hegel's *History of Philosophy*. Despite later
progress in the editions of the Greek texts to which Hegel refers, it
is striking that none, or virtually none, of the points he makes about
ancient philosophy need now be abandoned for philological reasons.
Indeed, this is not unexpected. If the relative independence of philosophy from historical scholarship, well known to Hegel, is not a
philosophical platitude, it ought to become one. Obviously, the deepest and most far-reaching philosophical criticism rarely, if ever, de-

pends on the kind of critical apparatus that has become the omnipresent guarantee of scholarly status in the age of the journal article. Husserl's objection is clearly related to a supposed decline of the critical impulse contained in the views of Descartes, Kant, and Fichte. This impulse is manifested in the triple concern with true beginnings, decisive formulation of problems, and correct method. According to Husserl, the decline of philosophical rigor in the Romantic School and in Hegel's thought unwittingly leads to skepticism.

If this is a fair statement of Husserl's objection, then I see three points at issue. First, there is the general problem of the relation of Hegel's thought to romanticism; and the question of that movement's relation to preceding views. Second, there is the more restricted series of queries concerning "scientificity" and the critique of reason in Hegel's thought, including its relation to Kant's. Third, there is the effect of Hegel's view in two areas: on the rise of naturalism [*Naturalismus*], what we would now also call realism or positivism in natural science, and on the emergence of the theory of the world view [*Weltanschaungsphilosophie*]. Since these three points concern the relation of Hegel's thought to the history of philosophy, the intrinsic character of the position, and its later fate, Husserl's objection despite its general nature, goes to the heart of the Hegelian philosophy.

As concerns "romanticism," the generality of Husserl's reference, which includes no qualification of this ambiguous term, makes it difficult to interpret. It is, of course, equally difficult to describe "romanticism" briefly.[5] The term is widely used to refer to literature, the arts, and philosophy. Artistic and literary romanticism concerns the reaction against neo-classicism, beginning at the end of the eighteenth century. This reaction features stress on imagination and emotion, rather than on formal criteria, for instance in Goethe's early period.

In philosophy, romanticism refers to the reaction against eighteenth century Enlightenment thought. In a broad sense, philosophical romanticism might include thinkers as disparate as Rousseau, Schopenhauer, and Nietzsche. In a narrow sense, it refers to the initial phase of German idealism, perhaps including such figures as the Schlegel brothers, Novalis, Fries, Schelling, and Schleiermacher. From the latter perspective, romanticism provides a renewed emphasis on man and nature, and perhaps the most typical figure is Schelling. A central doctrine of philosophical romanticism is the stress on *Naturphilosophie*, or philosophy of nature.

We are not concerned here with the precise description of romanticism; we are concerned with the accuracy of Husserl's attempt to link Hegel to the proposed epistemological weakness in the Roman-

tic School. We can usefully distinguish between the term and Hegel's use of it. The term "Romantic School" is not employed by
Hegel and seems first to have been used by H. Heine, his pupil,
after Hegel's death.[6] Broadly speaking, Hegel was critical of all the
thinkers included under the heading of German philosophical romanticism. Schelling is the only one among them whom he even
recognizes as a representative of philosophy, as differentiated from
non-philosophy.

The most congenial example for a positive relation between Hegel
and romanticism, in the absence of a specific understanding of the
concept, is provided by Hegel's adoption of a modified form of
Schelling's philosophy of nature. It is harder to demonstrate a positive relation between Hegel's thought and romanticism in terms of
the claimed absence of a critique of reason, especially in Hegel's
thought.

The absence of a critique of reason is suggested in Husserl's second point, which we can paraphrase as the assertion that Hegel's
position lacks the necessary critique of its instrument which alone
can provide and guarantee its scientific status. Husserl almost certainly has in mind theoretical reason, although he does not mention
the different forms distinguished by Kant. He seems to have understood theoretical reason as possessing a practical function, in a quasi-
Platonic sense, later restated by Kant, for instance in the concept of
the *Weltbegriff*, or *conceptus cosmicus*.[7] And he seems never to have
been interested in aesthetic reason as such.

The relation of Husserl's view to Kant's *Vernunftkritik* requires
mention. It is well known that Husserl's understanding of the critical
philosophy changed greatly in the course of the evolution of his
thought. We know that his initial, strongly critical reaction to Kant's
thought was largely mediated through the eyes of Natorp, a leading
neo-Kantian.[8] Later, as Husserl began to teach Kant's thought, and
became more familiar with it, he became more positive towards the
critical philosophy and began to perceive important parallels between it and his own thought. His main, remaining reservation was
that Kant did not think his position through to the end, as witness
his silent presupposition of what Husserl called the "life-world."

In the insistence here on a critique of reason and the realization
in fact of philosophy as a rigorous science, we can perceive Husserl's
immanent restructuring of phenomenology on a transcendental basis. This reworking of phenomenology is, I believe, implicit in the
Göttingen lectures (1907). It becomes explicit in *Ideas I* (1913), which
brought Husserl closer to the critical philosophy, and which remained a permanent feature of his later thought.

We can note, since it is important for the discussion, that Husserl never accepted Kant's *Vernunftkritik* in an uncritical manner. He follows Kant in the rejection of psychologism as early as his initial phenomenological breakthrough. From this perspective, in the present text he goes beyond Kant in two ways: in his emphasis on the relation of psychologism and skeptical relativism; and in the associated rejection of historicism and the *Weltanschauungsphilosophie*, which, according to Husserl, follows from historicism. The tension between Kant and Husserl is evident, for instance, in Fink's "authorized" rejection of the neo-Kantian criticisms of Kreis and Zocher.[9] But Husserl, despite other differences, is clearly adopting a quasi-Kantian perspective in his stress on the necessary relation between *Vernunftkritik* and rigorously scientific philosophy, which provides the basis of his objection to Hegel's thought here.

For Husserl, the claimed lack of a critique of reason in Hegel's thought is closely related to its purported inability to justify claims to know. This criticism is not incidental; it is intended to negate the viability of absolute idealism as an approach to the problem of knowledge. To respond, it will be necessary to discuss Hegel's concept of reason.

I believe that it is hopeless even to attempt a capsule summary of Hegel's view of reason in a few well chosen words. No fundamental philosophical doctrine can be adequately described in that way, and any philosophical concept that can successfully be described in rapid fashion is not of far-reaching importance. To answer Husserl, it will be convenient not to undertake a lengthy discussion of Hegel's *Vernunftkritik* at present. This is unnecessary. Husserl's point is not that Hegel's critique of reason is unsatisfactory; his point is that it is lacking [*fehlt*] in the position. To meet this charge, it will suffice to establish that Hegel does offer a critique of reason, something no close student of Hegel has ever doubted. It will further be useful to comment on the relation of Hegel's *Vernunftkritik* to the problem of justification. This is a side of his thought that even his most assiduous students often ignore, but one which is highly significant.

Husserl's claim of the absence of a critique of reason in Hegel's thought is in basic and obvious contradiction with Hegel's writings, in which *Vernunftkritik* is a central theme from beginning to end. To stress this point, I will now describe Hegel's intent broadly in terms of the critical philosophy. Hegel is sometimes regarded as the antithesis of Kant, which is a profound error. This kind of interpretation is not only mistaken; it is pernicious, since it effectively conceals the positive relation between the two positions.

In general terms, it is accurate to say that Hegel's position originates in the course of the debate concerning the reconstruction of the results of the *Critique of Pure Reason* in fully systematic form.[10]

Specifically, Hegel's initial aim, which I believe he never abandoned, was to complete the philosophical revolution begun by Kant in a manner consistent, if not with the letter, then with the spirit of his thought. Thus, like Husserl, Hegel's relation to Kant's *Vernunftkritik* was always critical. More precisely, Hegel shares Husserl's belief, for different reasons, that the critical philosophy stops short and fails to complete its critique of reason.

The general outline of Hegel's extension of the Kantian critique of reason is already present in the *Differenzschrift*, his initial philosophical publication. In this text, Hegel criticizes Kant's view of reason in a way he later develops, but never decisively alters or abandons. In the systematic portion of this text, especially in the account of "Reflection as Instrument of Philosophizing," Hegel characterizes the critical philosophy as a philosophy of the understanding. Understanding, he insists, can lead merely to antitheses, which it is the purpose of reason, unfairly neglected by Kant, to overcome in the form of an articulated synthesis. Hegel amplifies this objection in the historical portion of the text through the description of the views of Kant and of Fichte as subjective philosophies, which require supplementation by a philosophy of objectivity, or nature. This same critical approach to the foreshortened form of reason in evidence in the critical philosophy is later restated at length in the *History of Philosophy*, particularly in the discussions of Kant, Fichte, and Schelling.

For the mature concept of reason in Hegel's thought, we need to turn to the *Encyclopedia of the Philosophical Sciences*, the twice revised presentation of his systematic position. The continuity in Hegel's critique of reason with his earlier discussion is clearly in evidence in this text. Hegel here embeds his critique of the critical philosophy in the important discussion of three basic "Attitudes of Thought to Objectivity." In his approach to Kant's position as a form of empiricism, Hegel insists that the necessary outcome of the restriction of knowledge to appearance, as distinguished from essence, is skepticism. Knowledge in the full sense requires that the essence appear and that the distinctions of the understanding be sublated by reason. Hegel further supplements his critique of what he regards as mere philosophy of the understanding by a detailed philosophy of nature.

I have to this point done no more than indicate the clear and constant presence of a critique of reason in Hegel's thought, without any comment on its adequacy. Husserl's claim that Hegel's position lacks this dimension is meant to indicate a basic difference with his own thought. We can also note that, with the exception of the French discussion, little attention is devoted in the phenomenological literature to a possible positive relation between Husserl and Hegel.[11]

That there is a positive relation can be inferred from the interest of both thinkers in *Vernunftkritik*.

As this account is rapid, it is not complete. But merely on this basis, a series of four parallels concerning the critique of reason can be distinguished in the views of Hegel and Husserl, as follows: First, both agree that Kant's *Vernunftkritik* is insufficiently radical, but that the attempt should not be abandoned, and each tries to carry the enterprise beyond the point at which Kant left it. Second, both insist that knowledge is possible only if its object is immanent to consciousness. Accordingly, each rejects the traditional approach to knowledge as knowledge of an external object. Third, each argues that philosophy must take shape as a science of the experience of consciousness, in other words as phenomenology. This is self-evident in Husserl's position and in Hegel's *Phenomenology*. To show that Hegel's position retains a phenomenological dimension, we would need to enter into an account of the relation between the *Phenomenology*, the *Encyclopedia*, and the *Science of Logic*. This is not the place for such an account. It will suffice here to state without further discussion that I believe the phenomenological and logical aspects of Hegel's thought to be inseparable dimensions of a single philosophical project. Fourth, each rejects Kant's formulation of the basic distinction between appearance and essence, which follows from his stress on understanding. In different ways consistent with their respective positions, Hegel and Husserl maintain that the condition of knowledge is that the essence be given in conscious experience.

In response to Husserl it is insufficient to note the presence of a critique of reason in Hegel's thought; we need to demonstrate further the relation of that critique to the justification of claims to know. Husserl's objection is closely related to the widely held view that Hegel's position lacks an epistemology.

Although Hegel's critics are often not well versed in his thought, this is not the case for his students. Unfortunately for Hegel, his students often interpret his position so as to illustrate his insight that what is familiar is, for that reason, not recognized. If "epistemology" is understood as "a fully Kantian, transcendental analysis of knowledge," then perhaps neither Hegel nor Husserl possesses an epistemology. If the definition is widened to include the effort to justify the claim to know, then in Hegel's position we have one of the deepest, but least known theories of knowledge.[12]

Hegel's theory of knowledge is often overlooked because he neither presents it explicitly not describes it in purely systematic form in isolation from historical considerations. In my opinion, Hegel's strategy for the justification of claims to know follows from a reversal

of the "linear" approach to epistemology, which has been dominant
in the philosophical tradition roughly since Aristotle's critique of
circular reasoning. According to what I will call the "linear epistemological strategy," later elements of a theory are justified through
their relation to earlier elements, from which they follow rigorously,
and the theory itself, in its strongest version, derives seamlessly from
an initial principle known to be true.

The "linear" approach to knowledge is widely present in modern
philosophy, especially in rationalism, and above all in Descartes'
position. Fichte is frequently studied as a neo-rationalist, particularly
in relation to Descartes. There is a clear relation between the views
of Fichte and Descartes, as Hegel, for instance, shows in his *History
of Philosophy*. But there is a clear difference as concerns the justification of claims to know.

Fichte rejects the "linear" approach to knowledge on the grounds
that since a position's initial principle cannot be demonstrated within
it, thought is necessarily circular. Hegel carries this idea further in
his suggestion, as early as the *Differenzschrift*, that the consequences
of a theory justify its claims to knowledge. What I call a "circular
epistemological strategy" accordingly rests its claim to knowledge on
what would now be regarded as a quasi-pragmatic appeal to consequences. This is the basic insight behind Hegel's rarely thematized,
but profound view of philosophy as the circle of circles. The plausibility of the "circular" form of epistemology in part rests on the
evident impossibility of the linear alternative, and in part presupposes the quasi-pragmatic justification of claims to know in terms of
consequences, as distinguished from presuppositions.

We need to differentiate Hegel's critique of reason and its reception in the succeeding intellectual tradition. Husserl raises the latter
point in his remark on the weakening or falsification of the drive
towards the constitution of rigorous philosophical science, which
was widespread in the post-Hegelian period. Among the points at
issue here, we can note the general character of post-Hegelian
thought both on the philosophical and non-philosophical planes,
especially including natural science, and the responsibility of romanticism and Hegel's position for the later evolution of the intellectual
tradition.

This phase of Husserl's criticism raises an exceptionally wide range
of issues. As an aid in discussion, it will be helpful to narrow the
range of issues in two ways: through bracketing the accuracy of
Husserl's description of post-Hegelian thought, and through refrain-
ing from discussion of the role of romanticism. In a sense, Husserl's
observation about the decline of the impulse towards the constitution of rigorous philosophy after Hegel does not go far enough. It is

well known that numerous thinkers in this period, for a variety of reasons, even declined to regard their own work as philosophy. We can safely bracket further consideration of the problem of romanticism since our topic here is Husserl's critique of Hegel.

The basic question Husserl raises concerns the attribution of responsibility to a given idea or philosophical position. This is a difficult area at best. Since Anaxagoras, a number of writers—including Hegel, but also including such non-philosophers as Victor Hugo— have affirmed the power of reason and by extension the capacity of ideas to realize themselves. This doctrine is not quite the same as an attribution of historical responsibility. We must not confuse the claim that a given idea, or its interpretation, can or has moved an individual to act in a certain way with the quite different claim that an idea or its author is responsible for what is done in its name. In what sense is an author responsible for the interpretation, or even the misinterpretation, of ideas? Is responsibility attributable to the person who formulates an idea, to the person who acts upon it, or to both in different ways?

I believe that Husserl's objection presupposes an analysis of the general question of the historical role, or motive force of ideas, upon which it depends. But his immediate concern is limited to Hegel's influence on the evolution of later thought. More precisely, he is concerned with the role of Hegel's view in what he evidently regards as the specific causal sequence leading to the appearance of naturalism and historicism in the post-Hegelian period.

In my opinion, Husserl overestimates the causal influence of Hegel's position on the rise of naturalism and historicism. Certainly, it is an error to use such terms as "Verfälschung" or "Schwächung" concerning Hegel's contribution to the concept of rigorous philosophy; as our brief review has shown, diametrically opposed terms would be more appropriate. Obviously, it is insufficient to claim causal responsibility for Hegel's position in virtue of mere temporal priority. But it is difficult to make a stronger claim since Hegel clearly opposed in his own thought both historicist and naturalist tendencies.

Hegel's relation to these two later movements is not the same in both cases. We need to remember that when he was writing, the distinction between natural science and philosophy of nature had not yet been sharply drawn. Clearly, as the distinction was being made, proponents of natural science, who tended towards naturalism, tended to regard theoreticians of the philosophy of nature as at best misguided. Indeed, this is still the case. But there is no reason to attribute specific responsibility to Hegel or to such other philosophers of nature as Schelling or Goethe. On the contrary, naturalism

is the general result of the ongoing separation of natural science
from philosophy begun, as Husserl points out in the *Crisis*, by the
rise of Galilean science. On the other hand, despite the espousal of
the *Weltanschauung* approach by Dilthey, a fine Hegel scholar, it is
clear that Hegel consistently sought to surpass historical relativism
for truth.[13] Whether he was successful in that attempt has no bearing
on the direction of his thought. At most, we can say that *Weltanschauungsphilosophie* arose in Hegel's wake; what we cannot show is
that Hegel's position tended in that direction.

The aim of this discussion was to examine Husserl's critique of
Hegel. Husserl objects that Hegel's thought lacks a *Vernunftkritik* and
cannot justify its claims to know, but I have shown that the objection
is unfounded through remarks on Hegel's profound critique of reason and his equally profound epistemology. Husserl's critique presupposes a basic dissimilarity between his view and Hegel's. In part
this is an accurate assessment, since the views do differ radically,
although there is a limited similarity. This similarity resides in the
independent awareness—since we cannot suppose that Husserl knew
Hegel even that well—that Kant's account of the possibility of knowledge could best be carried forward through a radical deepening of
his *Vernunftkritik* and a turn to phenomenology.

The interest of this similarity is not only historical; it offers an
important lesson for later thought, particular for post-Husserlian
phenomenology. In general, we find in the writings of Heidegger
and Gadamer, Sartre and Merleau-Ponty, Ricoeur and Derrida, a
decline of *Vernunftkritik*, a turn away from questions of methodology
and epistemology, and, in the attack on the metaphysics of presence,
an overt rejection of the tradition of occidental rationalism.

But a decision to ignore epistemology is misconstrued as a resolution of this central philosophical theme. It is rather a symptom of
the inability to approach the problem of knowledge that results from
the turn away from reason, evident most recently in the attack on
subject philosophy.[14] Despite the important differences in their views,
from this perspective the similarity is perhaps more significant: in
their respective commitment to reason, to its critique, to the problem
of knowledge from a phenomenological standpoint, to philosophy
from the subject's angle of vision.

NOTES

1. See A. de Waelhens, "Phénoménologie husserlienne et Phénoménologie
hégélienne," in *Revue philosophique de Louvain*, L II, 1954, p. 235.

2. See Herbert Spiegelberg, *The Phenomenological Movement: A Historical
Introduction* (The Hague: Martinus Nijhoff, 1982), p. 13.

3. Edmund Husserl, *Philosophie als strenge Wissenschaft* (Frankfurt a.M.: Vittorio Klostermann, 1965), p. 11. My translation.

4. For a close anticipation of Husserl's desire to begin again, which is widespread in modern thought, see Descartes, *Les passions de l'âme*, in *Descartes: Oeuvres philosophiques*, ed. F. Alquié (Paris: Garnier, 1973), III, pp. 951–952: ". . . je serai obligé d'écrire ici en même facon que si je traitais d'une matière que jamais personne avant moi n'eût touchée."

5. For a discussion, especially of romanticism in philosophy, see Harald Höffding, *A History of Modern Philosophy*, trans., B.E. Myer (New York: Dover, 1955), II, *passim*, esp. Bk. VIII, pp. 139–293.

6. Apparently this term was not used before 1836. See Herbert Schnädelbach, *Philosophy in Germany. 1831–1933* (New York: Cambridge University Press, 1984), p. 238n6.

7. See Immanuel Kant, *Kritik der reinen Vernunft*, B 866–868.

8. For a complete discussion, see Iso Kern, *Husserl und Kant* (The Hague: Martinus Nijhoff, 1964).

9. The criticisms concerned Husserl's intuitionism and supposed ontologism [*Ontologismus*]. See Eugen Fink, "Die phänomenologische Philosophie Edmund Husserls in der gegenwärtigen Kritik," in *Kant-Studien*, XXXVIII, 1933, pp. 319–383.

10. For a discussion, see my "La systématicité et le cercle hegélien," in *Archives de philosophie*, XLVIII, no. 1 (1985), pp. 3–20.

11. For a typical example, see H. Spiegelberg, *ibid.*, pp. 12–14.

12. For a reconstruction and critical evaluation of Hegel's epistemology against the historical background, see my *Hegel's Circular Epistemology* (Bloomington: Indiana University Press, 1986).

13. See Wilhelm Dilthey, *Die Jugendgeschichte Hegels*, Berlin, 1905.

14. For a recent example, see Jürgen Habermas, *Der philosophische Diskurs der Moderne. Zwölf Vorlesungen* (Frankfurt a.M.: Suhrkamp, 1985).

Commentary on Tom Rockmore's "Husserl's Critique of Hegel"
David A. Duquette

In reading Professor Rockmore's paper the first time through I found myself surprised at the direction that it eventually took. For up to approximately the first third of the paper I was quite sure that he was going to offer a defense of Husserl's criticism of Hegel, but quite the opposite turned out to be the case. Although I basically agree with what Professor Rockmore has to say in his evaluation of this criticism, nonetheless, in light of this evaluation, I still wonder why he begins by citing from Husserl as a possible example of an "interesting" criticism of one major thinker by another. Isn't it shown, rather, that Husserl's quite general and non-specific criticism is ill-informed? Indeed, isn't Husserl's concern with philosophical rigor somewhat ironic given his very inadequate reference to Hegel's view of romanticism, his failure to recognize Hegel's own evident critique of reason and his overestimation of Hegel's influence on the rise of naturalism and historicism. When all of this is acknowledged it is difficult to understand how the general and non-specific manner of Husserl's criticism could be considered helpful or insightful, even if by some chance it happened to be correct, which it is not.

Be that as it may, I think that Professor Rockmore is quite correct in holding that Husserl has no grounds for including Hegel under the heading of romanticism and in showing that there is in fact both a critique of reason and a justification of claims to knowledge in Hegel's "circular epistemological strategy." Also, the suggestion that the causal influence of Hegel's position on the rise of naturalism and historicism is a complex issue involving significant counterevidence appears sound. I am less sure, however, about the significant similarity Professor Rockmore finds between Hegel and Husserl in their "turn to phenomenology." Accordingly, I would like to direct my comments to what I find are the important dissimilarities between the philosophies of Hegel and Husserl and their significance in the wake of Kant's *Vernunftkritik*.

I will begin by noting that any discussion of the concept of rigorous science in either Hegel or Husserl must consider the issue of presuppositions in a philosophical science. This issue can be seen as the hallmark of the modern period in philosophy, and, as we know, it is Descartes who gives direction to its main developments with his claim for the self-certitude of the *Cogito*. With this move we have the beginning of what might be called the "epistemological turn" in philosophy, which sets the agenda for many of the succeeding thinkers of the period, empiricist and rationalist alike, and which comes to a climax in Kant's "Copernican Revolution." It seems to me that some of the most important systematic features of the philosophy of this entire period involve the attempt to make the basic presuppositions of philosophical science fully explicit, to limit the number of these presuppositions to the bare minimum and to demonstrate or show their intuitive self-evidence.[1] Both Hegel and Husserl can be viewed as responding to the project of modern philosophy in criticizing the use of presuppositions and in calling for presupposition-free science.

Now, to some extent, the transition to presupposition-free science is already under preparation in Kant's critical philosophy and in particular with the idea that knowledge is to be accounted for not by reference to the properties of the object but rather in terms of the constituting activity of the subject. This turn to the subject of knowledge as the point of reference for the explanation of knowledge—a project only incompletely or inconsistently carried out by Descartes—and the establishing of the domain of the transcendental as the proper field within which knowledge can be grounded and justified is of tremendous importance for the limiting of presuppositions. For all Kant must do is presuppose experience and then go on to articulate the conditions that make experience possible. Moreover, unlike Hume's conception of experience, Kant does not presuppose that experience need by analyzed into atomic simples and the complexes out of which they are formed. Kant's notion of *Phaenomena* is just that epistemic notion that the discipline of phenomenology will later appropriate.[2]

We are all well aware of Hegel's critical response to Kant's project and I will mention the most notable objections: (1) that Kant's transcendental philosophy is overly formalistic and (2) that in spite of his attempt to limit reason Kant is never able to liberate himself from the presupposition of the thing-in-itself. I take it that the first objection is related to Kant's employment of the categories of cognition.

These are rooted in the unity of apperception, the nexus of mediation of subject and object as an act of self-constitution, an act which
for Hegel remains abstract since this reflection-into-self never gets
properly displayed or articulated at the level of the particular phenomena.[3] The second and related objection is aimed at Kant's claim
that the concept of appearances requires the concept of things in
themselves, the latter of which we can have no knowledge whatsoever. For Hegel this is effectively to divorce thought from reality and
make truly objective thought and knowledge impossible.[4]

The transition from transcendental philosophy to phenomenology
requires that one concretize the process of the constitution of the
object of knowledge in the subject and also that one transcend the
dichotomy between reality and appearance. In this I think that Husserl follows Hegel and I would agree with the four parallels concerning the critique of reason that Professor Rockmore distinguishes in
the views of these two thinkers. However, it seems to me that on
certain crucial points Husserl, though not uncritical of Kant, is yet
still closer to Kant than one might expect given Husserl's own phenomenological turn. Indeed, I would claim, although I cannot fully
defend it here, that, unlike Hegel, Husserl is not fundamentally post-
Kantian in his treatment of philosophical presuppositions.

In order to give my hypothesis some semblance of plausibility it
will be useful to consider two controversial issues that have been
discussed by post-Husserlian phenomenologists. The one has to do
with the validity of the Husserlian *epoche* and the other with the
Husserlian intuition of the Transcendental Ego. I submit that the
question of the validity of each of these strategies in Husserl is
related in a parallel manner to the two previously mentioned problems that Hegel found in Kant.

First, notice that Husserl's *epoche* is a suspension of the "natural
standpoint" from which things are viewed as existing independent
of consciousness, not a denial that such things exist. The strategy is
simply to avoid the presupposition of a transcendent object by reducing the field of the subject-object relation to the immanency of
pure consciousness, thereby achieving that very apodicity sought
after by Descartes.[5] But is the *epoche* itself without presuppositions?
Does it not, similar to Kant, presuppose that which it brackets out
while, curiously, at the same time it is also simply assumed that
consciousness is self-contained and closed?

Second, falling under the *epoche* are a series of phenomenological
reductions that lead ultimately to the pure subject. This pure subject
is the Transcendental Ego and it cannot be made into an object of
experience but is only intuited correlatively to the objects of experience.[6] Thus, we have a primordial and apodictic consciousness of

the Ego that does not take the form of a subject-object relation. But despite the fact that Husserl arrives at the intuition of the Ego as a residuum of the *reduction* of experience, as distinct from Kant's *deduction* of the Ego from experience, is the former any less formal and abstract than the latter?[7]

Despite Husserl's important influence on later philosophers such as Heidegger, Merleau-Ponty and Sartre, it is interesting to note the relative agreement that occurs among them in the criticism of these features of Husserl's philosophy I have just outlined. If my hypothesis about Husserl is correct, then this is no accident for it is precisely these above mentioned features that keep Husserl wedded to the presuppositions of modern philosophy. By this I mean that Husserl is unable to overcome the subjectivism and formalism that characterize much of the modern period in its failure to ground adequately the concept of objectivity. To put it in Hegelian terms, Husserl has made the activity of the constitution of objects a function solely of consciousness (the object is *Gewusstsein*) and not a function of the self-relation of the object itself. Accordingly, Husserl's phenomenology is purely analytical, with its mathematical-like conception of eidetic intuition and self-evidence, whereas Hegel's phenomenology is dialectical in its conception of reflection into self as the activity of the concept—*der Begriff* understood as the unity of form and content.

In the Preface to his *Phenomenology of Spirit* Hegel distinguishes between "ratiocinative thinking," in which "the self is an ideally presented subject to which the content is related as an accident and predicate," and "conceptual thinking," where "the content is in truth no longer the predicate of the subject; it is the very substance, is the inmost reality, and the very principle of what is being considered."[8] I wonder, given Hegel's delineation of the difference between *Verstand* and *Vernunft*, if Husserl might well be characterized as remaining within the domain of the merely ratiocinative because of inability to get beyond a subjective presentation of truth.

This brings me to a final point about post-Hegelian naturalism and historicism. There is no doubt that the importance of the philosophy of nature and philosophy of history in Hegel's system has to do with his program for the concretizing of philosophy in a manner unparalleled by previous modern philosophy. This importance is in no way vitiated by the fact that nature and history, while intrinsic moments of *Realphilosophie*, lose their truth when they become isolated in an extreme and one-sided manner from the overall context of absolute philosophy. Again, if my hypothesis is correct then Husserl's charge of Hegel's responsibility for the rise of naturalism and historicism is based not only upon a lack of familiarity with Hegel's texts but also on a fundamental discordance between the Husserlian

project of rigorous science, which maintains an ambivalence if not
skepticism towards the place of nature and history in philosophy,
and the Hegelian project of actualizing philosophy in the concrete.[9]
This suggests that, despite the similarities between Hegel and Husserl in their deepening of the *Vernunftkritik*, the difference are perhaps more significant after all. It also indicates that the value of
Husserl's criticisms of Hegel lies not in their casting light on Hegel
but in what they reveal about Husserl's own limited project for
philosophy.

NOTES

1. Hume may appear to be an exception here, but underlying his "academic" skepticism is the unargued presupposition, apparently to be taken
as intuitively self-evident, that "nothing can be present to the mind but an
image or perception." *An Enquiry Concerning Human Understanding* (Indianapolis: Hackett, 1984), p. 104.

2. Cf. Kant, *Critique of Pure Reason*, trans. Norman Kemp Smith (New York:
St. Martin's Press, 1965), p. 265 (A 249).

3. Cf. Hegel's remark about the Kantian categories in the *Phenomenology of
Mind*, trans. J. B. Baillie (New York: Harper and Row, 1967), p. 112. See also
the *Logic*, trans. W. Wallace (Oxford: Oxford University Press, 1978), p. 70
(§ 42, *Zus*).

4. Cf. *Logic*. p. 67 (§ 41, *Zus*).

5. Cf. *Ideas*, trans. W. R. Boyce Gibson (New York: MacMillan, 1975), pp. 99–100.

6. Cf. *Ideas*, pp. 156–157. See also *Cartesian Meditations*, trans. Dorion Cairns
(The Hague: Martinus Nijhoff, 1973), pp. 65ff.

7. Cf. Sartre's *Transcendence of the Ego*, trans. F. Williams & R. Kirkpatrick
(New York: Noonday Press, 1972), pp. 35–54 for a critique of Husserl's
Transcendental Ego.

8. *Phenomenology*, pp. 118–119.

9. Although in his *The Crisis of European Sciences* Husserl speaks of the
necessity of historical reflection and the pregivenness of the "life-world," it
is not clear how this can be made compatible with his original program of
presupposition-free science. In any case, this is a problem for a separate
discussion.

Chapter Twelve

HEGEL VERSUS THE NEW ORTHODOXY

Richard Dien Winfield

I. The New Orthodoxy In Philosophy

A new orthodoxy[1] has taken hold of contemporary philosophy, repudiating "Cartesianism" and "Foundationalism" and espousing a theoretical and practical holism. It maintains that self-reflection always proceeds within a historical linguistic and cultural context conditioning its knowledge and that all philosophical reasoning operates with foundations that can never be justified because no argument can proceed unless there is already an accepted conceptual scheme providing shared parameters of rationality. Hence the new orthodoxy concludes that all knowledge claims and principles of right are contextually grounded in coherence with conceptual schemes rooted in historically given practices. With this verdict, the new orthodoxy embraces naturalized epistemology and ethics, relegating the distinctions between a *priori* and *a posteriori*, subjectivity and objectivity, norm and behavior, and theory and practice to constructs of empirical contingent conventions. In place of the Cartesian, foundationalist image of "philosophy as a mirror of nature,"[2] representing what world, consciousness, and language are in themselves from some timeless "view from nowhere,"[3] the new orthodoxy offers the picture of a corrigible, historical reason operating within pragmatically adopted frames of reference. Whether it be called "hermeneutics," "deconstruction," "internal realism," or "post-analytic philosophy," the new orthodoxy condemns reason to doxology, leaving philosophers with little to do but chronicle the practices and conceptual schemes underlying historical philosophical positions, foster an edifying awareness of how our theories are laden with assumptions, and engage in a reflective equilibrium determining the coherence of given theories inhabiting the same philosophical paradigm.

Not surprisingly, the spokesmen for the new orthodoxy have turned to Hegel for much of their inspiration. His phenomenological critique of the claims of consciousness offers them a source for radical anti-Cartesianism. His attack on all appeal to givens provides the cutting edge for their radical anti-foundationalism. His development of categories as elements of a logical totality, whose truth resides in categorical immanence, gives their holism its basis. And lastly, his concrete conception of spirit, wherein consciousness figures as an embodied subject, embedded in interaction with others, requiring language for the expression of thought, and participating in institutions of right arising in history, serves to support the historicized holism of their "naturalization" of epistemology and ethics.

While appropriating these Hegelian achievements, the new orthodoxy has jettisoned Hegel's pursuit of a presuppositionless science as a vestige of foundationalism, from which Hegel never successfully escapes. In the eyes of the new orthodoxy, Hegel absolutizes logical totality and the reason that conceives it, the practice of the modern age, the history of nations leading to modernity, and the history of Western philosophy. All this, the new orthodoxy asserts, must be purged to retrieve the rational kernel within the mystical shell.

Yet can the truncated Hegelianism of the new orthodoxy stop short at theoretical and practical holism? And if it cannot, how can Hegel's embrace of categorical immanence and the concreteness of spirit be reconciled with his pursuit of a foundation-free, yet systematic philosophy?

*II. Can The Critique of Epistemology Result In
A Naturalized Epistemology?*

To answer these questions, it makes sense to consider first the new orthodoxy's use of the critique of epistemology it finds in the *Phenomenology of Spirit*. Hegel describes this work as an attempt to free discourse of the opposition of consciousness, where knowing remains captive to a structure of reference in which some putative given always provides the standard for truth.[4] The new orthodoxy, however, views the *Phenomenology's* critique of consciousness as testimony to knowing's captivity to historically given standpoints and conceptual schemes.

Admittedly, the incessant inversions of consciousness described in the *Phenomenology* do show how the epistemological project of consciousness can never succeed. Since whatever consciousness appeals to as its standard of truth is accessible only as something for consciousness' own awareness, there is nothing against which to test knowledge claims other than representations of an equally subjective character. As Hegel is well aware, this Achilles heel of the representational model of knowledge is equivalent to the dilemma of foundationalism, to the extent that foundational arguments always appeal to some privileged given as the standard of knowledge.

What the new orthodoxy finds so noteworthy in Hegel's account are the exhaustiveness and concreteness of its gallery of different foundational projects. Its exhaustiveness suggests that there can be no shape of knowing that does not operate in terms of a self-defeating appeal to givens. Hegel may claim to have reached a final shape of consciousness whose knowing is absolute. Nonetheless, so long as such knowing measures its knowledge against any putative given, as it must do to retain the reference constitutive of consciousness, the new orthodoxy has good reason to regard "absolute knowing" as a misnomer, designating but one more shape of corrigible cognition.

As for its wealth of content, the progress of shapes from self-consciousness through spirit has an unprecedented concreteness documenting how the foundational knowing of consciousness involves intersubjective practices, approximating the institutions of different historical epochs. For the new orthodoxy, this provides the key insight leading the critique of epistemology to naturalized epistemology—the revelation that the frameworks of reference characterizing shapes of knowing are not *a priori* schemes rooted in some timeless structure of consciousness, but transient paradigms embedded in historical practices.

On this account, Hegel has little choice but to redeem the incorrigibility of absolute knowing by arguing for the absolute character of the historical epoch through whose practices his own standpoint is constituted. If, however, as the new orthodoxy claims, the phenomenological analysis of spirit shows how historical practices frame the givens and modes of reference by which knowledge claims are adjudicated, it is impossible for any historical formation to engender an absolute standpoint in which knowing is freed of the limits of representation. So long as given practices provide knowing with foundations determining what it accepts as valid, every historical epoch and every frame of reference is equally tainted. Hence, Hegel's critique of epistemology undermines his own claims of wisdom, leaving behind the naturalized epistemology that transforms philosophy into edifying deconstruction.

Bracketing out whether Hegel's *Phenomenology* actually has this as its outcome, it bears asking whether the critique of epistemology can stop short at the naturalized epistemology with which the new orthodoxy aborts philosophy. In upholding the naturalization of epistemology, the new orthodoxy makes three claims. First, in acknowledgment of the critique of epistemology, it maintains that representational or foundational knowing can never succeed in justifying its knowledge claims. Secondly, it maintains that knowing is embedded in historical practices. Thirdly, it affirms that all knowing is foundational in character, reflected in the fact that knowing's immersion in historical practices straps it with frames of reference predetermining its standards of truth.

There is nothing incoherent about the first two theses. Significantly, they do not imply the third. In order to arrive at the last thesis, they must be supplemented by arguments establishing that all knowing is foundational and that the historical practices in which knowing is embedded not only make knowing possible, but juridically determine what counts as knowledge. Without these additional arguments, the critique of epistemology does not result in naturalized epistemology.

Although it can be debated whether the new orthodoxy seriously attempts to supply these further arguments, what cannot be denied is the utter absurdity of the third thesis, on which their whole position is anchored. In advancing the third thesis, the new orthodoxy offers a suprahistorical, incorrigible claim concerning the character of knowing. Yet, to do so, the new orthodoxy must somehow occupy a standpoint free of the historically conditioned, foundational character its own position ascribes to cognition. If it seeks to escape this contradiction by regarding its own theoretical claims as burdened by foundational assumptions rooted in the practices of its time, it must admit that its naturalized epistemology has no more authority than any other competing picture. For it must confess that the corrigible character it ascribes to knowing precludes any objective knowledge about the practices of this or any other time, or, for that matter, about the new orthodoxy's own conceptual framework or that of any other standpoint.

For these reasons it makes no sense to claim that all knowing is representational, that is, foundational, or that the historical practices underlying knowing determine what counts as true or false. If any coherent argument is to follow from the critique of epistemology, it will have to be that there is a knowing free of foundations, and that the historical practices that make knowing possible leave undetermined all juridical questions of knowledge.

Can the *Phenomenology* be in concord with these conclusions, or does it result in the incoherent naturalized epistemology that the new orthodoxy finds nascent in Hegel's critique of epistemology? If we return to the three theses that underly the turn to a naturalized epistemology and examine whether the *Phenomenology* is really committed to them, it becomes evident that Hegel does not condemn himself to the dilemmas of his latter day followers.

Admittedly, the new orthodoxy is correct in maintaining that the *Phenomenology* testifies to the truth of the first thesis, that representational knowing can never ground its knowledge claims. Further, the shapes of consciousness observed under the heading of "Spirit" may stand as evidence for the second thesis, that knowing is embedded in historical practices, provided two propositions hold true. First, all the prior shapes of consciousness must be incorporated within and grounded by those of "Spirit," since otherwise, not all, but only some modes of knowing will be historically embedded. Second, the *Phenomenology* must comprise a systematic doctrine of consciousness, rather than a positive science addressing a given subject matter whose own status is taken for granted. The second proviso is particularly suspect, since the *Phenomenology* can serve its propaedeutic role as introduction to science only if it refrains from making truth claims in its own right and restricts itself to observing how the stipulated structure of consciousness makes and tests its own truth claims en route to exhibiting the futility of its own epistemological project.[5]

However, what decides the issues is whether the third thesis, that all knowing is foundational and historically conditioned, is embraced by the *Phenomenology*. To some extent, this question depends upon whether the *Phenomenology* is a scientific doctrine of knowing. If the *Phenomenology* is only the observation of how a certain stipulated structure of knowing fails in its quest for knowledge, no conclusions can be drawn from the *Phenomenology's* outcome about knowing per se. Hegel repeatedly maintains that the problems besetting consciousness' search for truth are not representative of knowledge in general, precisely insofar as the *Phenomenology* carries out its introductory service of freeing discourse from the opposition of consciousness by which foundational knowing is defined. As has been noted, the new orthodoxy dismisses all talk of such liberation by interpreting "Absolute Knowing" as just another shape of consciousness, carrying within itself the same representational opposition of knowledge and what is given in itself. However, Hegel emphasizes that "Absolute Knowing" is not a privileged standpoint from which knowing conceives what is in itself, in the fashion of the contemplative intelligence of pre-critical metaphysics. It rather comprises a self-dissolution of representational knowing, where the quest to ground knowledge in something in itself is beset by an inability to distinguish representing from what is given, eliminating the foundational project altogether.[6] Hence, Hegel characterizes the outcome of his

phenomenological critique of epistemology as a collapse of representational, that is, foundational knowing.[7] Far from rendering the foundational dilemma an inescapable fate, this collapse results in an
indeterminacy from which Hegel launches a philosophical cognition
that will refrain from conceiving its categories either in reference to
what is given or as representations of some underlying structure of
knowing.[8] Whether or not such a philosophical cognition can function remains to be seen. What is already clear is that the *Phenomenology* is not committed to the third thesis, on which the naturalization
of epistemology rests.

*III. Is Holism The Answer To The Logical
Requirement of Categorical Immanence*

By exhibiting the internal collapse of the foundational project of
representational knowing, the *Phenomenology of Spirit* confirms how
the critique of epistemology need not, and indeed, cannot result in
a naturalized epistemology. Nevertheless, Hegel's own sequel to the
Phenomenology, the *Science of Logic*, still seems a harbinger of the new
orthodoxy's theoretical holism.

Since the *Science of Logic* comprises Hegel's positive alternative to
the dilemmas of representational knowing, the categories whose
development it presents can no longer have their truth in correspondence with some putative given that they are supposed to mirror.
Because logic consists in thought thinking itself, Hegel recognizes
that a proper science of logic must involve a self-exposition of categories that refer to nothing but themselves. Their content will have
to be at one with their presentation, allowing what is first for thought
to be first in thinking.[9] Only then can logical science avoid taking for
granted the categorical method it is supposed to establish. Further,
such a self-exposition of categories will satisfy the requirements of
rational autonomy and presuppositionless science by both avoiding
any references to extraneous givens and relying on its categories to
determine themselves. In so doing, it will provide philosophy with a
new beginning, leaving behind foundationalism and the correspondence theory of truth entailed by any appeal to privileged givens.

Granted these basic features of Hegel's *Science of Logic*, it is not
hard to see how it could be used to buttress a coherence theory of
truth in which all categories of thought are holistically determined.
Since logic can escape reliance upon given foundations only if its
categories are their own exposition, determined exclusively through
themselves and one another, it would appear that each one will be
what it is through its place in the whole immanent development of
categories. On these terms, every category will stand defined by

incorporating the categories preceding its development and by being a component element of those that follow. Furthermore, because the development of categories will have to be self-determined, what it is that determines itself will be at hand only at the conclusion of the development as a final category incorporating all other logical categories as features of its self-determination.[10] Although this categorical whole can be thematized only at the conclusion of the development, after all its elements are explicated, its component categories are fully intelligible only in terms of their incorporation within it. This seems to signify that the truth of putative categories will reside in their coherence with logical development, a coherence consisting in their integration into the conceptual totality with which logic concludes.

Although Hegel maintains that this categorical immanence is the mark of a foundation-free, presuppositionless science, the new orthodoxy understands it as testimony to the holistic character of reason. Far from signaling a break from foundations, it rather reflects how rational thought always operates in terms of a conceptual framework in coherence with which concepts have their true meaning. By showing how categories are fully intelligible only as moments of a categorical totality, Hegel's logic demonstrates the impossibility of his own vestigial yearning to exercise an incorrigible thinking that takes nothing for granted. Although Hegel may maintain that science must begin with an indeterminacy independent of any conceptual framework, the integration of all categories within the Absolute Idea signifies that the logical whole must be assumed from the outset. So, in any event, concludes the new orthodoxy, enlisting the *Science of Logic* in support of the two theses of its theoretical holism: (1) that truth resides in coherence, rather than correspondence, and (2) that all thought operates in terms of a given conceptual scheme.

Yet can truth reside in coherence, as the new orthodoxy affirms? The turn to the coherence theory of truth is motivated by the inability of correspondence theory to establish how there can be any access to what is in itself, which knowledge should mirror. The coherence theory of truth is intended to overcome this problem by avoiding all immediate reference to a standard of truth, the defining pitfall of representational knowing. However, in asserting that truth lies in coherence, the new orthodoxy falls into a dual dilemma. According to theoretical holism, all objects of knowledge have their intelligibility in coherence with some encompassing theoretical context. Yet, if this is so, what is the status of the coherence theorist's reference to the theoretical context in coherence with which knowledge claims have their truth? If knowledge of it and its privileged role is obtained by referring directly to it, irrespective of some encompassing context, this knowledge violates the coherence theory of truth. If, however, reference to what knowledge is in coherence with is obtained in accord with the coherence principle, then the context it knows cannot be the ultimate context, but must instead be known through another in terms of which it is intelligible. But then, knowledge of the latter context presents the same difficulty, leading either to an infinite regress in which no context can be known as that in coherence with which knowledge is true, or else to an admission that the ultimate context must be accessible through a direct reference, placing coherence dependent upon an ultimate truth known through correspondence. Either way, the coherence theory of truth self-destructs, demonstrating the impossibility of knowing through coherence what the context is in coherence with which knowledge lies or, for that matter, of knowing that truth lies in coherence.

This incoherence of the coherence theory of truth has fatal implications for the holist idea of a conceptual scheme. Through the critical work of Davidson, the new orthodoxy has come to recognize the absurdities of maintaining the incommensurability of conceptual schemes.[11] However, in doing so, the new orthodoxy has not abandoned the idea of a conceptual scheme. Instead, it has accepted what it takes to be the Hegelian notion of our having one all-encompassing conceptual scheme circumscribing everything that can be intelligible to us. In embracing this idea, the new orthodoxy falls into the same trap besetting its advocacy of the coherence theory of truth.

Logically speaking, this trap is a very common one, reflecting the foundationalism of any transcendental argument. It consists in the incoherence of grounding all intelligibility in some given cognitive condition. Although such grounding should preclude any immediate cognition, it rests on prior knowledge of the condition of intelligibility and its privileged role. Transcendental knowledge is therefore impossible because it involves the incoherence of what Hegel diagnosed as attempting to know before knowing.

The idea of a conceptual scheme involves just this fallacy. By affirming that all intelligibility lies grounded in a given conceptual scheme, the new orthodoxy presumes to have transcendental knowledge both of what that conceptual scheme is, at least in some minimal sense, and how it serves as the condition of all meaning and knowledge. Yet how can the conceptual scheme be known? To be consistent with its grounding role, it must be known in terms of its own scheme. That is, it must be determined by itself as an object of knowledge. Yet, if it lies at the root of all intelligibility, how can one be certain that the idea of a conceptual scheme that it presents to us is equivalent to the conceptual scheme itself as it underlies intelligibility? To be certain would seem to require access to what the conceptual scheme is in itself, prior to what it makes intelligible to us. Direct access of that sort must be precluded, however, since it would contradict the grounding role of the conceptual scheme. Hence, the very idea of a conceptual scheme precludes any knowledge of what it is, or that it has the grounding role ascribed to it. All that can be done is assume that our conceptual scheme grounds intelligibility such that what we know as our conceptual scheme corresponds to what it is in itself. Making that assumption, however, is tantamount to embracing the dogmatic faith of the correspondence theory of truth, which the idea of a conceptual scheme is supposed to overcome.

It can be questioned whether that assumption could possibly be true. In order for the conceptual scheme to determine itself, as the new orthodoxy must ultimately assume, it would have to be a oclf determined framework. However, to be self-determined, the conceptual scheme could not have any given character by which it could stand as the antecedent ground to all intelligible content. If it did have such a nature, prior to the constitution of all intelligibility, it would have a content that it had not constituted for itself and thus fail to be self-determined. If, on the other hand, it was self-determined, generating its own intelligibility by means of its self-exposition, it would no longer comprise a ground of intelligibility, fundamentally prior to everything it grounded. Either way, the idea of a self-constituting conceptual scheme is incoherent.

Nevertheless, the idea of a self-determined conceptual development, making intelligible only itself, is precisely what allows Hegel's *Science of Logic* to escape the perplexities of the coherence theory of truth and its associate notion of a conceptual scheme. Admittedly, Hegel does acknowledge that the logical development of categories concludes in an all-encompassing category, the Absolute Idea, providing the method or principle of intelligibility for all the preceding ones contained within itself. However, he emphasizes that the Absolute Idea can only be as a result.[12] This is because it does not have any given character, in the manner of a conceptual scheme serving as the foundation of intelligibility. Instead, what it is is mediated by the categorical development it consummates. It cannot be otherwise, for it is the established subject matter of a logic of self-determination, which, as such, can have no antecedent nature, but must be what it determines itself to be. Accordingly, there can be no conceptual framework already operative at the outset of the *Science of Logic*, rendering intelligible the parade of categories that follows. If that were so, the work would be just one more version of foundationalism, determining its concepts through a given set of assumptions. If, on the contrary, logic is to establish the categories and their interrelations without taking them for granted, if, in other words, logic is to be the self-exposition of the categories, it must operate through a categorical immanence, where their order and intelligibility are produced as results rather than presupposed as dogmatic givens. Hence, the truth of the categories will not reside in their coherence with any given scheme, but in their total freedom from determination by any prior principles, given standpoints or other extraneous factors. Although they may achieve integration in the categorical whole that determines itself through their development, that integration does not underlie their exposition as an antecedent condition. For these reasons, the *Science of Logic*, to its own credit and viability, offers anything but support for the theoretical holism of the new orthodoxy.

IV. Can The Concrete Practices of Spirit Historicize Knowledge and Ethics

The *Phenomenology of Spirit* and the *Science of Logic* resist their enlistment by the new orthodoxy, but can the same be said of Hegel's Philosophy of Spirit? At every one of its levels, the Hegelian doctrine of spirit seems to offer an unshakeable basis for the new orthodoxy's turn to historical practices.

In the analysis of subjective spirit Hegel sets the stage by arguing three points: (1) consciousness is irreducibly an embodied subject in the world, (2) self-consciousness has an intersubjective dimension, and (3) language is the necessary medium of thought. All have important significance for the new orthodoxy.

Hegel's argument that consciousness is an embodied awareness, presupposing nature and individuated through a spatio-temporal being in the world[13] provides a first step away from the Cartesian picture of a disengaged ego, whose pure self-reflection is a source of knowledge independently of time and place and worldly practices. If, as Hegel argues, consciousness is a being in the world, wedded to a body caught in metabolism with nature, and thereby endowed with a concretely embedded perspective framing all its internal and external sensations, is this not an almost Heideggerian encouragement to view cognition as something already conditioned by a pretheoretical practical engagement with the world?

This practical conditioning of knowing only seems to be confirmed when Hegel turns from consciousness to self-consciousness and analyzes it in terms of desire, the domination of nature and a master-slave relation.[14] Here Hegel's argument seems to testify that self-consciousness is predicated upon not only a practical involvement with nature, but one involving relations between selves. Many view Hegel's master-slave discussion as if it shows how self-consciousness is constituted through intersubjectivity. However, since the subjects who interact as master and slave can only do so by already bearing desire and recognizing their difference from one another, it would seem that they must already be self-conscious in some respect.[15] Hence, what Hegel's argument would suggest is that the intersubjectivity of the master-slave relation establishes further forms of self-consciousness, if not self-consciousness per se. Nevertheless, even in this weakened form, the relation permits intersubjective practice to gain a foothold in the formation of awareness, a step which is fundamental for the new orthodoxy.

What seems to seal intersubjectivity's role as an indispensable condition of knowing is Hegel's analysis of language's contribution to thought. Treating thinking like consciousness and self-consciousness as a topic of *Realphilosophie*, he argues that thought is a real activity presupposing not only nature and the existence of embodied, practically engaged self-conscious individuals, but language as well.[16] Language is necessary for thinking, Hegel argues, because only words can provide the universal representations, freely generated by intelligence, that thought requires as the medium for its expression.[17]

For the new orthodoxy, this involvement of language is doubly fundamental. On the one hand, it signifies that thinking is conditioned by linguistic usage, which is itself an intersubjective practice arising within history and subject to historical change. Hence, thinking is historically grounded. On the other hand, because language presupposes conscious intelligence to create signs, retain their meaning, and generate intelligible and understood speech, thinking remains bound to the foundational dilemmas of consciousness. Consequently, thought is not only historically framed, but perennially dependent on assumed standards of truth.

For the new orthodoxy, Hegel's appeal to history in his doctrines of objective and absolute spirit offers a final corroboration of this corrigibility of reason. Although Hegel discusses the historical development of art and religion just as prominently as the history of freedom and the history of philosophy, it is his treatments of right and philosophy that bear directly upon the character of theoretical and practical reason.

Although Hegel conceives objective spirit as the philosophy of right, detailing the institutions of freedom of which justice is composed, he views them as non-natural conventions, and accordingly concludes their analysis with an account of what must occur in history for them to arise. That account consists in a history of freedom that, by definition, concludes with the emergence of the institutions of right. Hence, the end of the history of freedom does not signify any halt to actual history.

Similarly, when Hegel addresses the reality of philosophy as the final cultural phenomenon of absolute spirit, he conceives a development of philosophical systems comprising the theoretical history by which his own system arises. Consequently, the history of philosophy he depicts comes to an end that does not signify the close of philosophical debate, but rather the emergence of the form of philosophy the Hegelian system represents.

For the new orthodoxy these dual histories express how systems of justice and philosophies are creatures of parallel institutional and intellectual developments where each new system arises through determinate negation of the tradition from which it springs. Since practical and theoretical systems thereby have their own problematics grounded in overcoming the antecedent dilemmas of their heritage, each is a product of its age. Hence, every system of justice and philosophy has its norms predicated on a foundation given in history, a foundation consisting in the negation of preceding theory and practice. Hegel may wish to celebrate his own philosophy and the institutions of modernity as historical results that can never be bettered, but this is idle boasting, if their principles are grounded in the equally conditioned practices of the past. A more honest appraisal would consist in recognizing that all practical and theoretical achievements are only final in respect to their own genesis. Because that historical genesis gives each ethic and philosophy its bearings, none can lay claim to an unconditioned validity. Therefore, the new orthodoxy concludes, Hegel's theory of objective and absolute spirit only reaffirms the lessons of subjective spirit: that reason and justice are corrigible conventions grounded in historical practices as transient as they.

Does this make any more sense than the coherence theory of truth and logical holism? Whether we turn to subjective spirit or the histories of objective and absolute spirit, the problem is the same.

Thinking may be an activity of a living individual, conscious of his own representations, self-conscious in virtue of certain relations to other individuals, and linguistically able to express his thoughts. Yet can any of these preconditions of thought be known to determine what counts as knowledge? To claim that either the structure of consciousness, intersubjectivity, or language predetermine the standards of objectivity requires some account of how we can have objective knowledge of what these conditions are and that they play their privileged role as foundations of knowledge. If, however, any of these putative foundations do determine what we know as true and right, how can we have any certainty that our knowledge of them is not a distorted vision that they themselves impose? So long as they underlie all our cognition, we can never remove their blinders and gain immediate access to what they or any other objects are in their own right. Conversely, if what they determine as true or false regarding their own role is true unconditionally, then what they contribute to the formation of this knowledge is of no consequence to its validity. But this means that in this instance, they do not function as foundations of knowledge, which is to say, that they contradict the privileged character ascribed to them. Hence, either way, it is impossible to know that consciousness, intersubjectivity or language are juridical conditions of knowledge. They may well be necessary preconditions of knowing, without which knowledge is impossible, but it makes no sense to argue that they play any role in the adjudication of knowledge claims.

Instead of treating any of these factors as foundations of knowledge, one must conceive them as conditions of knowing that leave utterly undetermined what can be known on their basis. Contrary to the interpretation of the new orthodoxy, this is precisely how Hegel addresses each one in his doctrine of subjective spirit. In conceiving consciousness as a being in the world, Hegel carefully refrains from ever asserting that the physical engagement of consciousness or the categories of its understanding enter in in distinguishing which of the representations they make possible are true or false. Similarly, when he analyzes the master-slave relation, he acknowledges the type of self-knowledge it contains, but he never claims that its intersubjectivity decides what else counts as knowledge for the mode of self-consciousness it makes possible. Finally, when Hegel turns to language, his whole point is to show how it provides a medium for thought precisely by leaving thinking free of any dependence upon privileged givens. Language provides this service by furnishing signs, representations whose reference is freely determined by intelligence itself. Far from restricting thought to thinking representations tied to givens from whose bondage reason can never escape, language allows the conscious individual to have representations whose referent is a product of thought, or more accurately, a self-determination of thinking. Hence language neither predetermines what can be thought, nor which of the possible thoughts it can express are true or false. Language may have a given grammar and vocabulary, established in the practices of an historically situated linguistic community. Nevertheless, every language is and must be such as to allow any of its speakers to create whatever new meanings they choose without violating grammatical rules or current usage. By the same token, semantic analysis can never determine the truth of meanings which any language allows to be expressed. For if grammatical language can express not just novel ideas, but true and false theories, then linguistic structure leaves utterly undetermined which of its possible communications convey knowledge. Not only does the character of signs make this so, but it is impossible to argue the contrary with any coherence.

Hegel, unlike the new orthodoxy, grasps the true lesson of subjective spirit, that consciousness, intersubjectivity and language all leave thought free of any limits other than those it imposes upon itself. And despite all appearances, Hegel does not lose sight of this lesson in his histories of freedom and philosophy.

By conceiving the genesis of the institutions of right after determining them in their concept, Hegel strictly demarcates the legitimation of these institutions from the historical process by which they emerge. What gives the institutions of right their exclusive justice is that they are structures of self-determination. As such, they have no antecedent foundations from which their character derives. Hence, the history from which they arise can contribute nothing to their validity, neither by providing prior standards for justice nor by imposing external limits upon what can count as right and wrong.[18]

If, on the contrary, one were to adopt the new orthodoxy's view that standards of justice are rooted in historically conditioned practices, as MacIntyre argues,[19] there is no way to escape the nihilist conclusion that all ethics are corrigible conventions relative to prevailing institutions. If one tries to circumvent nihilism by holding that history has an absolute character, leading to practices whose ethics are unconditionally valid, then one admits that at the end of history, an ethics emerges whose validity is no longer historically conditioned, a conclusion contradicting the claim that right and wrong are historically relative categories. Hence, it makes little sense for a new orthodoxy pundit like MacIntyre to denounce contemporary morals as the work of new barbarians, as if his appeal to historical practice still left room for objective ethical judgments.[20]

If this leaves the new orthodoxy in the clutches of nihilism, what undermines that embrace is the untenability of its claim that no practice can have its juridical character unconditioned by history. That claim is destroyed by Hegel's philosophy of right, which shows how the institutions of justice are structures of freedom, determined through their own practices, and hence grounded on themselves. Although nature and a plurality of choosing individuals are prerequisites for any institutions of right, they are conditions for just as well as unjust activity. Consequently, neither they nor any other enabling conditions comprise juridical foundations determining which of the practices they make possible are right or wrong.

The case of the history of philosophy is no different. Admittedly, Hegel seems to describe the genesis of his own system as if all prior philosophical history were guided by an internal necessity, logically linking each successive system to its predecessor in a continuous march towards true wisdom. If this be taken at face value, it leads to the new orthodoxy's view that every philosophical system is founded upon a conceptual result that is the product not of its own argument, but of a prior incommensurable system. This condemns all philosophizing to foundationalism save perhaps for the very first philosophy, which, if not grounded on assumptions generated by preceding philosophers, may still be founded on a conceptual framework rooted in some pre-philosophical practice. In any event, since the new orthodoxy must regard its own theory about philosophical development as something other than the first philosophy, it is at pains to account for the validity of its own philosophical position. Once again, if it admits that its metaphilosophical theory is itself conditioned by past philosophical history, then its view will be relativized unless that past history is an absolute development leading to an incorrigible wisdom unlike any prior theory. In that case, however, the truth of the new orthodoxy's position will not be conditioned by its genesis, but will be unconditionally valid, with the result that it will contradict the very view about philosophy that it advocates.

Despite first appearances, Hegel's doctrine of philosophy can escape this dilemma once it is no longer assumed to be a theory about how the actual history of philosophy is governed by a necessity mandating what can or can not be conceived at any stage. To be consistent with Hegel's own claims concerning the presupposition-less, self-grounding character of his system, it must rather be understood as a rational reconstruction of theoretical history, showing how the greatest past thinkers have explored the possible options of thought, doing something that nothing compels them to do, namely, recognize the conceptual limits of their predecessors and then strike ahead on their own with what overcomes those limits in the most direct fashion. Whether thinkers repeat the errors of the past or blunder into forgettable novelties is up to them. But if they are to make any abiding mark on the history of philosophy they must go beyond all past developments, while offering something that must be retained. If, further, the options of philosophical thought are logically limited and logically connected, then it should come as no surprise that one can order the history of philosophy in terms of the self-ordering of the different logical categories. That ordering is not an external necessity compelling philosophers how to think, but testimony to how the autonomy of reason need not be without a logic of its own.

It is here, in philosophy's own development, that the new orthodoxy meets its Waterloo, freeing Hegelian theory from the truncated dogma to which it has been reduced. For us, this signifies both a liberation and an inexorable bondage. While we may escape enslavement to a corrigible, historical reason, the collapse of the new orthodoxy shows how no arguments can ever free us from the temptations of a systematic philosophy without foundations.

NOTES

1. Because the new orthodoxy has a unified position that can most fruitfully be discussed in its own right, independent of an analysis of its particular representatives, it is here addressed as an argument, without textual references to the innumerable presentations it has been given. For this reason, all subsequent references to the Hegel interpretation of the new orthodoxy consist in explorations of how the new orthodoxy can and must interpret Hegel to buttress its position. Since it is the logic of this interpretation that counts, citations from representatives of the new orthodoxy are not and need not be provided.

2. Richard Rorty, *Philosophy and the Mirror of Nature* (Princeton: Princeton University Press, 1980).

3. Thomas Nagel, *The View from Nowhere* (Oxford: Oxford University Press, 1985).

4. G.W.F. Hegel, *Phenomenology of Spirit*, trans. A.V. Miller (New York: Oxford University Press, 1977), p. 49; G.W.F. Hegel, *Science of Logic*, trans. A.V. Miller (New York: Humanities Press, 1969), pp. 49, 51, 69.

5. See Kenley R. Dove, "Hegel's Phenomenological Method," *The Review of Metaphysics*, XXII, No. 4, June 1970; William Maker, "Hegel's *Phenomenology* As Introduction To Science," *Clio*, No. 10, 1981; Richard Dien Winfield, "The Route To Foundation-Free Systematic Philosophy," *The Philosophical Forum*, Vol. XV, No. 3, Spring 1984.

6. Hegel, *Phenomenology of Spirit*, pp. 21, 51; Hegel, *Science of Logic*, p. 49.

7. Hegel, *Phenomenology of Spirit*, pp. 479–480, 485–486, 487; Hegel, *Science of Logic*, p. 69.

8. Hegel, *Science of Logic*, p. 73.

9. *Ibid.*, pp. 43ff., 68.

10. *Ibid.*, pp. 72, 829, 838.

11. Donald Davidson, "On The Very Idea of A Conceptual Scheme," in *Inquiries into Truth and Interpretation* (Oxford: Oxford University Press, 1984), pp. 183–198.

12. Hegel, *Science of Logic*, pp. 70–72, 829, 838.

13. G.W.F. Hegel, *Philosophy of Mind*, trans. William Wallace and A.V. Miller (Oxford: Oxford University Press, 1978), §'s 413–423.

14. *Ibid.*, §'s 424–435.

15. *Ibid.*, § 430.

16. *Ibid.*, § 465.

17. *Ibid.*, § 459.

18. See Richard Dien Winfield, "The Theory and Practice of The History of Freedom: On the Right of History in Hegel's Philosophy of Right," in *History and System: Hegel's Philosophy of History*, ed. Robert L. Perkins (Albany: SUNY Press, 1984), pp. 123–144.

19. Alasdair MacIntyre, *After Virtue* (Notre Dame: Notre Dame Press, 1981).

20. *Ibid.*, p. 245.

Commentary on Richard Winfield's "Hegel Versus the New
Orthodoxy"
Drucilla Cornell

There may be no philosopher more difficult than Hegel to borrow
from partially. The grandeur of his system demands that we come to
terms with the whole. Yet, the dialectical richness of his narration of
the development of human consciousness in the *Phenomenology*, his
incisive critique of representational thinking and the correspondence
theory of truth, and his brilliant deconstruction of the philosophy of
substance and of constituted essences in the *Logic* make his thinking
so timely that the temptation to endorse a version of pragmatic
Hegelianism which picks and chooses from within Hegel's system is
great indeed. By pragmatic Hegelians, I mean to indicate the group
of philosophers whose Hegelianism rejects the philosophical demonstration of the ascension to Absolute Knowledge, even if they do
not necessarily reject absolute knowledge as a redemptive perspective. I am adopting "pragmatic Hegelians" as a replacement for
Winfield's "the new orthodoxy." I do so to indicate that Winfield has
thrown his net very wide in his designation of diverse writers as the
new orthodoxy, many of whom do not make the mistakes that Winfield critiques as inherent in the tendency to absolutize the appeal to
objective spirit. Winfield, in other words, rightfully critiques one
brand of pragmatic Hegelianism, but he throws the net too wide and
as a result, he too narrowly draws our choice, either Hegel or the
new orthodoxy and downplays the power of the pragmatic challenge
to Hegel's absolute idealism.

Hegel, as Winfield correctly notes, would reject the absolutization
of the appeal to objective spirit not only because as Winfield suggests
the unleashing of the full force of subjective spirit is key to Hegel's
understanding of the *Sittlichkeit* of modernity, but also because
Hegel's own appeal to objective spirit is given meaning within the

encompassing immanence of absolute knowledge. The institutions of right in Hegel are not only justified because they are self-determining, but because they are the self-determined conditions of the actualization of relations of reciprocal symmetry. One should read the *Philosophy of Right* against the *Logic's* systematic unfolding of the truth of all of reality as one of mutual co-determination and reciprocity. Within the circumstances of absolute knowledge reality would have found its substantive truth and thus become fully real . . . everything would be relatio to such an extent that the relata would not retain their separateness as independent entities or constituted essences. On one reading this is what Hegel means by absolute knowledge or self-recognition in absolute otherness. Such a normative standard—of course Hegel would never have put it that way—of "self-recognition in absolute otherness" is assumed in the *Philosophy of Right* as the truth of the actual.

Within Hegel's own system the institutions of freedom that comprise justice are not reduced to conventions valid only in respect to the antecedent conditions of their own genesis, nor as Winfield argues, are they justified solely as the pure structures of self-determination, "that have no antecedent foundations from which their character derives." Of course Winfield is right that Hegel himself would reject the derivation of the structures of freedom from antecedent historical conditions. Such an approach would deny the categorical immanence on which Hegel's presuppositionless philosophy is based. The structures of freedom are instead the concretization of the concept of freedom as it has been actualized in the world. Hegel's structures of freedom are not self-legitimating; they are instead legitimated through the Hegelian system itself which shows them to be the actualization of the idea of freedom in history. Hegel narrates the justice of what has been done to counter the claims of revolutionary governments to a self-generated legitimacy because of the identification of their institutions with the self-determination of the will of the people.

As an account of the actual, the narration of the *Philosophy of Right* is inevitably retrospective. "The owl of Minerva flies only at dusk." Yet, within Hegel's own system, the actualization of the ideal in history prevents the reduction of ethics to the perpetuation of order. The institutions of freedom are not justified simply because they are there; they are legitimated because they are the embodiment of the very idea of freedom and of reciprocal symmetry, the "we that is I and the I that is we." Removed from the circle of immanence of absolute knowledge, the appeal to objective spirit can easily, as Winfield wisely reminds us, degenerate into a new kind of positivism in which what is, is reified as the condition for its own justification.

In the recent debates in American legal literature over the crisis in interpretation, we can find a good example of the conservative holism inherent in the absolutization of the appeal to objective spirit. Writers such as Ronald Dworkin, Stanley Fish, and Owen Fiss have all relied on an appeal to our immersion in an already established linguistic community with its embodied *sittlich* commitments to counter the danger of subjectivism in interpretation, more dramatically called nihilism. In particular, the argument made by Fish, who prides himself as an anti-foundationalist, exemplifies "internal realism." Fish, unfamiliar with Hegel, has picked up the new orthodoxy by osmosis, but the errors that Winfield points to are only too evident. Our reality of historical understanding is appealed to as a self-enclosed whole with which the subject is completely identified. Fish, in other words, falls into the philosophical incoherence of the conceptual schema. Hegel long ago in his dialectic of the limit brilliantly demonstrated the contradiction in such an appeal. In order to determine the boundaries of our reality of historical understanding, we would already have to be beyond them. Fish also exemplifies the failure to grasp the force of subjective spirit in the effectuation of *Sittlichkeit*. The I, separate from social role, does have meaning in our form of life. As Hegel reminds us, the subject is an aspect of our objective spirit. Ironically the abstract negation of the subject denies what it purportedly affirms: the embodiment of social reality in and through language.

Derrida has repeatedly shown us that the attempt to reduce the subject to contextuality fails. I deliberately bring up Derrida's name. I do not wish to make a defense of deconstruction here, but I want to show that Derrida not only does not replicate Fish's errors, his entire repertoire of deconstructive exercises can be understood as an attempt to undermine the new orthodoxy and more specifically the coherence theory of truth. Yet, because Derrida has borrowed so heavily from Charles Peirce and because his challenge to objective idealism so sharply delineates the issues at stake in the pragmatic rebellion against Hegel, I want to turn now to the critique of Charles Peirce. What I offer here, is of course a translation, since Peirce never spoke directly to the new orthodoxy.

For Peirce, the central error of Hegel's objective idealism is that it reduces the triadic structure of reality to one dimension of what Peirce would call Thirdness. Peirce, on the other hand, distinguishes between Firstness, Secondness, and Thirdness, as the ultimate categories of experience, reality, and being. The category of Secondness is key to understanding Pierce's break with objective idealism. Secondness is the real that resists, what Peirce refers to as the outward clash. With his category of Secondness, Peirce does not deny the mediation of all human knowledge of reality. Secondness is what is left over, that which can never be captured by any system of signs. Derrida's materialism on which he insists and which he uses to disrupt the appeal to the immanent meaning of a self-enclosed context can be understood implicitly to incorporate Peirce's category of Secondness. Secondness, in other words, is Derrida's constitutive outside that disrupts the claim to self-identity or full presence of a reality of historical understanding. Fish's mistake is to deny Secondness. We are left instead with a self-enclosed context that provides us with a fully determined internal reality.

But we can also understand the mistakes of the new orthodoxy vis-à-vis Peirce's category of Thirdness. For Peirce, all human knowledge is triadic. Knowledge is enfolded in the habits, rules, signs and modes of conduct that Peirce designates thirds. For Peirce, the condition of generality pervades all thirds. The element of the principle of generality implicit in all thirds goes beyond anything that can ever be done or has happened. The future-oriented dimension of Thirdness yields an essential indeterminacy that cannot be theoretically or indeed practically closed.

The error of the new orthodoxy is that it continues to give actuality privilege over possibility, as Hegel ultimately did but now without the appeal to absolute knowledge. In Hegel real potential finds its fulfillment. Potential no longer serves as the more than this inherent in reality itself. The error of the new orthodoxy very simply put, is to reduce the conditional generality of Thirdness to a finite set of past and present regularities and by so doing to deny implicitly the reality of potential. The new orthodoxy chains us to the rock of the past in the appeal to the determining power of established commitments. It is particularly ironic that Rorty, who claims to be a strong proponent of American pragmatism, makes this mistake. If there is a common thread that holds the diverse writings of Dewey, James, Peirce, and Rorty's contemporary Bernstein together, it is precisely the shared orientation to the future as the horizon for the effectuation of meaning. We can then not only correct the mistakes of the new orthodoxy vis-à-vis Hegel, we can do so with the help of the best writings of American pragmatism itself. If, of course, the Hegelian system is true, we need to go no further. To make such a claim we need a full defense of the *Logic*, a project that has to my mind yet to be accomplished. As Hegel himself reminds us, we must show the truth of the *Logic*, not simply assume it. To quote Hegel:

> For science cannot simply reject a form a knowledge which is not true, and treat this as a common view of things, and then assure us that itself is an entirely different knowledge, and hold the other to

be of no account at all, nor can it appeal to the fact that in this other, there are pre-stages of the better. By giving that assurance it would declare its force and value to lie in its existence; but the untrue knowledge appeals likewise to the fact that it is, and assures us that to it, science is nothing. One barren assurance, however, is of just as much value as another.

It is not enough to confront the "barren assurance" of the new orthodoxy with the countervailing assurance of the truth of Hegel's system. Winfield eloquently critiques the errors inherent in bad historicism, but he downplays the significance of the pragmatic Hegelians' challenge to Hegel's claim for his system that it is the ultimate *Wissenschaft*. The pragmatic rebellion against Hegel's absolute idealism confronts us with indeterminacy. We are opened to the force of unrealized potential and to our responsibility for actualizing it. Hegel's speculative statement, what is rational is real and what is real is rational, articulates a task for each individual. But once that task is articulated, we must go further and take it up. The pragmatists remind us that reason will only be realized in history through our commitment to so orient our praxis.

INDEX

241